4.25

THE JOHN HARVARD LIBRARY

Bernard Bailyn
Editor-in-Chief

AMERICAN PROSE MASTERS

COOPER–HAWTHORNE–EMERSON
–POE–LOWELL–HENRY JAMES

By

W. C. BROWNELL

Edited by Howard Mumford Jones

THE BELKNAP PRESS OF
HARVARD UNIVERSITY PRESS
Cambridge, Massachusetts
1963

Distributed in Great Britain by Oxford University Press, London

Library of Congress Catalog Card Number 63-11415

Printed in the United States of America

CONTENTS

AMERICAN PROSE MASTERS

COOPER

HAWTHORNE

EMERSON

CONTENTS

POE

LOWELL

HENRY JAMES

INTRODUCTION

The present generation is not prepared to grant importance to movements of culture in the United States during the thirty or forty years preceding our entrance into World War I. Indeed, except as a technical term among anthropologists culture has fallen into disuse. Literary specialists, it is true, admire the critical essays of Henry James (who spent most of these years abroad); the *Huckleberry Finn* of Mark Twain (who, we are discovering, was a tortured personality); the novels of Melville (who virtually disappeared from view in the period); and the work of Whitman (who, dead in 1892, contributed nothing of value after *Passage to India* and *Democratic Vistas,* both in 1871). Specialists also admit with an air of patronage that Howells "fought for" the younger realists, but as between the fiction of Howells and that of James, they concentrate on James. That Howells, like James, was striving to destroy American parochialism; that Edmund Clarence Stedman, George Edward Woodberry, Lewis E. Gates, Hamilton Wright Mabie, Richard Watson Gilder, Brander Matthews, James G. Huneker and William Crary Brownell were trying to make the Atlantic community a cultural whole; that American writing profoundly needed the discipline of form and American readers the enrichment of culture; that the whole period needs sympathetic re-examination—these considerations are ignored.

What was the literary situation when *Huckleberry Finn* appeared in 1884? A leading American romantic—Poe—had possessed craftsmanship, but lacked culture. Another leading American romantic—Lowell—possessed culture but lacked craftsmanship. A third romantic—Longfellow—possessed both culture and craftsmanship but lacked force. A fourth romantic—Whitman—possessed force, lacked culture, and displayed a mercurial uncertainty in craftsmanship that his admirers have been struggling ever since to explain away. The brilliance of Emerson's *sententiae* is unequaled but his essays, it is notorious, are paragraphs on a string and his books are invertebrate except for *Nature* and *English Traits. Walden* is fascinating, but has no real architecture.

Cooper had information, narrative drive, political and religious earnestness—and a style so uncertain he has been classed among both the worst and the best of nineteenth-century writers. Irving was diffuse. The novels of Melville are medleys. Aside from *The Scarlet Letter* Hawthorne never constructed a perfect book as *Adolphe* or *Mlle. de Maupin* or *Frankenstein* or *Madame Bovary* is, each in its special category, perfect—that is to say, a novel in which every word cumulates towards a predetermined central impression of aesthetic truth. Sentimentalism, that illegitimate sister of romanticism, haunted the footsteps of her kinswoman, and was a more pervasive element in American writing between Irving and 1890 than any other. In his picturesque way Emerson might declare: "I would write on the lintels of the doorpost, Whim" (adding, however, the Yankee caution: "I hope it is somewhat better than whim at last"), but "genius" in the arts too often came out as "inspiration," as amateurishness, as wilfulness, as contentment with what is shapeless, fragmentary, maudlin, facile, flamboyant, or melodramatic. In literature this sentimentalism shapes most of the contributions to the "elegant" giftbooks and annuals, the equally elegant magazines like *Godey's Lady's Book,* the "tales" that satisfied the "feminine fifties," and such popular fiction as *The Wide, Wide World, St. Elmo, Ramona,* and *He Fell in Love with His Wife.* The author of the last was the Rev. E. P. Roe; and it is a cultural datum of significance that he abandoned his pulpit in Highland Falls, New York, in 1874, bought an estate at Cornwall on the Hudson, and enjoyed an income of $15,000 a year from his seventeen successive best sellers, all triumphs of the sentimental muse. *The Gilded Age* by Warner and Twain gives us a picturesque phrase; the book to which the phrase is attached is possibly the worst-built novel ever put together by two intelligent men.

American literature had gone through successive stages of evolution to reach this point. In the first of these, the epoch of exploration, discovery, and settlement, writing in and about the New World by Englishmen had something of the large discourse of the Jacobean world—witness the works of Captain John Smith. In the next phase, that of the colonial and provincial periods, American writing was content to be a subordinate and inferior province of the British muse. In the third, American Revolutionary prose rose to a perfection admired by Pitt and capped by the haunting felicity of Jefferson, but sentimentality overcame the novel and sham neoclassicism produced innumerable lines of mediocre verse. In the fourth, the radical republic was determined to produce a radically new literature in response, so to speak, to the taunt of Sidney Smith's question: "In the four quarters of the world, who reads an American book?" A thousand essays, addresses, and fourth-of-July orations demanded, as Emerson did, that we abandon the courtly muses of Europe. The results were illogical and surprising. Romanticism was domesticated in America by the Hudson River School, by writers from Irving to Poe, from Bryant to Longfellow, and by musicians such as Stephen Foster. But romanticism, as I have indicated, was also shadowed by the sentimental, and a really moving success like *Uncle Tom's Cabin* is characteristic in its fusion of these two elements.

The national could not always be distinguished from the parochial, just as the romantic could not always be divorced from the sentimental—the romantic sentimentalism Howells denounced in a vastly misread volume, *Criticism and Fiction* (1892). Against decayed romanticism, against a low satisfaction with the sentimental and the parochial, the better brains of the genteel tradition set their faces. Again we have an unfortunate term. In a day when even such a phrase as "a gentleman of the old school" has disappeared, nobody wants to be genteel; and ever since Santayana's tendentious *The Genteel Tradition at Bay* (1933), it has been difficult for a modern to comprehend either the age of Howells or the work of William Crary Brownell. *Lolita, The Tropic of Cancer, Light in August,* criticism on the myth-and-metaphor assumption, and the vogue of Freud and post-Freudian psychology get in the way. Perhaps the simplest way to understand the true work of the genteel tradition is to look through the first volume of the *Atlantic Monthly* (1857) and then through volume 79, published forty years later. The first volume has a good deal of honest, if mediocre, local color, minor contributions by Longfellow, Whittier, and their contemporaries, a few notable pieces by Europeans (for example, Arthur H. Clough), and a great deal of undistinguished non-fictional prose. The chief memorable pieces by Americans are Fitzjames O'Brien's Hoffmann-

esque "The Diamond Lens" and the opening third of *The Autocrat of the Breakfast Table,* the intellectual gaiety of which does
not conceal its whimsical lack of structure. The *Autocrat* sparkled
then, and it sparkles now. Volume 79 has nothing as good. Nevertheless, forty years later we are moving in a maturer, a more cosmopolitan universe of discourse. In the single category of non-
fictional prose, for example, contributions by Charles W. Eliot,
John Fiske, Irving Babbitt, Bradford Torrey, John Jay Chapman,
Henry Van Brunt and Daniel Coit Gilman, among others, are
firm, ordered, articulate, planned. Something has intervened to
discipline prose. That something was the contribution of the
genteel critics: a discipline of craftsmanship in the context of
Western culture. Doubtless Poe had undertaken a similar task
earlier, but his legend got in the way of his criticism, and it remained for the genteel critics to rediscover the meaning of "The
Philosophy of Composition."

The return into the context of Western culture had little to
do with the courtly muses of Europe. The Americans no longer
found it necessary to fight off the superiority of British genius,
especially after Lowell's successful tour of duty as minister to
the Court of St. James (1880–1885). The British classics became
firmly established in American schools and colleges, and the
rising generation of critics were by no means unsympathetic to
British writers—one of Brownell's best books is his *Victorian
Prose Masters.* But the genteel critics took with admirable seriousness the injunctions of Goethe and Arnold that, if one wished to
avoid provinciality, one must become a good European. Arnold,
indeed, who was the most powerful single influence upon this
group, led the way to France. In painting, in architecture, in the
theatrical arts, in the principles of naturalism, in a theory of
criticism that was, paradoxically, in flat contradiction to naturalism, the practitioners and critics of the arts in America looked to
Paris rather more than they did to London. Paris had become the
capital of modern painting. The Ecole des Beaux Arts educated
American architects, triumphing at the World's Columbian Exposition. Brander Matthews' first book was *The Theatres of
Paris* (1880) and his second, *French Dramatists of the Nineteenth Century* (1881). Frank Norris, Stephen Crane, and others
admired Flaubert and Zola, on whom Henry James wrote an

admirable essay. And, finally, Sainte-Beuve, Taine, Schérer and Brunetière became familiar names in literary criticism.

The genteel critics (how one detests the phrase!) portioned out their tasks almost as if they were members of a single English department. Edmund Clarence Stedman in *Poets of America* (1885) and *The Nature and Elements of Poetry* (1892) insisted with Rossetti that poetry means fundamental brainwork, and applied the standards of a rational classicism to American verse. George Edward Woodberry, more successful as a teacher than as a critic, went back to Plato to assert that art is a succession of glimpses into a divine order, thus supplying the emotional afflatus Stedman lacked. Now best remembered as the teacher of Frank Norris, Lewis E. Gates denied that the "momentary shiver" of impressionism was valid and insisted upon the place of form in art. Mabie educated readers through volumes such as *Books and Culture* (1896), and if his comments on somebody like Goethe seem to us jejune, they were not jejune in the year when Charles M. Sheldon published *In His Steps*. Like Horace E. Scudder, Richard Watson Gilder was a great editor. In charge of *Scribner's Monthly Magazine* after 1887, he made it one of the ten or twelve best periodicals in the entire Atlantic community. In classroom and in article Brander Matthews insisted upon craftsmanship. James G. Huneker, it is true, mistook gossip for scholarship and the journalistic for the critical, but he seemed to have all the seven arts, he seemed to have all of Europe at his fingertips. America had produced nobody like him. Whether he was writing about wine or Wagner, Shaw or Chopin, he appeared to restore the *uomo universale* to modern discourse, he revived in Philadelphia and New York the Renaissance of Florence and Rome. And there were, of course, others. By and by the values represented by these critics were to freeze and become bellicose in the writings of the neohumanists. But the most intelligent, the most flexible, the maturest of these men was William Crary Brownell.

II

William Crary Brownell (1851–1928) was born into the Establishment, had all his life ample means, and knew virtually nothing at first hand about North America beyond the Hudson River.

Except for a few boyhood years in Buffalo, he spent his life in Rhode Island, New York, and Europe, principally in Paris. He was educated at private schools and at Amherst College. At twenty-one he was made city editor of the New York *World,* then in a period of literary glory. From 1879 to 1881 he was associated with *The Nation,* under E. L. Godkin, who raised that weekly to a pitch of intellectual eminence it has since recovered only intermittently. He was for a time on the *Philadelphia Press,* a paper that was to know the first work of members of the Ashcan School. He married the first time Virginia Swinburne of the Swinburnes of Newport; the second time, Gertrude Hall, a translator of Verlaine and Rostand. He was so much at home in Newport he could in 1896 publish a book about Newport as it was before the millionaires wholly took over. In New York, after 1888 he was a member of The Century Association: the range and power of the influence of the Centurions upon American thought, education, publishing, art, and public policy have still to be estimated. In New York he was the friend of the sculptor J. Q. A. Ward, in Philadelphia of the painter Thomas Eakins, in Paris of Rodin, and in Williamstown, of "two small Armenians, with midnight eyes, long-lashed like the gazelle's" and of the Negro elevator boy, with whom he gravely discussed prize fighting, for he had, as Maxwell Perkins said, no condescensions. Beginning in January 1888, he was for forty years the chief literary adviser to Charles Scribner's Sons, where his influence was powerful, gracious, and conservative. Said Robert Cortes Holliday:

I regarded him as omniscient. The calm, unconscious nobility of his presence, the classic sculpture of his head and greying beard, the philosophic detachment of his bearing, suggested to my mind a . . . blend of Socrates and Marcus Aurelius.

In an era when book publishing was still a profession and not an industry, Brownell treated it as a branch of the fine arts. Possibly he was *too* "cultured": his wife, in a fragment of biography, writes that "summing up his noble joys" at the end of day, he said, "To-day I have heard the Fifth Symphony and seen 'Hamlet.'" She once persuaded him to go with her to see Charlie Chaplin in "Shoulder Arms," but he did not laugh. Why not?

"He explained thoughtfully, with eyes absorbed in the picture, 'He is so charming!' " This is sound cinematic criticism; nevertheless one wishes Brownell had guffawed. But it is easy to be unjust. Bliss Perry wrote of his "witty comments on the galley proofs," Robert Bridges of his "humor and personal irony," Edith Wharton of his generous nature.

III

If one puts the book about Newport aside, Brownell's other volumes fall symmetrically into two groups of four titles each. It is perhaps significant that all the books in the first group were published before World War I, and that all the other four were published in 1914 or after, and deal with an Atlantic community so changing or so changed, Brownell could not feel at home in it. The first group is made up of *French Traits* (1889), *French Art* (1892; a new and enlarged edition came out in 1908), *Victorian Prose Masters* (1901) and *American Prose Masters* (1909). The second group comprises *Criticism* (1914), *Standards* (1917), *The Genius of Style* (1924) and *Democratic Distinction in America* (1927). These later books are attempts to codify the literary and cultural philosophy he had drawn from his earlier experiments in criticism, and the last volume attempts to apply this philosophy to America of the Twenties. One might say smartly that Brownell could find no democratic distinction in America, but this would be unfair, for he believed in democracy, he believed in distinction, he thought we were neglecting our cultural opportunity, and he was far more good-humored about his analysis than were the neohumanists. Inasmuch as the characteristic complaint against Brownell has been that his style is unnecessarily difficult, *The Genius of Style* is not persuasive and, moreover, suffers from divided aims: part of it is devoted to an historical analysis of style, and part of it to lamenting "the diminution of personal dignity" in our time. In general Brownell's endeavors at theory are less successful than his work in criticism, and the four books of the first group contain about all that is vital and influential in his writing. It is evident upon inspection that *American Prose Masters* comes at the climax of the best phase of Brownell's interpretative career.

American Prose Masters profits from its three great predecessors. I use the word "great" advisedly. *French Traits* is the first book about a foreign culture by an American after Emerson's *English Traits* to reach the plane of that admirable work. It is a study so excellent as to justify William James's inquiry to Burlingame of Scribner's:

Who the deuce is Brownell? His article on French character is *wonderful* in all respects. The best thing of that sort ever done about any nation, if I mistake not; and you may tell him I say so.

James added that he thought Brownell was "a bit off the mark with the painters," an amusing observation in view of *French Art,* which followed. The France of Brownell is, it is true, Paris. His pages have little or nothing to do with provincial or rural life, he never looks into the appalling gulfs of greed from which Balzac fished up Gobseck and Grandet, nor into the swamps of misery from which Zola drew *L'Assommoir, Germinal* and *La Terre.* His discussion in his chapter on morality, of sexual relations among the French is of a delicacy that would seem uproariously funny to Mr. Henry Miller, nor would one suspect from the lengthy essay on French women that the Parisian *cocotte* is in the world's eye a standard French type. But nothing is gained by blaming our author for what he had no intention of doing. His France is the France of tradition, of intelligence, of the social graces, of wit, of clarity and light; the France, if one likes, of the *noblesse* and the *haute bourgeoisie* and, certainly, of the intellectuals; and this France is the center of Atlantic culture where Paris is perpetually the city of light. France for him is Molière, Daudet, Voltaire, Houdon, Pascal, the great painters, and the great critics; and in a final chapter, "New York after Paris," he makes the point that he has undertaken this minute and laborious analysis for the benefit of America:

. . . one's last word about the America emphasized by contrast with the organic and *solidaire* society of France, is that, for insuring order and efficiency to the lines of this advance, it would be difficult to conceive too gravely the utility of observing attentively the work in the modern world of the only other great nation that follows the democratic standard, and is perennially prepared to make sacrifices for ideas.

The passage makes clear what one means by saying that the genteel critics strove to reunite the severed parts of the Atlantic community.

French Art, even in its revised form, has, like *French Traits,* its limitations. Brownell discusses Bouguereau, and he does not discuss Seurat, Van Gogh, or Gauguin, but, it must be said, he discusses Bouguereau with no perceptible enthusiasm. He is capable of prophesying that "whatever the painting of the future is to be, it is certainly not to be the painting of Monet," though he is excellent on Monet. We no longer take Millet *au grand sérieux,* the sculptures at the opera house in Paris now awaken only a limited interest, and a defense of Rodin against academicism now seems to us a work of supererogation. All this, however, is only to say that, writing in 1892, Brownell could not adopt the values, possibly transient, of 1962. He is surveying the whole history of French painting and sculpture, and his book is a model of organization, sympathy, and clearness. It required unusual historical insight to write that

French painting really began in connoisseurship . . . It arose in appreciation, that faculty by which the French have always been, and still are, unrivalled. Its syntheses were based on elements already in combination. Its first practitioners were men of culture rather than of feeling; they were inspired by the artistic, the constructive, the fashioning, rather than the poetic, spirit.

He insists that the romantics did not break the essential French tradition in art (one thinks of Tocqueville's parallel view of the French Revolution), but he also is capable of saying of Manet that "his is the great, the very rare, merit of having conceived a new point of view" and that "it is impossible to exaggerate the way in which the sense of reality has been intensified" by him. True, Brownell thinks of impressionism as exhibiting "a kind of undertone of frivolity" and thus betrays his own neoclassical sympathies, but he also notes that "it is not a way of looking at things, but of rendering them"; and when one remembers that *French Art* was published just a year before Hovenden's "Breaking Home Ties" was to prove the most popular canvas at the World's Columbian Exposition, one acquires a new and startled respect for Brownell. He surveyed all of French painting and French sculpture under four large categories in a book at once more solid, informed and subtle than anything in American art criticism before 1892.

IV

The first two titles in the Brownell quadrilateral deal with a Romance culture, with a Continental social life, and with the fine arts. The remaining two discuss Anglo-Saxon culture on both sides the Atlantic, and English literature, particularly the literature of English prose in the nineteenth century. If one of Brownell's "masters" writes verse, Brownell does not ignore it. *Victorian Prose Masters* takes up Thackeray, Carlyle, George Eliot, Arnold, Ruskin, and George Meredith. Doubtless the critic could have discussed others—Dickens and Mill, for example, are omitted—but he settled on these six, and on six comparable writers in *American Prose Masters*. He assumes that the work done on one side of the ocean is on the same plane of merit as that done on the other, and that is why I have spoken of him and of his contemporaries as engaged in reuniting the Atlantic community. In fact Brownell gently ridicules American chauvinism. Among these twelve authors he has of course his favorites—Thackeray and Arnold in one book, Cooper and Emerson in the other—and he is less sympathetic with some of the rest. Perhaps in 1901 it required no critical daring to reduce Carlyle and Ruskin to eccentrics of genius, but in 1909 it took courage to deflate Poe to our present estimate of him and to declare that Hawthorne wrote but one perfect book. Moreover, our current passion for James and the current revival of interest in *Middlemarch* may lead the reader to find a good many blind spots in Brownell's discussions. The reader may also be inclined to dismiss his lengthy analysis of James Russell Lowell as so much waste matter. But the essays on James and George Eliot are by no means negligible, and, concerning Lowell, one has to remember that he loomed larger on the American literary horizon in 1909 than he does in 1962.

The important consideration, however, is not whether Brownell is right or wrong in this or that essay, the important consideration is the grave dignity of his criticism. It is in the first place informed —he gives the impression of having steeped himself in each of his prose masters before writing about him—and it is in the second place mature and cosmopolitan. To say there is no flag-waving in *American Prose Masters* is not to pay Brownell much of a compliment; one must remember, to be frank, how many schoolbooks, how much magazine criticism in 1909 talked about "our authors" as if authorship were part of the national defense. Brownell is the least chauvinistic of critics. He sat at the feet of great European practitioners of the art, but he was not over-whelmed by any one of them, not even his favorite Arnold. He is aware of the *race, milieu et moment* of Taine, whom he some-times cites, and the milieu and the period have their important places in his estimates—for example, the essays on Cooper and Hawthorne—but he does not erect these concepts into a "scien-tific" system. He is aware of the doctrine of literary evolution, particularly the evolution of genres one associates with Bru-netière, but though the word "evolution" sometimes appears, it is not an absolute; and if Brownell occasionally estimates the worth of a novel by considering its genre, he makes no sacrifices to consistency. As for the "laws" of art, though he sometimes appeals to "law" in establishing a judgment, with him the word is no more than a designating of some aesthetic norm experience has found illuminating. He is, to be sure, a judicious critic, but his judgments are flexible. This flexibility he learned from Arnold, to whom he more often appeals than he does to any other master in criticism. Again, however, Brownell, is no idolator. He at-tributes to Arnold's influence a vast improvement in the "critical aspect" of America and England, he admires Arnold's ideal of reasonableness, his capacity for analysis, and his desire to see the object as in itself it really is, he tries to clear Arnold's poetry from the charge of cacophony, and he even declares that

criticism is the pertinent characterization of great writers, in the mind and art of whom their works are co-ordinated with an explicitness and effectiveness not to be attained by any detailed and objective analysis of the works themselves,

which is virtually a summary of the purport of Arnold's *Essays in Criticism.* Nevertheless, he also flatly states that Arnold "lacked the edge at least of the aesthetic faculty," that he was "not happy" in dealing with America, that his attack on metaphysics in *Literature and Dogma* was unsuccessful, and that his prose, distinguished as it is for "limpidity," has also "a tincture of virtuosity" and is on the whole inferior to the prose of Thackeray.

But the essay on Arnold also contains in a nutshell a better statement of Brownell's theory of criticism than the statement in his little book, *Criticism* (1914). Literature for Brownell as for Arnold is literature teaching by examples. The examples are not, however, single literary works, but the outlook of leading literary figures. "To deal with life powerfully and profoundly is to deal with it critically." Criticism, to be sure, is directed at literature rather than at life, and therefore lacks the element of beauty, but in foregoing the element of beauty it concentrates upon truth. Its role is not that of exposition or of interpretation only, but of synthesis—the synthesis of the more or less heterogeneous work of its subject, the artist. It characterizes art as art characterizes nature. In criticism the thought of an era becomes articulate and coherent. Yet—and here the wheel comes full circle—the best criticism returns upon and becomes literature because it is the direct expression of ideas rather than the expression of ideas at one remove. Impressionist critics chronicle the effect of ideas in a work of art upon themselves; judicial critics weigh such ideas by some detached and objective standard of values.

Brownell's criticism was judicial without being systematic. By this I mean that his terms of reference were to the long tradition of Western culture but that he did not, like some of his European contemporaries and the neohumanists, his contemporaries and successors, sacrifice insight to system. In the background of his essays and in the back of his mind there was forever a general norm or set of norms that, because it was traditional and cosmopolitan in origin and application, can be called classical—if by classicality one understands, not Brownell's referring the bores in Cooper's novels to a Latin tag from Terence, but his larger meanings for words like "literature," "criticism," "art" and "reason." These terms, he felt, have a perennial life before and beyond transient literary fashions like realism and romanticism. It is true, he is inconsistent in the use he makes of these terms. For him "art" sometimes seems to refer to neo-Platonic idealities, sometimes to mere artifice; and reason and its cognates may imply whatever is convenient to his discussion at the moment. But his critical stance cannot be mistaken.

Certain other words are specially to be noted because they are idiosyncratic. Among these are "the ideal," the "actual," the "real," the "concrete," "style," "moral," "temperament," "energy," and "character." The ideal commonly implies either perfection or some variant of the Platonic doctrine of absolute form, but "actual" in most cases refers to what is sensorily present without reference to a work of art, whereas "real" often connotes a quality of illusion conveyed by the writer of a successful book. Thus Hester Prynne in *The Scarlet Letter* is "real," but Roger Chillingworth is not—he is too much an *ad hoc* creation. The "concrete" is, paradoxically, the special realm of art even when it is "ideal." Brownell cannot imagine a literature that does not live in a world of specificity. Hence he praises, condemns, or condones an author or a book because of the strength or flabbiness of his presentation of the concrete. Style is a special concern of his. An essay by him on any author invariably discusses style in the ultimate, penultimate, or antepenultimate section of the criticism. I think style had not been more maturely or meditatively discussed by any American critic before his time. "Moral" means for him neither bare morality nor crude didacticism. It has, rather, the French sense of ethical decision, of commitment, and is Brownell's parallel to the high seriousness of Arnold. Thus Poe, he thinks, has virtually no moral commitment whatever because he has no "philosophy of life," a term Brownell uses to mean: "simply to be profoundly impressed by certain truths. These truths need not be recondite, but they must be deeply felt." On the other hand Cooper is profoundly moral, not because he is an Episcopalian but because he had "a *large* nature" and sincere convictions, as Poe had not. "Temperament" is, for one so essentially classical, almost a romantic concept. It is personality, talent, the recognition of function, the unconscious sensibility or instinct that leads an artist in the right direction, whatever his philosophy or his training, his milieu or his audience. Then there is "energy," which is, I take it, about equivalent to our contemporary "creativity," or that unwearying interest in invention, in "shaping," without which art sinks into the dead level of mere commonplace. Above all and finally, Brownell is convinced that in art character is fate and that the great writer, whatever his philosophy, is he who produces characters that are "real" as Leatherstocking is real and Roderick Usher is not. In this connection the essay on George Eliot in *Victorian Prose Masters* is especially revealing.

Brownell was never a popular critic, and is not likely to become one. He was incapable of literary chitchat. He never let down. He was aloof, weighty, grave. He does not scintillate. He has no enthusiasms, or rather he does not think the conveying of enthusiasm a proper duty for the critic. Thus his admirable essay on Cooper—one of the best in the language—attempts neither to convert nor to crusade, and his obvious admiration for Emerson's idealism does not blind him to Emerson's irremediable artistic faults. He could not anticipate the post-Freudian turn in American literary criticism. Our talk about myth and metaphor would have seemed to him not merely nonsense but betrayal. He did not write about Mark Twain, but if he had, he would never have talked about Huckleberry Finn and that great brown god, the Mississippi River. He overlooked Melville; in the light of his dissection of Hawthorne, no essay by him on *Moby Dick* would have pleased the specialists. On the other hand it is virtually impossible to name an American critic stemming from the nineteenth century who possessed a surer instinct for writing of permanent worth. If his judgments are severe, they are commonly just—witness his evaluations of Hawthorne, Poe and James. Of the last he truly said: "His concern is to be precise, not to be clear." He was not hag-ridden by a thesis like Irving Babbitt, nor obsessed by a cloudy philosophy like George Edward Woodberry. He is one of the few Americans who were also, in the proper sense of the word, good Europeans in our literary world. He wrote with a large discourse; and if his prose was sometimes difficult and even occasionally uncouth, it became so in part because of his anxiety to be honest with the theme under his hand. His appeal was forever to the intelligence, not to the subrational; his belief was that culture is possible in a popular democracy, and in that spirit he tried to illuminate the darkness of the American reading public.

Howard Mumford Jones

Cambridge, Massachusetts
September 3, 1962

A NOTE ON THE TEXT

The text of *American Prose Masters* is a replica of the only edition in book form, published in October 1909 by Charles Scribner's Sons, and is here reprinted by their permission.

Brownell published the several essays earlier in periodical form, revising and expanding them for his book. "Cooper" appeared in *Scribner's Magazine*, 39 (April 1906): 455–469; "Lowell" in that magazine, 41 (February: 1907): 220–235; "Hawthorne" in the same, 43 (January 1908): 69–84; "Poe" in the same, 45 (January 1909): 69–84; and "Emerson" in the same, 46 (November 1909): 608–624. "Henry James" appeared in *The Atlantic Monthly*, 95 (April 1905): 496–519.

I have annotated almost all of Brownell's citations and allusions, even when they refer to familiar sources. Some twenty-five remain unassigned. I have hunted down Brownell's sources because to do so illumines the range and interest of his work and of his mind.

I desire to thank the staff of the Harvard College Library for their patience in fulfilling my many requests, and my colleagues for helping me run down references.

H. M. J.

AMERICAN PROSE MASTERS

COOPER–HAWTHORNE–EMERSON
–POE–LOWELL–HENRY JAMES

TO JOHN W. SIMPSON

COOPER

COOPER

I

THE literary standard of his countrymen is undoubtedly far higher than it was in Cooper's own day. No writer at present with a tenth of his ability would commit his literary faults—faults for which the standard of his day is largely responsible, since it was oblivious to them and since they are precisely those which any widely accepted standard would automatically correct. In other words, Cooper wrote as well as, and builded better than, any one required of him—and though genius, *ex hypothesi,* escapes the operation of evolutionary law, literary or any other artistic expression is almost as much a matter of supply and demand as railroads or any other means of communication; the demand, that is, produces, controls, and gives its character to the supply. The theory that art is due to artists leaves the origin of artists unexplained.

But it is a depressing phenomenon in current American letters that our standard, though satisfactorily higher, should be applied with so little intelligence and elasticity, so mechanically. It is widely held, and the puniest whipsters flourish it like a falchion when they play at soldiers—our popular literary game at present, it sometimes seems. It is not to deny that this diversion has its uses to assert that it has its limitations. To have popularized a high literary standard is an accomplishment of which American letters may well be proud. Indeed it is, perhaps, the result of which hitherto—a few eminent names excepted—it has most reason to be proud. And no doubt there is still reason to hope that our high popular standard may become even higher and more popular than it is! Meantime one would like to see its application more elastic, less mechanical. The way in which it has been applied to the detriment of Cooper's fame, has been not merely unintelligent but thoroughly discreditable. For Cooper, from any point of view, is one of the most distinguished of our literary assets, and there is something ludicrous in being before all the world—as, assuredly, we sometimes are—in recognizing our own merit where it is contestable and in neglecting it where it is not.

It is only superficially remarkable that Cooper should have been over thirty when he wrote his first story. Had he possessed the native temperament of the literary artist, he certainly would not have deferred experimentation so long. Nor would he, probably, if he had had to cast about for a livelihood, or if his environment had been other than it was. But to determine the literary vocation of a man of literary genius, yet nevertheless a man who had been occupied in wholly unliterary pursuits until so ripe a maturity as his, the accident of a whim was not only an appropriate but altogether the most natural cause. "Precaution" was the result of such an accident. It has no other merit, but it established the fact, which apparently he had never suspected, that he had the gift of improvisation; and when he found his material, in his next book, he produced a work that established his reputation as a writer of romance. He did much better, as he did far worse, afterward, but "The Spy" is eminently characteristic. It betrays his faults—very nearly all of them, I think—and most of his virtues. It signalized the entrance into the field of romance, in the fulness of untried but uncommon powers, of a born story-teller. This he was first of all. Some of his stories are dull, but they are never not stories. He belongs, accordingly, in the same category with Scott and Dumas and George Sand, and in general, the writers whose improvising imagination is a conspicuous if not their preponderant faculty—a faculty which, though it may sometimes weary others, seems itself never to tire.

To be one of the great romancers of the world is, in itself, a distinction. But there is more than one kind of romance, and Cooper's has the additional interest of reality. It is based on very solid substance. It is needless to say that it has no interest of literary form—such as distinguishes, though it may not preserve, the exhilarating sophistication of Stevenson. It quite lacks the spiritual fancy of Hawthorne, the inventive extravagance of Poe, the *verve* of Dumas's opulent irresponsibility, the reach and scope of Scott's massive imaginativeness, the richness and beauty of George Sand's poetic improvisation. It has, however, on its side a certain advantage in being absolutely native to its material. More than any other writer of "tales" Cooper fused romance and realism. His books are flights of the imagination, strictly so-called, and at the same time the human documents which it has been left to a later age thus to label. There is not a character, not an incident, in Cooper that could be accused of exaggeration from the standpoint of rationality. And yet the breeze of adventure blows through his pages as if he had no care whatever for truth and fact. Second, no doubt, to Scott in romantic imaginativeness, he is even his superior in the illusion which gives his books an unpretentious and convincing air of relating rather than of inventing, of keeping within bounds and essaying no literary flights —of, as Arnold said in eulogy of German poetry, "going near the ground." [1]

II

The circumstances of his life explain the characteristics of his books with even more completeness than circumstances—as has now become a commonplace—explain everything, and constitute as well as alter cases. He had little systematic education. His character was developed and affirmed before his mind was either trained or stored. His taste naturally suffered. Taste is the product of tradition, and of tradition he was quite independent, quite ignorant. Fortunately, he was also ignorant of its value, and when at thirty he began to produce literature his energy was unhampered by diffidence. But it was inevitable that the literature he produced should be extremely unliterary, and noticeably so in proportion to its power. The fact that he was thirty before he took up his pen is proof enough that he was not a literary genius, proof enough, indeed, that his talent was not distinctively a literary talent. He had not even a tincture of bookishness. Of the *art* of literature he had perhaps never heard. It was quite possible in his day—singular as it may seem in ours—not to hear of it. He indulged in no youthful experimentation in it, unlike Irving. He left school early and was a sailor, a man of business, a gentleman of more or less leisure—enough, at all events, to encourage a temperament that was aristocratic and critical, and not in the least speculative, adventurous, and æsthetic.

What encouragement the literary temperament could find, too, in the America of his youth is well known. The conditions drove Irving abroad, and made a recluse of Hawthorne. Cooper throve under them. They suited his genius, and when he had once started he worked freely in them. He was personally interested in life, in people, in social and political phenomena, in American history and promise, American traits as already determined, American ideas and "institutions," in the country itself, its lakes and woods and plains and seashore, its mountains and rivers, as well as its cities and "settlements"—as Leatherstocking calls them. At least until he began "The Spy" he had never thought of all this as "material," if, indeed, he ever did afterward—in the express and æsthetic sense in which, for example, Stevenson would have regarded it. He was its historian, its critic, its painter, in his own view. He classed his books as works of the imagination in the rather conventional and limited sense in virtue of which fiction is necessarily, and by definition, imaginative. His "art" was for him the art of story-telling, in which the characters and incidents are imagined instead of being real. That his fiction was imaginative rather than merely imagined, I mean, probably never occurred to him. He never philosophized about it at all, and as he began it by conscious imitation of convention, continued it conventionally, so far as his procedure was conscious. As he wrote "Precaution" to determine whether or no he "could write a novel," he wrote "The Pilot" to prove that he could write a more seamanlike tale than "The Pirate" of Scott. He continued to write story after story, because he had made a success of story-telling, and demonstrated it to be his vocation.

But story-telling did not absorb his interests. He wrote other things, too. He has decided rank as a publicist. And he spoiled some of his novels by his preoccupations of that kind—although, indeed, he gave value and solidity to others of them in the same way; "The Bravo" is, for example, as strong a story as "The Ways of the Hour" is weak. Distinctly what we should call "unliterary," however, his point of view remained, as it had been at the outset. Without the poetic or artistic temperament—at least in sufficiently controlling force to stimulate self-expression before almost middle life—he subsisted in an environment, both personal and national, so hostile to the æsthetic and academic as to color what manifestations of these it suffered at all with a decidedly provincial tinge. The conjunction was fortunate. If it was responsible for a long list of the most unliterary works by any writer of eminence in any literature—as I suppose Cooper's may be called —it nevertheless produced an author of acknowledged power and indisputable originality, whose force and vitality are as markedly native and personal as their various manifestations are at times superficial, careless, and conventional. In a word, Cooper was, if not a great writer, a man of conspicuously large mental and moral stature, of broad vision, of wide horizon, of independent philosophy.

His prolixity is perhaps his worst fault; it is, at all events, the source of the worst fault his novels have, the heaviest handicap a novel can have—namely, their tedium. To begin with, hardly one of them is without its tiresome character. Not a few have more than one. Few of his best characters avoid tedium at times; at times even Leatherstocking is a bore. Cooper must himself, in actual life, have been fond of bores. Perhaps his irascibility was soothed by studying this particular foible of his fellows. The trait is to be suspected in other writers of fiction; Scott, for example. For my own part, I recall no character in Cooper as tiresome as some of "Scott's bores," as they are proverbially called. Cooper, however, in this respect is, in general, unsurpassed. The Scotch doctor in "The Spy," the Dutch father in "The Water-Witch," the Italian disputants in "Wing-and-Wing," the crackbrained psalmodist in "The Last of the Mohicans"—but it is idle to specify, the list is too long.

It is true that to represent a bore adequately a novelist cannot avoid making him tiresome. That is his *raison d'être,* and for a novelist *nihil humani* can be *alienum.*[2] But Terence himself would have modified his maxim if he could have foreseen Cooper's addiction to this especial genus. And, as I say, some of the best and most interesting of his personages prose at times interminably: the Pathfinder talking about his own and Killdeer's merits at the prize-shooting, not a few, indeed, of the deliverances of this star character of Cooper's entire company are hard to bear. And both the bores who are—so explicitly and, thus, exhaustively—exhibited as such and the non-bores who nevertheless so frequently bore us have the painful and monotonous family resemblance of all being tiresome in one way—in prolixity. They are really not studied very closely as bores or as occasionally tiresome personages, but are extremely simplified by being represented merely as long-winded. No shades of character, no particular and individual weaknesses are illustrated by their prolixity. Their prolixity is itself the trait that distinguishes them.

The conclusion is inevitable that his characters are often so prolix and often such prolix characters because—which also we know to be the fact—Cooper himself was. Speaking of the unreadable "Mercedes of Castile," Professor Lounsbury truly says that the author is as long getting under way with his story as Columbus himself was in arranging for his voyage.[3] And though this inexplicable novel is probably his dullest, there are few others that do not contain long passages whose redundancy is remorseless. He has no standards. He feels no responsibility. He never thinks of the reader. He follows his own inclination completely, quite without concern for company, one must conclude. There was no tribunal whose judgments he had to consider; there was no censure to be dreaded, no praise he had to try to earn by being other than his own disposition prompted, by being more simple, more concise, more respectful of the reader's intelligence —no ideal of perfection, in short, at which the pressure of current criticism constrained him to aim. And of technical perfection in any but its broadest details—such as general composition and construction—he had no notion. His pace was leisurely, because such was his habit of mind, and there was nothing extraneous to hasten it. He lingered because he liked to, and his public was not impatient. He repeated because he enjoyed repetition, and there was no one to wince at it. He was as elaborate in commonplace as the dilettante can be in paradox because novelty as such did not attract nor familiarity repel either himself or his public. As to literary standards, the times have certainly changed since his day. In literary performance there is perhaps an occasional reminder that the tendency to prolixity still subsists. And in actual life!— but, of course, changes in the macrocosm are naturally more gradual.

Yet even our own time may profitably inquire how it is that Cooper's popularity has triumphed so completely over so grave a fault. Largely, I think, it is due to the fact that the fault is a "literary"—that is to say, a technical—defect, and is counterbalanced by the vitality and largeness of the work of which it, too, is a characteristic. It is far from negligible. On the contrary, it is, however accounted for, the chief obstacle that prevents Cooper from attaining truly classic rank—the rank never quite attained by any one destitute of the sense of form, the feeling for perfection which is what makes art artistic, however inane or insubstantial it may be. But Cooper's technical blemishes are in no danger of being neglected. As Thackeray said impatiently of Macaulay's, "What critic can't point them out?" [4] To point out Cooper's is so easy that his critics are singularly apt to sag into caricature in the process. Nevertheless, though it is indubitable that his prolixity is a grave defect, it is important to remember that it is a formal rather than a substantial one, and that in popular esteem it has been more than counterbalanced by compensations of substance. What is less evident, but what is still more worth indicating, is that there is, speaking somewhat loosely, a certain artistic fitness in his diffuseness, and that this is probably the main reason why it has so slightly diminished not only his popularity, but his legitimate fame. It is, in a word, and except in its excess, an element of his illusion. And in a sense, thus, it is rather a quality than a defect of his work. His illusion is incontestable. No writer of romance has more. It is simply impossible to praise him too highly here. And where the effect is so plainly secured one may properly divine some native felicity in the cause, however, abstractly considered, inadequate to anything such a cause may seem.

III

Cooper is usually called the American Scott in a sense that implies his indebtedness to Scott as a model and a master. His romances are esteemed imitations of the Waverley Novels, differing from their originals as all imitations do in having less energy, less spontaneity—of necessity, therefore, less originality. This is to consider mere surface resemblance. How much or how little Cooper owed to Scott is a question for the literary historian rather than the critic. Doubtless he copied Scott in various practical ways. Romance had received a stamp, a *cachet*, from Scott that, devoted to the same *genre*, it was impossible to ignore. Scott's own derivation may be defined quite as clearly, and the record of it is, like similar studies, one that has its uses. But for other than didactic purposes it is the contrast rather than the resemblance, even, between him and Cooper that is pertinent. It is misleading to compare them—in any sense which implies that Cooper's originality is in any way inferior. It is idle to characterize so voluminous a writer as imitative. Whatever its initial impetus imitation will not furnish the momentum for forty volumes. Cooper's inspiration is as genuine, his zest as great, his genius as individual, as Scott's own. He was less of an artist. He was nothing at all of a poet—at least, in any constructional sense. It is simply impossible to fancy him essaying verse. Even balladry, even rhyming, is beyond him.

> "Tunstall lies dead upon the field,
> His life-blood stains the spotless shield;" [5]

—there is not a note like that in his equipment. For a writer of romance the defect is grave. Nor did he know the world of society as Scott knew it. Any one who can take literally Scott's generous compliment to Miss Austen must never have read "St. Ronan's Well." [6] Neither did he inhabit the same world of the imagination. If he had far less temperament he had also far less culture. His environment forbade it; and he lived in the present. His conservatism was a rationalized liberalism—nothing akin to the instinctive toryism that made it natural for Scott to poetize history. And consequently his environment and his genius combined to confine him in the main to a field which, however interesting in itself, is incontestably inferior to the grandiose theatre of Scott's fiction. A splendid historical pageant winds its way through the Waverley Novels, with which nothing that the pioneer America of Cooper's day furnished could compare.

It is, indeed, in his material that Cooper presents the greatest possible contrast to Scott. It is vain, I think, for American chauvinism itself to deny that our civilization is less romantic than an older one, than that of Europe. To begin with, it has less background, and, as Stevenson pointed out, romanticism in literature largely consists in consciousness of the background.[7] Nothing, it is true, is more romantic than nature, except nature plus man. But the exception is prodigious. Nature in Cooper counts as romantically as she does in Scott, but it is nature without memories, without monuments, without associations. Man, too, with him, though counting on the whole as romantically, does not count as background. His figures are necessarily foreground figures. They are not relieved against the wonderful tapestry of the past. In a word, there is necessarily little *history* in Cooper. Of course, there is "The Bravo," as admirable a tale as "Mercedes of Castile" is an unprofitable one. But the mass of Cooper's most admirable accomplishment is thoroughly and fortunately American, and compared with Europe America has no history. Scott's material in itself, thus, constitutes an incontestable romantic superiority. For fiction history provides offhand a whole world for the exercise of the imagination.

It may undoubtedly be urged that a romantic situation is such in virtue of its elements and not of its associations; that the escape of Uncas from the Hurons in "The Last of the Mohicans" is as romantic as Edward Waverley's visit to the cave of Donald Bean Lean.[8] Or to consider more profoundly, it may be said that, looking within, Hawthorne found in the spiritual drama of New England Puritanism the very quintessence of the romantic, thrown into all the sharper relief by its excessively austere and arid environment—that is to say, by a featureless and thoroughly *un*romantic background. Still, in considering the mass of a writer's work its romantic interest is not to be admeasured mainly by its situations, or its psychology, but by the texture of its entire fabric. And owing to its wealth of imaginative association, the romance of the Waverley Novels is indubitably deeper, richer, more *important* than that of the Leatherstocking Tales. Bernardin de Saint Pierre passes for the father of French literary romanticism, for instance, but it can be only in a purely poetic or very technical sense that "Paul et Virginie" can be called as romantically important as "The Cloister and the Hearth."[9]

There is a quality in Cooper's romance, however, that gives it as romance an almost unique distinction. I mean its solid alliance with reality. It is thoroughly romantic, and yet—very likely owing to his imaginative deficiency, if anything can be so owing—it produces, for romance, an almost unequalled illusion of life itself. This writer, one says to one's self, who was completely unconscious of either the jargon or the philosophy of "art," and who had but a primitively romantic civilization to deal with, has, nevertheless, in this way produced the rarest, the happiest, artistic result. He looked at his material as so much life; it interested him because of the human elements it contained. Scott viewed his through an incontestably more artistic temperament, as romantic material. "Quentin Durward" is, it is true, a masterpiece and, to take an analogous novel of Cooper's, "The Bravo" is not; the presentation of the latter's substance is not masterly enough to answer the requirements of a masterpiece; the substance itself is far less important than the splendid historical picture, with its famous historical portraits, that Scott has painted in his monumental work. But Scott was inspired, precisely, by the epic potentialities for painting and portraiture of the struggle between Louis and Charles and its extraordinarily picturesque accessories. Cooper's theme was the effect of oligarchical tyranny on the social and political life of Venice at the acme of her fame and glory. Humanly speaking, "The Bravo" has more meaning. Historical portraiture aside, I do not think there is in "Quentin Durward" the sense of actual life and its significance that one gets from the tragedy of Jacopo Frontoni's heroic story and the picture of the vicious Venetian state whose sway corrupted "alike the ruler and the ruled" and where "each lived for himself." [10] The gist of the latter book is more serious; it is conceived more in the modern manner; it is not a mere panorama of mediæval panoply and performance, but a romance with a thesis—at least so much of a thesis as any highly concentrated epoch must suggest to a thinking and reflective, instead of a merely seeing and feeling student of its phenomena.

Cooper's genius was a thinking and reflective one. He was certainly not a meditative philosopher, but it was life that interested him and not story-telling as such, even if he might at times get less life and more convention into his books than a romancer *pur sang*. The essence of his romance is that there is no routine in his substance—only in its presentation. His central theme, his main substance, is, like Scott's, his native land. As a romancer his whole attitude toward the pioneer civilization he depicted was one of sympathetic and intelligent interest. He was an observer, a spectator, sufficiently detached to view his subject in the requisite perspective. Some of it he caricatured, and he was oppressively didactic in some of his poorer books. But that proceeded from his constitutional limitations as an artist. On the whole his general and personal interest in the life he depicted makes his account of it solider art, gives his romance even, as I said, more substance and meaning than Scott's historiography. It is more nearly "criticism of life" than the result of a romantic temperament dealing in a purely romantic way with purely romantic elements can be. It is true that Tory as he was, Scott held the balance very true in his pictures of the Cavalier and Roundhead, the Stuart and Hanoverian, contests. But there is more of the philosophy of the latter struggle in "The Two Admirals" than there is in "Waverley" itself.

In "Waverley" the romantic element of the struggle between the legitimist and the legitimate parties, as we may say, is powerfully set forth, the passionate ardor of the one and the practical good sense of the other effectively contrasted, though largely by indirection and in an accessory way. In "Wyandotte" the antagonism between Tory and patriot, between the British and the American partisan, is given far more relief. It is not used merely as a romantic element, tragically dividing a household as it does, but exhibited as a clash of states of mind, of feeling, of conscience, of tradition. *It* is the subject, or at least a part of the subject, not mainly a contribution to its color. The reader notes the reasons that made Major Willoughby a loyalist and Captain Beekman a patriot. The book is a picture of the times, as well as a story, in presenting not only the action but the thinking of the times. One remarks in it that there were "issues" then as well as events. And, of course, with Cooper's noteworthy largeness they are presented with due impartiality, and in this way, too, acquire a sense of verisimilitude and a value that treatment of them as solely romantic elements could not secure.

And in the way of pure romance—romance quite independent of any associations of time and place—there *are* novels of Cooper that are unsurpassed. For an example of this element, in virtue of which, after all, Cooper's tales have made the tour of the world, take the introductory book of the famous Leatherstocking Tales. "The Deerslayer" is, indeed, a delightful romance, full of imaginative interest, redolent of the woods, compact of incident, and alive with suspense. How many times has the genuine lover

of Cooper paid it the tribute of a rereading? For such a reader
every small lake in the woods is a Glimmerglass; around its points
might at any moment appear one of old Hutter's canoes; at any
moment down on yonder sand-spit Le Loup Cervier might issue
from the underbrush; in a clearing beyond the nearer tree-tops
the Deerslayer might so easily be bound to the stake, be looking
into the rifle barrel of his torturer—reassured by his expert knowledge and *sang-froid* to note its ever so slight deflection from a
fatal aim! "Treasure Island"? A literary *tour de force*, not only
suspiciously clever (aside from the admirable beginning), but
so easy not to go on with, so little illusory! "La Dame de Monsoreau"? [11] Pure melodrama, impossible of realization even on
the stage, its unreality certain of exposure even by the friendly
histrionic test. Quite without the aid of a "literary" presentation,
quite without the supplement of historic suggestion and a monumental background, the romance of "The Deerslayer" is, nevertheless, so intrinsic, so essential, and so pervasive as to give the
work commanding rank in its class. No tinsel, literary or other,
accentuates its simplicity, and no footlight illumination colors its
freshness. Cooper is hardly to be called a poet, as I have said. Yet
"The Deerslayer's" romance is, in the net impression it leaves, in
the resultant effect of its extraordinary visualization of wild and
lovely material, as poetic as Chateaubriand's,[12] and fully as effective as that of any work of Scott.

IV

The verisimilitude of Cooper's Indians has been the main point
of attack of his caricaturing critics. None of them has failed to
have his fling at this. It is extraordinary what a convention his
assumed idealization of the Indian has become. I say extraordinary, because it is the fact that the so-called "noble red man,"
whom he is popularly supposed to have invented, does not exist
in his books at all. Successful or not, his Indians, like his other
characters, belong to the realm of attempted portraiture of racial
types, and are, in intention, at all events, in no wise purely romantic creations.

If they were they would, of course, be superabundantly justified. Ethnology might be reminded that fiction is, to some extent,

at least, outside its jurisdiction. The claims of history are far higher, but only a pedant sneers at "Ivanhoe," in which Freeman asserted there was an error on every page,[13] though this is undeniably regrettable; and, in recent times, certainly, the great Dumas is not asked to be otherwise, though a reader here and there may be found who would give him higher rank had he been something other. The introduction into literature of the North American Indian, considered merely as a romantic element, was an important event in the history of fiction. He was an unprecedented and a unique figure—at least on the scale and with the vividness with which he is depicted in Cooper, for the Indians of Mrs. Behn and Voltaire and Chateaubriand [14] can in comparison hardly be said to count at all. They are incarnated abstractions didactically inspired for the most part; L'Ingénu, the virtuous, for example, being no more than an expedient for the contrasted exhibition of civilized vices. But Cooper's Indians, whatever their warrant in truth, were notable actors in the picturesque drama of pioneer storm and stress. They stand out in individual as well as racial relief, like his other personages, American, English, French, and Italian, and discharge their rôles in idiosyncratic, as well as in energetic, fashion. To object to them on the ground that, like Don Quixote and Athos, the Black Knight and Saladin, Uncle Toby and Dalgetty, they are ideal types without actual analogues would be singularly ungracious.

However, they are not ideal types, but depend for their validity in large degree on their reality of portraiture as well as on their romantic interest. As I say, they stand on the same ground as Cooper's other characters, and share with them the seriousness a close correspondence to life gives to fiction that has a realistic basis, however great its romantic interest may also be. They are not in the least "ideal" personages. Cooper does not, to be sure, take quite the cowboy view of the Indian, and people with a smattering of pioneering who regard the cowboy as an expert in Indians and echo his opinion that "the only good Indian is a dead one," may find him unduly discriminating. Still, the cowboy's ethnological experience is, after all, limited, and the frontiersman of recent years has had to deal not with the Indian of the time of Cooper's tales, but with his descendants demoralized by contact with his censors, to say nothing of the "century of dishonor." [15]

Cooper's view is certainly that the Indian is human. But the fact which is so generally lost sight of is that the "noble red man"—the fictitious character he is charged with inventing—is not to be found in his pages. In general he endows the Indian with traits that would be approved as authentic even by the ranchman, the rustler, or the army officer. His Indians are in the main epitomized in Magua. And in the mass the race is depicted pretty much as Hawkeye conceived the Mingoes of the Mohawk Valley and Leatherstocking the Sioux of the prairies—"varmints" one and all. The exceptions are few. There are the Delawares, Chingachgook and Uncas, Conanchet, and the Pawnee Hardheart—hardly any others of importance. And the "goodness" of these is always carefully characterized as *sui generis*. The difference between their moral "gifts," as Leatherstocking often enough points out, and those of the white man is always made to appear as radical. The most "idealized" of them is shown as possessing passions and governed by a code that sharply distinguish him from a white of analogous superiority to his fellows. Nor is his ability exaggerated. In spite of his special senses, developed by his life in peace and war, his woodcraft and physical prowess, when it comes to the pinch in any case his inferiority to the white man is generally marked. So far from being untruthful idealizations Cooper's little group of "good Indians" is in both quality and importance considerably below what a writer not actuated by the truly realistic purpose that was always his would be justified in depicting as representative of the best specimens of the Indian race. The history of this country abounds in figures from Massasoit to Brant, from Osceola to Joseph,[16] of moral and mental stature hardly emulated by any of Cooper's aborigines. The only approach to them is in the sage Tamenund of the Lenni Lenape, who is introduced at a great age, and with failing faculties almost extinct.[17] Chingachgook dies a drunkard as old Indian John. Uncas is slain when a mere youth, before his character is thoroughly developed. Conanchet proves untamable by the best of white influences. Wyandotte [18] preserves his fundamental treachery and vengefulness through years of faithful service to the family to which he is attached. Catlin,[19] who passed his life among the Indians, took a far more favorable view of them. The truth is that not only is Indian character not misrepre-

sented by Cooper, at least in being idealized, but his Indian characters are as carefully studied and as successfully portrayed as his
white ones. Their psychology even is set forth with as much definition. They are as much personalities and differ from each other
as much. Representatives of a single tribe have their marked individual differences. The Hurons Rivenoak and Le Renard Subtil [20]
have but a family resemblance. With the naturally greater simplicity of the savage they are, nevertheless, not represented without the complexities that constitute and characterize the individual. The Tuscarora who enters the room where a mortal struggle is taking place, extinguishes the light, and, one against a
dozen, slays the enemies of the white household he serves, in a
fray as dramatic as, and far more credible than, the famous fatal
fight of the Chevalier de Bussy,[21] is a genuine hero. Yet he is the
same man who, for injustice long since forgotten by all but himself, murders his benefactor in absolute cold blood. And the inconsistency is not an anomaly. It is an Indian trait. In short,
Cooper's Indians are at once Indians to the core, and thoroughly
individualized as well. The "stock" Indian is no more to be found
in his books than the "ideal" primitive hero. He has added to the
traditional material of romance an entire race of human beings,
possessing in common the romantic elements of strangeness and
savagery, but also illustrating a distinctive and coherent racial
character.

V

"If Cooper," said Balzac, "had succeeded in the painting of
character as well as he did in the painting of the phenomena of
nature he would have uttered the last word of our art." [22] The
phenomena of nature considered as material for literary art probably seem less important, less apt, at any rate, nowadays than
they did in Balzac's time.[23] In France especially the generation
to which Chateaubriand remained an inspiration esteemed them
in a degree that appears to us exaggerated. They were much more
of a novelty, to begin with. The eighteenth century, even in England, had certainly little minded them. And certainly they are
well handled by Cooper. Nowhere else has prose rendered the
woods and the sea so vividly, so splendidly, so adequately—and

so simply. Too much can hardly be said of this element of the sea stories and the Leatherstocking Tales. But there is a peculiarity in Cooper's view and treatment of nature. Nature was to him a grandiose manifestation of the Creator's benevolence and power, a vision of beauty and force unrolled by Omnipotence, but a panorama, not a presence. There was nothing Wordsworthian, nothing pantheistic in his feeling for her—for "it" he would have said. No flower ever gave him thoughts that lay too deep for tears. He was at one with nature as Dr. Johnson was with London. There is something extremely tonic and natural in the simplicity of such an attitude, and as a romancer the reality and soundness of it stood Cooper in good stead. It is due to it that nature in his books is an environment, an actual medium, in which his personages live and move rather than a background against which they are relieved, or a rival to which their interest yields. It is the theatre of their action. It simply never occurs to Cooper to "paint the phenomena of nature" except as thus related to his people or their story—though generally more closely related than an accessory, and never less so than an atmosphere. But he knew the sea and the woods, and felt them as no other romancer has ever done, and he made such distinguished use of them as abundantly to merit Balzac's eulogy.

To say, however, that he did not succeed in the painting of character as in a domain wherein he was unrivalled is not to depreciate his portraiture. And certainly Balzac's meaning is merely that in the one field his excellence was unique and in the other it was not. Balzac, moreover, exaggerated, as I have intimated, the value for fiction of painting the phenomena of nature; he meant his praise to be very high praise indeed, and it would greatly have surprised him, we may be sure, to have had any one, as has since been done, take his reference to Cooper's powers of portraiture as depreciatory, as a putting of his finger on Cooper's weak point. He adored Cooper. His admiration of him was not undiscriminating—any more than any other of his admirations. But his enthusiasm for him at his best—even at his second best—was unbounded. "The Pathfinder," says his latest biographer, M. André Le Breton, *"lui arrachait de véritables rugissements de plaisir et d'admiration."* [24] It is idle to refer Balzac's *"rugissements de plaisir"*—at any rate as late as 1840—altogether to the "painting of the phenomena of nature." It is true that what captivated him especially perhaps was the *life* in general that Cooper depicted— the wild, free, savage life of the frontier, easily paradisaic (in idea!) to a Parisian. "Oh," he says in a letter of 1830, "to lead the life of a Mohican, to run over the rocks, to swim the sea, to breathe the free air, the sun! Oh, how I have conceived the savage! Oh, how admirably I have understood the pirates, the adventurers, their lives of opposition and outlawry! There, I said to myself, life is courage, good rifles, the art of navigating in the wide ocean, and the hatred of men." [25] And ten years later his enthusiasm was quite as great. But it is naive to suppose that what made this "life" so attractive to Balzac was in the last analysis anything else than the people who lived it. In "Jack Tier," for example, the phenomena of nature are as effectively depicted as in the somewhat analogous "Red Rover." What makes the book itself less effective? Mainly the comparative inferiority of the characters, though the story, it is true, is less heroic and though some of the characters are very good indeed. However, here is Balzac's own estimate of Leatherstocking: *"Je ne sais pas si l'œuvre de Walter Scott fournit une création aussi grandiose que celle de ce heros des savanes et des forêts."* [26] And though, in speaking of Cooper and Scott, he says *"l'un est l'historien de la nature, l'autre de l'humanité,"* the antithesis is doubtless due to the greater prominence of nature in Cooper's works as in his material, to Cooper's artistic inferiority, and to the vaster stage of the Waverley drama—to say nothing of the charms for Balzac of antithesis in itself. Cooper, continues M. Le Breton, after citing the above phrase, is not less than Scott "a great painter of manners," and "I fear," he says, later, "that the usurers of Balzac, his lawyers, bankers and notaries, owe too much to the sojourn his imagination had made in the cabin of Leatherstocking or the wigwam of Chingachgook, and that there are in the *Comédie Humaine* too many Mohicans in spencers or Hurons in frockcoats." [27]

The criticism of Balzac is sound enough, but the compliment to Cooper is equally clear. To have shared with Scott the derivation of "the master of us all," as Mr. Henry James calls Balzac [28] (who has other titles to fame, but in the light of a provenience from Cooper none so piquant), of itself constitutes a position in the hierarchy of fiction. And in so far as Balzac does derive from Cooper, he does so in virtue of Cooper's realism. His Mohicans in spencers and Hurons in frock-coats really testify to the vivid reality of Cooper's characters, which so impressed the great French realist as to lead him to transfer to the boulevards in unconscious caricature the types which in their native environment possessed a vitality energetic enough to impose imitation even on a romancer of whose greatness originality is a conspicuous trait.

Interesting testimony, however, to the force and truth of Cooper's characters as Balzac's authoritative approval and their influence on his own are, it is interesting only in an authoritative way, and as counterbalancing the judgment of critics of less weight. The characters are there to speak for themselves—to any reader, as they spoke to Balzac. Sainte-Beuve praises them without reserve. In reviewing an early work he speaks enthusiastically of Cooper's "faculté créatrice qui enfante et met au monde des caractères nouveaux, et en vertu de laquelle Rabelais a produit 'Panurge,' Le Sage 'Gil Blas,' et Richardson 'Clarissa.' " [29] They certainly differ in value and solidity, and not only because the types they represent or the conceptions they incarnate so differ, but in what for the sake of clearness may be called the un-Shakespearean way of being characterized with varying effectiveness. Balzac notes the inferiority of his secondary personages to those of Scott—which is true only of his *conventional* secondary personages, I think. For these he had not the zest that the true *artist* has in all his creations. His personages interested him personally or not at all. And when he has no interest he is the last word of the perfunctory. But it is certainly true that he is nowhere less perfunctory than in the creation of character, and that as a rule even his secondary characters adequately fill the rôle assigned to them. Even if they are not made much of, even if he does not, as the French expression is, *les faire valoir,* they are real enough. They are the exact analogues of the negligible folk one meets in life.

There are, however, those who, appreciating Cooper's success with Leatherstocking, with Long Tom Coffin, with Betty Flanagan, and others, have maintained that it is with low life only that he is successful, and that he fails when he attempts to depict the

higher social types. The view is a superficial one. It is in general
a superficial or else an insignificant view when taken of a writer
of conspicuous distinction in character portrayal. Character is
character. There are not two kinds of it, high and low, except in
the sense in which youth and old age, for example, may be said to
differ in character. There is as much and as little of it at one end
of the social scale as at the other. What types a writer with an eye
for it and a faculty for effectively embodying his conception of it
will best succeed in depends upon his experience. When Cooper
wrote his experimental English novel "Precaution" he was writing
of something he knew nothing about. In "The Spy" and "The
Pioneer," which followed it, the gentry are as good as the humble
folk. Leatherstocking and Betty Flanagan are effective largely
because they are picturesque, and it is in the lower walks of life
that the picturesque is especially to be found. And romance deals
largely in the picturesque.

Of course temperament is to some extent a factor in determining the types that an author treats most successfully. So great a
writer as Dickens, it is true, has sometimes been said to have succeeded best with characters from low life. If one contrasts Lord
Frederick Verisopht with Sam Weller [30] one perceives that the
author's genius is most at home in the society of the latter. And
whatever Dickens's experience his temperament, undoubtedly,
led him to depict the lower, with more zest than the upper, ten.
He depicted them, however, for the benefit of the upper. And,
whatever his feeling for character, his high spirits irresistibly impelled him toward caricature. Naturally a novelist producing
caricature for the benefit of the reading classes finds the material
readiest to his hand in another class. Naturally, too, a writer of
romance and adventure finds most effective what is, except in
its outlines and saliencies, least familiar. Stevenson's readers
would find John Silver rather flat if he were a titular gentleman. [31]
Readers aside, morever, the more civilized, the higher in the social scale, the character is, the less accentuated it is, externally.
For romantic purposes, at least for the purposes of realistic romance such as Cooper's, it is normally of inferior interest, for less
is apt normally to happen to it. In ideal romance, of course, neither this nor any similar consideration matters. No one expects a
character in Dumas or in Disraeli to be *in* character otherwise

than to be consistent with itself. The ends of realistic romance are better served by the more elemental natures that have not been smoothed and polished into conformity and are independent of convention. The passions that agitate aristocratic bosoms are more sophisticated and their dramatic result is in the domain rather of the novelist of manners or of the psychological novelist than of the realistic romancer.

Any preponderance of low over high life personages, therefore, among Cooper's successful characters might very well be accounted for by the kind of fiction he wrote. Certainly beyond such as may be thus accounted for no such preponderance exists. He had simply no talent at all for caricature. His failures when he attempted it are grotesque. For example, the vulgar American journalist in "Homeward Bound." He could no more have invented a Dick Swiveller than he could have imagined Hamlet.[32] But within his range of experience and imagination, one of his characters is as good as another, so far as the class to which they belong is concerned. The "blue" admiral in "The Two Admirals" is quite as fine in his way as Long Tom Coffin is in his. His type is simply less picturesque. Perhaps, indeed, a fo'castle reader, were there such, would think him equally picturesque. In all the nautical novels, in fact, the quarter deck people are quite as well done as the able seamen. Lord Geoffrey Cleveland, the midshipman favorite of Admiral Bluewater, is a charming character. There are a score of lieutenants, most of them of gentle birth and breeding, that are extraordinarily good, each one of them an individual and no more mere types than the actual people of one's acquaintance. Griffith, Barnstable, Winchester, Yelverton, Griffin —I have my own idea, I confess, of how each of them looks. When "The Pilot" appeared Miss Mitford wrote: "No one but Smollett has ever attempted to delineate the naval character; and then his are so coarse and hard. Now this has the same truth and power with a deep, grand feeling. . . . Imagine the author's boldness in taking Paul Jones for a hero, and his power in making one care for him."[33] This is very true. Cooper does on occasion combine truth, power, and a deep, grand feeling. He was the manliest of men himself and he had a sympathetic sense for what is noble and elevated in character. He found it, to be sure, in the humbler social types, but I think not disproportionately. His pa-

tricians are, on the whole, as good as his plebs, so far as verisimilitude is concerned. To find him exclusively or mainly successful in the characters belonging to "low life" is, I think, to miss his
chief distinction—that is to say, his genius for the portrayal of
character as character, within the limits of his experience and the
types his observation suggested to his imagination.

If he had imagined no other character than Leatherstocking,
this creation alone would set him in the front rank of the novelists
of the world. It is singular that this feat, as it may in justice be
called, has brought him so little purely literary recognition. Perhaps it is because every one makes Leatherstocking's acquaintance in childhood, and acceptance of him is accordingly perfunctory and unthinking, like that of Robinson Crusoe, for example. No one seems really to reflect on the extraordinary nature of
Cooper's accomplishment. Merit in American literature is the
last thing, one would say, that escapes notice—at least at home.
We have apparently a national disposition to create our geniuses
out of hand. Our criticism is geniality itself. It assigns us great
writers—poets, historians, novelists, critics—with the utmost im-
perturbability, and on the slightest provocation. Certainly in no
country, at any epoch, has appreciation of its own men of letters
been as ready or, as one may say, so energetic. The predisposition
in their favor is perhaps the most persistent survival from days—
pungently depicted by Cooper, who seems, in this respect, too,
to have few successors—in which it was a wide-spread belief that
on any battlefield we could "lick all creation." Yet here is an
American literary possession that really ranks with all but the
greatest, who is never thought of when our literary auctioneers
are extolling and exalting our stock. Not long ago one of our
acutest and most careful critics was coupling Leatherstocking
with Irving's Knickerbocker and speculating about the ideal or
mythical character of both. *They* were this and not that, *et
cætera.*

Thackeray wrote literary criticism lightly and had an instinctive repugnance to curbing his prejudices. But in the matter of
fiction his authority is unimpeachable. No one ever—and others
have tried—parodied Cooper so well. His "Leatherlegs" [34] is an
amusing figure. His serious judgment, however, is as follows: "I
have to own," he says, "that I think the heroes of another writer,

viz., Leatherstocking, Uncas, Hardheart, Tom Coffin, are quite
the equals of Scott's men; perhaps Leatherstocking is better than
any one in 'Scott's lot.' *La Longue Carabine* is one of the great
prize men of fiction. He ranks with your Uncle Toby, Sir Roger
de Coverley, Falstaff—heroic figures all, American or British—
and the artist has deserved well of his country who devised
them." [35] He has indeed.

From the point of view of literature the drama itself is finally
assayed for character rather than action. This is true even of
Greek tragedy, where everything revolves about the action,
where the action is altogether the overwhelming *motif*. The
Greeks were nothing if not didactic, one may say, and the gospel
of art for art's sake would be understood no more on Parnassus
than on Olympus, would seem equally aloof from the vital interests of man to the audiences of Menander and to the pupils of
the Platonic Academy, where no one entered who was ignorant
of geometry, and where the basis of æsthetics was assumed to
be ethical and utilitarian. Even in a drama which—in the best of
taste, of course, and in the most serious artistic sense—preached,
as we may be sure "The Coëphori" preached to the trembling
Felixes [36] of its day, a drama of which the thesis is so tremendously concrete as to make the characters seem abstract, the
vigor of the presentation is due to the force with which the characters, however traditional, are conceived and portrayed. And the
same thing is true of romance. What gives the story vital rather
than transient interest is the personages to whom the events happen. It is the human nature in the "Arabian Nights," in the "De-
cameron," in "Gil Blas," that secures their perennial interest. Just
as this element in Balzac usually counteracts the effect of his occasional melodrama, and in Dumas often palliates his essential
levity, and in Hugo endues with grandeur what else would be
insipid. An example of romance deprived of this element is Stevenson's "Price Otto." Story, style, everything is there but character. The personages are the toys of the dilettante. "The Prisoner
of Zenda" [37] is a more considerable performance precisely because, inferior in other respects, its characters are felt and rendered with more energy. It is far less "literary," it is true, but so
far as it goes it is solider literature. What is it that gives such a
romance as "Ivanhoe" its value as literature—in other words, its

enduring interest? Not the tourney, the attack on Front de Bœuf's castle, the bout between Friar Tuck and the Black Knight, the archery exhibition of Locksley, but the character of Rebecca of York and the warfare between good and evil in the passionate soul of the Templar, as truly the protagonist of the book as Lucifer is of "Paradise Lost," or Hector—who has infinitely more *character* than Achilles—of the "Iliad." What would the ultraromantic "Rob Roy" be without Di Vernon and Rashleigh Osbaldistone? What would "Robinson Crusoe" be without the autobiographer's account of his interier experiences as well as his adventures? Could anything more insipid be imagined than the mere adventures of Don Quixote recounted by a Dumas or a Stevenson? Gautier's "Le Capitaine Fracasse" [38] is a delightful imaginative work, but the defect that has probably prevented its ever being reread is that its figures are feeble. On the other hand, the character interest of "Hamlet" or "Macbeth," for example, is so overwhelming as to obscure for most readers, probably, the splendidly romantic setting in which it is fixed. But the point is too obvious to dwell upon. The most inveterate lover of the story for the story's sake must admit that what makes literature of romance is the element that distinguishes its classic examples from the excellent stories of Horace Walpole and Mrs. Radcliffe—the element of character, namely. On any other theory that now forgotten masterpiece, "The Three Spaniards," [39] a veritable marvel of purely narrative romance, should still be in every one's hands.

Even in romance, therefore, what gives the story vital rather than transient interest is the personages to whom the events happen, and the function of the most romantic events is largely to elucidate the actors in them. A main excellence of romance as a literary form is that it elucidates a range of character with which only the imagination can adequately deal, traits and personalities which lie outside the realm of the novel of manners. Its environment has thus its own peculiar advantages, but when it exalts its environment at the expense of its figures it proportionately loses value as literature. What, accordingly, sets Cooper by the side of Scott is his instinct and practice in precisely this respect. He always has a story and always tells it well. Whatever its defects it moves, and it never lacks incident. No tedium of disquisition or digression, no awkwardness of construction, prevents it from being a series of events, a succession of pictures organically inter-related and tending cumulatively toward a climax. He accepted the story quite unconsciously as the essential condition of his pro-duction, and developed it not only loyally but enthusiastically with all the energy of remarkable powers of invention and an attentive conformity to what he conceived to be its general char-acter and import. This is why the young will always read him. He is, in fact, one of the great story-tellers of literature—so much so, indeed, that the narrative probably absorbed most of his con-scious effort in all his books. He thought of these, and often de-scribed them on his title-pages as "tales." In his day the narrative had not become "a slender thread." Things happened in it. Whether it followed the most commonplace traditions of the novel, and continued the practice of slipshod contradictions and inherent improbabilities, or whether it exhibited a nice sense of constructive propriety and singleness of effect (as in "Wing-and-Wing," or "The Deerslayer"), it was invariably his preoccupation.

But if his characters, on the other hand, show no particular care, it is because they are the direct products of his genius. They probably "came to him in his sleep." They are not "studied" from life or worked out from a central imaginative conception. They are thoroughly realistic and yet imaginatively typical simply be-cause Cooper had a remarkable instinct for character. He could read it and divine it in life, and when he came to create it and put it in situations of his own imagining he knew how it would act and what traits it would develop. For the time being he undoubt-edly lived with his creations as if they were actual people. His acquaintance with actual people was very large. He alludes in "The Two Admirals" to "the course of a chequered life in which we have been brought in collision with as great a diversity of rank, profession, and character, as often falls to the lot of any one individual," [40] and the multifarious variety of personages with which his novels are peopled proceeds from this circumstance—plus, of course, his genius in transmuting through his imagination his experience into his creation. And not only was his experience wide—both in his native pioneer civilization and in the more highly developed European world—but he was conspicuously endowed with the philosophic temperament. On what he saw he reflected. The individuals he met did not merely impress him with their peculiarities, they taught him human nature. He had the great advantage, associated with his deficiency of not being a writer from the first, of having been first a man. No writer of romance has been, as indisputably Cooper was, distinctly a publicist also. Scott's politics, for example, are negligible; Cooper's are rational, discriminating, and suggestive. He knew men as Lincoln knew them—which is to say, very differently from Dumas and Stevenson.

Consequently, the world of his creation is above all a solid one. Romantic as it is in form, its substance is of the reality secured by confining the form, the story, to its office of creating the illusion and not constituting the *primum mobile*. Slipshod as his story is now and then in disregarding probability and consistency so far as incident is concerned, the characters are never compromised by this carelessness, and where they are concerned he always checks his romance by the law of the situation, so to speak. *They* never share the occasional improbability or inconsistency of the events in which they participate, and the latter, accordingly, in any large sense, count no more than a self-correcting misprint. The consistency of Leatherstocking's character, for example, is hardly affected by his being represented as eighty years old on one page of "The Prairie" and eighty-odd on another. In "The Deerslayer" a single set of chessmen is provided with five castles. But such carelessness does not destroy the illusion of the story sufficiently to impair the integrity of the characters. These surely triumph over even a superfluity of chess castles, and like their congeners in all, or nearly all, the other books, establish the solidity of the world they inhabit by the definiteness, completeness, and comprehension with which they are portrayed.

No writer, not even the latest so-called psychological novelist, ever better understood the central and cardinal principle of enduing a character with life and reality—namely, the portrayal of its moral complexity. The equal in this vital respect of the New Hampshire man, Ithuel Bolt, in "Wing-and-Wing," hardly exists in Scott, and must be sought in Thackeray or George Eliot. An essay could be written on him as on a character of history. As a New England type, too, he is a masterpiece of great representative value. Having him end his days as a deacon of his especial denomination, after a lifetime of chicane and deceit, notably self-deception, was an inspiration, which must have been appreciated, even, or perhaps particularly, in New Hampshire itself. Spike in "Jack Tier" is a scoundrel, but he has, nevertheless, a side in virtue of which his wife clings to him—far otherwise explicably than Nancy to Bill Sikes,[41] for example. The struggle between good and evil impulses in the breast of the Red Rover is a truly heroic portrayal. The internal conflict that paralyzes the will of the "blue" admiral in "The Two Admirals" is treated with truly psychologic insight. To open any of the more important "tales" is to enter a company of personages in each of whom coexist—in virtue of the subtle law that constitutes character by unifying moral complexity—foibles, capacities, qualities, defects, weakness and strength, good and bad, and the inveterate heterogeneity of the human heart is fused into a single personality. And the variety, the multifariousness of the populous world that these personages, thus constituted, compose, is an analogue on a larger scale of their own individual differentiation. Cooper's world is a microcosm quite worthy to be set by the side of those of the great masters of fiction and, quite as effectively as theirs, mirroring a synthesis of the actual world to which it corresponds, based on a range of experience and framed with imaginative powers equalled by them alone.

VI

Cooper's women are generally believed, I suppose, especially to illustrate his limitations as a novelist of character. They are usually decried if not derided. His heroines are deemed the woodenest of conventional types, and their sisters the most mechanical of foils. Their creator's practice of referring to them as "females" is found amusing, for though it was a common enough practice of his day it has certainly become so obsolete as to seem singular to the reader of current books exclusively. Professor Lounsbury, who is the wittiest of writers, and in consequence a little at the mercy of a master faculty, has a good deal of fun with these "females" in his model biography. He pictures for them all "the same dreary and rather inane future," as members of Dorcas societies, as "carrying to the poor bundles of tracts and packages of tea," as haling ragged children into the Sunday-school and

making slippers for the rector. He says that "in fiction at least
one longs for a ruddier life than flows in the veins of these pale
bleached-out personifications of the proprieties," though "they
may possibly be far more agreeable to live with" than the "women
for whom men are willing or anxious to die." As regards not by
any means all but a certain class of Cooper's "females," one can
but "feel what he means." [42] Tastes differ, and in the quiet scho-
lastic closes of New Haven no doubt they like a little more ginger,
"in fiction at least," than palates more accustomed to it demand.
In the dustier and more driving world at large the simplicity and
sweetness of these natures may be considered to make in an
equivalent way the same appeal of novelty. However what "one
longs for, in fiction at least," is not the measure of a novelist's
success in character portraiture. To say that his characters are
conventional is, if they are, a just reproach. To say that they are
insipid is not. Professor Lounsbury may very explicably sigh for
"the stormier characters of fiction that"—as he conceives—"are
dear to the carnal-minded," and the carnal-minded may in turn
perversely delight in Arcadian innocence; but the business of the
novelist, and of the realistic romance writer such as Cooper, is to
"pander" to the desires of neither, but to "feel" his characters as
individuals,[43] whatever their nature, and to depict them with
personal zest and attention.

It would, of course, be idle to deny that some of Cooper's "females" are conventional, but I think they are far fewer than is
popularly imagined. Some, at all events, of those gentle and
placid beings that he was fond of creating are very real. It is possibly because they are measured by the standard provided by
more modern fiction rather than by actual life that they are found
conventional. They would appear truer according to this paradoxical standard if they were more exceptional. But the very definite forecast that Professor Lounsbury makes for them shows how
real they seem to him, after all. The reader, he says, "is as sure as
if their career had been actually unrolled before his eyes of the
part they will play in life." They are types of a kind of woman
probably far more persistent in life than in fiction and more persistent in life than is generally suspected at the present perhaps
transitional crisis in mankind's view of woman. In fiction we
have, for the moment at least, and except in such rare instances

as the fiction of Mr. Howells, lost sight of that side of the "female" in virtue of which she used to be called "the weaker vessel." The rise and education, the enormous increase and differentiation of the activities of woman at the present time, have in life also somewhat obscured this side of her nature. It is, however, too essential and integral a side to be more than temporarily forgotten, and it would not be surprising if, in the not remote future, some disquietude at woman's failure to take very significant advantage of her very signal opportunities should qualify the current conviction that her insignificance hitherto has been wholly due to her subjection. "Educate them as much as you please and give them all the privileges they want," observed an empirical philosopher once, "you will still have to take care of them." Woman herself would probably still agree that when pain and anguish wring *her* brow the male of her species is called upon to be a ministering angel of extremely energetic efficiency. Cooper's women certainly have to be taken care of, but this fact does not demonstrate them to be wooden and conventional, and is apparently not inconsistent with the nature of the *ewig Weibliches*,[44] however tame the resultant fiction, as fiction, may be found.

At any rate, these types existed in abundance in Cooper's day, and were not perfunctorily adopted by him from the characterless religious and other contemporary novel. It is in range rather than in quality that his portraiture of women is deficient. He portrayed the types he knew as realistically as he did his men, but his knowledge of women was not wide. He was eminently a man's man. The domestic affections probably taught him most of what he knew of woman, and of women in general he probably met comparatively few. And of these, of course, he "studied" none, that particular exercise of the literary artist's faculties being in his day but imperfectly developed. His clinging weaklings are as good as Scott's, I think. But he had nothing like Scott's social experience, and his women are less varied in consequence. Possibly, also, they are less varied because he had less ideality; for Scott was a poet and Cooper was not; though I think he shows a very charming ideality in his treatment of his women—not only is not one of them brutally limned, but there is a marked chivalry in his treatment of all of them. Moreover, in some of them there is a spiritual strength that qualifies their softness very nobly as well as very truly. There is scarcely in all Scott the equal in this respect of Ghita Caraccioli, in "Wing-and-Wing"—a tale which, aside from its adventurous interest and the admirable art that makes it exceptional among Cooper's works, is a particularly moving love story.

And the range of Cooper's female characters is far wider than is commonly appreciated or than is common in romance. Romance in general does not very insistently demand the feminine element—except, of course, the romance that demands nothing else—such as "Paul et Virginie." In the romance of adventure woman, almost of necessity, plays a subordinate part. She is almost inevitably reduced to the type, in order to count as a dramatic factor. The realism of Cooper's romance appears here as elsewhere. There are few of his women who are purely lay figures even among the insipid ones, as I have said, at least if we except the inferior novels—novels which, in Cooper's case, ought not to be considered at all; he wrote enough good ones to earn negligibility for such books as "Mercedes of Castile" and "The Ways of the Hour." Even such effaced characters as Alice Munro in "The Last of the Mohicans" are real enough. In almost every case, however insignificant and insipid they may be, they have the effect of being thoroughly alive—of having been felt and definitely visualized by their author. To this extent and in this way they bear, perhaps, even more striking witness to his master faculty, the faculty of creating character, than their more accentuated sisters.

But these latter are, for romance, as distinguished from the novel of character and manners pure and simple (which Cooper essayed, to be sure, but in which certainly his success was not notable), unusually numerous and varied. Compare the women of "Ivanhoe" and "Waverley," for example, with those of "The Last of the Mohicans" and "The Deerslayer." The background of the two former books has more dignity and importance than the woods of America in the middle of the eighteenth century could possibly provide. But the characters of the four American "females" and the contrast between the members of each couple of them are at least as firmly drawn, as vivid, and as effective; they do not so markedly function merely as antagonistic influences on the heart of the hero or the action of the tale. Cora

Munro, with her strain of negro blood appealing so strongly to both of her redskin admirers, her inevitably hopeless passion for Heyward and her truly tragic predestination, is an original and admirable creation. The two girls in "The Deerslayer" are masterpieces. Judith Hutter particularly is a character worthy of a place among the important figures of fiction. Her beauty, her worldliness, her exotic refinement, set off against the rude and vulgar background of her family environment and blending exquisitely with the wild beauty of her lacustrine surroundings, her sensibility to such simple elevation as she finds in the Deerslayer's character, the delicacy of her wooing of him and acquiescence in his rejection of her, and her final acceptance of her inevitable fate, compose a portrait with accessories rare in fiction of any kind and particularly rare in romance.

The feeble-minded Hetty, who serves superficially as her foil, is portrayed with equal attentiveness and great delicacy. There is something very gentle and attaching in the art with which Cooper, quite without the consciousness of doing anything unusual, and as simply as if it were the most natural thing in the world, achieves the difficult task of making convincing and interesting a character whose rectitude and fearlessness of nature enable her to play a rôle of pathetic dignity hardly hampered by a clouded mind. Here his touch, so heavy in generalization, in humor, and in broader portraiture often, is lightness itself. Some sympathetic strain in his nature endued him, too, with an analogous felicity in portraying such Ariel-like women as the masquerading mistresses of the Red Rover and the Skimmer of the Seas. These characters with him are the very converse of conventional, both in conception and in presentation, and they are at the same time perfectly embodied and realized with a definiteness and verisimilitude such as Scott in vain labored to impute to his tricksy Fenella in "Peveril of the Peak." They have the touch of fancy and the magic of strangeness, but they are understood as women in a way quite beyond the reach of a writer to whom the sex is the sealed book it is sometimes asserted to have been for Cooper.

Katharine Plowden in "The Pilot" is a breezy and even a brilliant girl. The heroine of "The Bravo" is extremely winning and pathetic. Mildred Dutton in "The Two Admirals" has as much dignity and resource as gentleness. The Wept of Wish-ton-Wish is a unique study, or at least sketch, of a white girl with an Indian soul. Maud Willoughby in "Wyandotte" is a charming beauty with a reserve of force such as Kingsley [45] might have conceived. And of Betty Flanagan in "The Spy" it is perhaps enough to record Miss Edgeworth's testimony in a letter to the author asserting that no Irish pen could have drawn her better. In fine, to my own sense, at least, Cooper drew well in the main such women as he drew. Of some of them he made memorable successes. That he drew no great variety of them and essentially duplicated his "females" now and then was very largely due to the limitedness of his experience, so generally confined to his acquaintance with his own sex save for a circle probably without much variety. The wide experience of people he speaks of in "The Two Admirals" in the passage I have already cited refers exclusively to men. Of course if he had been a sufficiently imaginative writer, if rather his imagination had not been less spiritual than romantic, he would have been less dependent on experience. But the romantic writer with a spiritual imagination is apt to be as insubstantial as he is rare, and in his portraits of women, as elsewhere, Cooper's romanticism is thoroughly realistic, and with whatever modification due to the sex of its subjects, thoroughly substantial and robust.

VII

There is one aspect of his contribution to literature that makes American neglect of Cooper's merits and his fame incomprehensible on any creditable grounds. That aspect is as varied as it is salient, but from its every facet is reflected *the rational aggrandizement of America*. Quite aside from the service to his country involved in the fact itself of his foreign literary popularity—greater than that of all other American authors combined—it is to be remarked that the patriotic is as prominent as any other element of his work. To him, to be sure, we owe it that immediately on his discovery, the European world set an American author among the classics of its own imaginative literature; through him to this world not only American native treasures of romance, but distinctively American traits, ideas and habits, moral, social, and political, were made known and familiar. He first painted for Europe the portrait of America. And the fact that it is in this likeness that the country is still so generally conceived there eloquently attests the power with which it was executed. The great changes that time has wrought in its lineaments have found no hand to depict them vigorously enough—at least in fiction—to secure the substitution of a later presentment for Cooper's. But in speaking of the patriotic element in his work, I refer only indirectly to its service in exalting American literature in European eyes and acquainting European minds with American character. Mainly I wish to signalize—what indirectly this proceeds from—the truth that in a large sense the subject of Cooper's entire work is America, nothing more, nothing less.

The substance of it, of course, is, materially speaking, preponderantly American. But what I mean is that even when he was writing such books as "The Bravo," "The Headsman," and "The Heidenmauer," he was distinctly thinking about his own country as well as his more immediate theme. In each of these novels the theme is really democracy. The fact has been made a reproach to him, and charged with the assumed "inartistic" intrusion of preachment into his romance. Doubtless a picture of Venice at the time when her sinister oligarchy was most despotic painted by a pure literary artist like Théophile Gautier, for example, might be spectacularly more "fetching." Cooper's, however, has the merit of being significant. One gets a little tired of the fetich of art, which is, nowadays, brought out of its shrine on so many occasions and venerated with such articulate inveteracy. Art in any other sense than that of a sound and agreeable way of doing things in accordance with their own law might sometimes, one impatiently reflects, be left to itself, to its practitioners, and to the metaphysicians. One may wish incidentally there were more of it! But to reproach such a work as "The Bravo" with a quality that secures its effectiveness is not at all credibly to assert that it would have been a masterpiece of pure beauty had it lacked this quality. As it is, it is an extremely good story made an extremely effective one by the fact that Cooper's democracy gave him a point of view from which the mockery styled the Republic of Venice appeared in a particularly striking light. These novels show at any rate how good a democrat Cooper was, how firmly grounded were his democratic principles, how sincere were his democratic convictions. They show him also as an American democrat—believing in law as well as liberty, that is to say—and not in the least a visionary. The preface alone of "The Headsman" demonstrates the intelligent enthusiasm with which he held his social and political creed. Europe, which nevertheless he thoroughly appreciated, did not disorient him. Nor on his return, whatever may superficially be inferred from his splenetic expressions of disgust with its defects, did his own country disillusionize him.

The undoubted aristocratic blend of his temperament and his traditions did not in the least conflict with his democracy, his Americanism. There is nothing *a priori* inconsistent in the holding of democratic convictions by the most aristocratic natures. The history of all religions, for example, is conclusive as to this; and from Pericles to the Gracchi, from Montaigne to Emerson, the phenomenon is common enough in politics and philosophy as well. Nor are Cooper's later American books *a posteriori* evidence of his defection. The excuses and perversions, the faults, and even the eccentricities of democracy, and the way in which these were illustrated by the democracy of his day, are certainly castigated—caricatured on occasion—with vigor, with zest, with temper, indeed. But the wounds are the faithful ones of a friend [46]—an extremely candid friend, of course—in a period of American evolution when candor of the kind was apt to be confounded with censure. His candor, however, was merely the measure of his discrimination. His censure is always delivered from a patriotic stand-point. The things, the traits, he satirizes and denounces are in his view the excrescences of democracy, and infuriate him as perversions, not as inherent evils. There is not the remotest trace of the snob in him. His often trivial and sometimes absurd excursions into the fields of etiquette and etymology, his rating of his countrymen for their minor crudities and fatuities, are the naive, and sometimes elephantine endeavors of a patriotic censor conscious of the value of elegance to precisely such a civilization as our own. We can see readily enough to-day that it is calumny to attribute his democracy in Europe to pure idealism, and his disgust with demagogy after his return to an irascibility that changed his convictions. The discriminating

American—Lowell, for a prominent example—is naturally an advocate of democracy abroad and a critic of it at home. And Cooper's temperament was not more irascible than his mind was judicial. There is, apparently, a native relation between irascibility and the judicial quality. Breadth of view, unless it is combined with the indifference of the dilettante, is naturally impatient of narrowness.

Defects of temper, at all events, which were conspicuous in Cooper, certainly coexisted with a fair-mindedness equally characteristic. Not a great, he was distinctly a large, man in all intellectual respects. Professor Trent in his "History of American Literature" [47] recurs to this central trait again and again, one is glad to note, in his exceptionally appreciative characterization. He was peppery, but not petulant, iracund without truculence. His quarrels with his encroaching Cooperstown neighbors, and with the unspeakable press of his day, undoubtedly lacked dignity, but in all cases he was in the right, and his outraged sense of justice was at the bottom of his violence. And his fair-mindedness so penetrated his patriotism as to render it notably intelligent, and therefore beneficent. In his day intelligent patriotism was not thorough-going enough to be popular. Partisanship was exacted. The detachment which Cooper owed to his experience and judicial-mindedness was simply not understood. It seemed necessarily inconsistent with patriotic feeling. Such scepticism is, in fact, not unknown in our own time! But in Cooper's, appreciation of foreign, and criticism of native, traits was in itself almost universally suspect. Yet such candor as his in noting excellence in men and things of other nations and civilizations is even nowadays rarely to be encountered. France, Italy, England, the Irish, Swiss, Germans—every nationality, in fact, that figures in his pages—are depicted with absolute sympathy and lack of prejudice. In "Jack Tier," written during the Mexican War, the Mexican character at its best is incarnated in the most polished and high-minded, the most refined and least vulgar of personalities. In the matter of national traits it is still more or less true that, as Stendhal observed, *"la différence fait la haine"*; [48] but to no writer of the English tongue at all events, even since his time, could the reproach be addressed with less reason than to Cooper. "Wing-and-Wing" is a text-book of true cosmopolitanism, and "Wyandotte" a lesson in non-partisanship at home.

No doubt it is only logical to be cosmopolitan and liberal when one is lecturing one's countrymen on their narrowness and provinciality. But the disposition to lecture them on this particular theme itself witnesses Cooper's genuine fair-mindedness and his desire to communicate it to his readers. Moreover, the quality appears in his writings quite as often instinctively as expressly; it pervades their purely artistic as well as their didactic portions. And there are two manifestations of it that are particularly piquant and certainly to be reckoned among Cooper's patriotic services. One is his treatment of New England, and the other that of the Protestant "sects" as distinguished from the Episcopal "Church."

Upon the New England of his day Cooper turned the vision of a writer who was also a man of the world—a product of civilization at that time extremely rare within its borders. He was himself an eminent example of what used to be called in somewhat esoteric eulogy by those who admired the type, a conservative, and New England was the paradise of the radical, the visionary, the doctrinaire. He had no disposition, accordingly, to view it with a friendly eye or to pass by any of its imperfections. The narrowness, the fanaticism, the absurd self-sufficiency and shallowness, the contempt for the rest of the country, the defects of the great New England qualities of thrift and self-reliance characteristic of the section, were particularly salient to him, and to signalize them was irresistible to an emancipated observer who could contemplate them from a detached standpoint. It would be idle to pretend that he interpreted New England types with the intimate appreciation of Hawthorne. On the other hand, his detachment being more complete, his portrayal of them often gives them the relief which can only be brought out by the colorless white light of cold impartiality. Occasionally, without doubt, he satirizes rather than depicts them—though more rarely than his heavy touch leads the reader to imagine. But from "Wing-and-Wing" to "Satanstoe" the New England contingent of his company of characters is portrayed with a searching and self-justifying veracity, at least as to its essential features; and, as was his habit, discriminatingly portrayed. Ithuel

Bolt is certainly one of the notable characters of fiction, and yet he could no more have been born and developed outside of New England than Leatherstocking could have hailed from Massachusetts. If the Rev. Meek Wolfe in "The Wept of Wishton-Wish" is a caricature, he is fully offset by the fine portrait of the Puritan head of the household.

It is difficult now to recall the New England of Cooper's day. Never, perhaps, in the world's history was so much and so widespread mental activity so intimately associated with such extreme provinciality. For a miniature portrait of it consult the first pages of Lowell's essay on Thoreau. At present we need to have the eminence of the section recalled to us. Professor Barrett Wendell's engaging "Literary History," [49] in which he not only limits American literature of much value to New England, but even tucks it into the confines of Harvard College, is an interesting reminder of days that seem curiously distant. Between 1825 and 1850, at all events, New England, always the apex, had become also the incubus of our civilization, and called loudly for the note-taking of a chiel [50] from beyond its borders. Cooper performed that service. And, as I say, it is to be counted to him for patriotism. To him we owe it that not only American authorship but American literature has been from his day of national rather than sectional character. The world he represented to the Europe of his day was a comprehensively American world, and the country as a whole, with the theretofore false proportion of its different sections duly rectified, first appeared in effective presentation in the domain of art.

His analogous hostility to ecclesiastical sectarianism was, perhaps, a corollary of his view of the New England whence largely this sectarianism came. English non-conformity transplanted added to its own defects those inseparable from an establishment, which practically it enjoyed. Its contentiousness became tyrannous, and its virtual establishment, destitute of traditions, served mainly to crystallize its crudities. Cooper's episcopalianism was in a doctrinal sense, no doubt, equally narrow. And his piety was strongly tinctured with dogma. Some of his polemic is absurd, and when he is absurd he is so to a degree only accounted for by his absolute indifference to appearing ridiculous. "The Crater" is an extraordinary exhibition of denominational fatuity. But in his day his churchmanship gave him in religious matters the same advantage of detachment that his treatment of New England enjoyed. It gave him a standard of taste, of measure, of decorum, of deference to tradition and custom, and made him a useful and unsparing critic of the rawness and irresponsibility so rife around him, in a field of considerably more important mundane concern to the community of that time than —owing largely to its own transformation—it has since become. He knew the difference in the ecclesiastical field, as few in his day did, between "a reading from Milton and a reading from Eliza Cook." [51] The intellectual mediocrity of the Episcopal pulpit did not blind him, as it did others, to "the Church's" distinctive superiorities, secular and religious. A ritual, a clergy (however triturate as a hierarchy), a sense of historic continuity, the possession of traditions, the spirit of conformity in lieu of self-assertion (a spirit so necessary to "the *communion* of saints"), set off the "Churchmen" of that day somewhat sharply from the immensely larger part of their respective societies. And Cooper's criticism of the more unlovely traits of the descendants of the Puritans and the Scotch-Irish immigration on the whole made for an ideal which, socially considered, must be regarded as superior to that he found defective. His "conservative" spirit, in a word, enabled him to perform a genuine and patriotic service to our civilization in this respect, as it did in the case of its portrayal of New England types of character. And as in the latter case he is not to be charged with a provinciality equivalent to that which he exposed, but really judges it from an open-minded and cosmopolitan stand-point, so, too—though naturally in a distinctly lesser degree, in consequence of his own ecclesiastical and theological rigidities—he exhibits the defectiveness of American non-conformity from a distinctly higher plane than its own. The proof of this and of his large tolerance in religious matters— where his controversial spirit is not aroused—is the fact that Catholicism and Catholics always receive just and appreciative treatment at his hands. Even atheism itself he treats with perfect and comprehending appreciation. In this respect the scene in "Wing-and-Wing" where Raoul Yvard is about to be executed as a spy forms a striking contrast to the somewhat analogous one in "Quentin Durward," where Scott uses the death of the unbelieving Hayraddin Mograbin to point a series of perfunctory commonplaces.

I come back in conclusion to Professor Trent's epithet. Cooper's was above all a *large* nature. Even his littlenesses were those of a large nature. Let us refine and scrutinize, hesitate and distinguish, when we have corresponding material to consider. But in considering Cooper's massive and opulent work it is inexcusable to obscure one's vision of the forest by a study of the trees. His work is in no sense a *jardin des plantes;* it is like the woods and sea that mainly form its subject and substance. Only critical myopia can be blind to the magnificent forest, with its pioneer clearings, its fringe of "settlements," its wood-embosomed lakes, its neighboring prairie on the one side, and on the other the distant ocean with the cities of its farther shore—the splendid panorama of man, of nature, and of human life unrolled for us by this large intelligence and noble imagination, this manly and patriotic American representative in the literary parliament of the world.

HAWTHORNE

HAWTHORNE

I

Hawthorne was so exceptional a writer that he has very generally been esteemed a great one. In America such an estimate has been almost universal. He won his way slowly, but his first solid achievement met with ready appreciation and thenceforward fame awaited his subsequent, and retroactively rewarded his earlier, performances. We stood in much need of great writers at the time; and, though our literary pantheon is now more populous, it would occur to no one, probably, to displace his figure from the niche where it was speedily installed, and where even a lesser one would have been welcome. His works never having been supplanted among us, it is hardly surprising that with us they stand where they did. Comparisons are in their favor. They are thoroughly original, quite without literary derivation upon which much of our literature leans with such deferential complacence. Even the theme of many of them —the romance of Puritan New England—was Hawthorne's discovery. They are works of pure literature and therefore in a field where competition is not numerous. They altogether eschew the ordinary, the literal, and they have the element of spiritual distinction, which still further narrows their eminence and gives them still greater relief. Withal they are extremely characteristic, extremely personal. They represent, one and all, their author and no one but their author, whom, therefore, they have the effect of making a very precise, a very definite figure. He was himself a very definite, even a unique, figure and one that harmonized obviously—or to employ the prevailing tone of Hawthorne criticism, exquisitely and beautifully—with their exceptional quality. He unquestionably dwelt apart, and partly, perhaps, for this reason his soul was generally believed to be like a star. At the same time there is nothing eccentric, no excess, in his genius to disintegrate his enduring reputation with the alloy

45

of the transient and the meretricious. His writings satisfy academic standards and appeal to the conservatism of culture. And their style, clear, chaste, and correct, is of the preservative order. They form a large constituent portion of our classics—our somewhat slender sheaf of truly classic production. As such they are read—more precisely, have been read—by everybody. Up to the present time at least they have been universally part of the "required reading," so to speak, of youth and the recollection of eld—a recollection always roseate if afforded half a chance, and in Hawthorne's case, one suspects, enjoying practical immunity from the readjustments and rectification of later re-reading.

On the whole, Hawthorne and his country are quits. If he enriched its literary treasure and contributed generously to its literary glory, as incontestably he did, it furnished him with both a comparatively clear field for the exercise, and a comparatively undistracting background for the exhibition, of his genius. In no literature would his works have been unobserved or even obscured by competition. But, as contributions to American literature they have abroad undoubtedly achieved success by an ampler margin, and have at home been awarded an importance commensurate with their originality. Hitherto, at all events, among ourselves their lack of substance has been deemed a quality instead of a defect and, indeed, their "airy and charming insubstantiality" their chief title to fame. We have had so few poets! The temptation has been great to eke out the roll with Hawthorne, and, sometimes, not to mince matters, to call him the greatest of them all. "The rarest creative imagination of the century, the rarest in some ideal respects since Shakespeare,"[1] says Lowell in his hearty wholesale way. We shall see as time passes. But one thing is certain. If Hawthorne's importance is to remain at its present evaluation it will not be because of his "insubstantiality." It will be, as it is in the case of every writer who makes no sensuous appeal, because of the amount and quality of significant truth effectively expressed in his writings.

II

This was not quite his own view, it may be said. And what his own view was he made perfectly plain. Though not an expansive,

Hawthorne's was a perfectly candid nature. A recluse in life, he overflows to the reader. He does not tell very much, but apparently he tells everything. His confidences are not ample. Nothing is ample in his writings but the plethora of detail and the fulness of fancies. But he has no reticences. If he communicates little, he has nothing to conceal. He discourses of his stories, of their particular *genre*, with admirable good sense and is very far from overvaluing them; of the kind of man he is, without coquetry or other self-consciousness. He is, however, passably complacent, at least in the sense that resignation is complacent. He is never dissatisfied. He does not strive or cry, or emulate or regret. He would gladly be more popular if he could, but, like Luther, he can do no other. Not that he blames the public in the least. He "rather wonders how the 'Twice-Told Tales' should have gained what vogue they did than that it was so little and so gradual." [2] He is a little perverse about his talent at times. He half wishes it were not so gloomy, but feels that it is irremediable, that he is under the spell of a rather mournful and melancholy inspiration. He finds his things lack sunlight, that they in a sort turn out that way without his cooperation. One of the most naïve performances in literature is due to this feeling. He writes an altogether inapt introduction to his one masterpiece to relieve and lighten its dark tone—in which it wholly fails, since it has nothing to do with the story, and in which, if successful, it would have been calamitous. But at heart he is altogether reconciled to his moonlight shadows and low tones. It is only in the interest of the public that he laments them. He looks upon "The Scarlet Letter" as a "volume," not as a production. It needs piecing out, being scant, being in short a longer "Twice-Told Tale." Hence the "Custom House" prologue —a graceful, pleasant, not very genial essay which used to be thought a marvel quite eclipsing "Elia," [3] and which he designs to secure the balance as well as increase the bulk of a story otherwise slight and sombre considered as a volume. He paid off some old scores in the process. Otherwise, it is doubtful if he would have had the zest to make the requisite effort. He could not be made to take any of it back. He was as implacable as he was upright, and as unyielding as he was straightforward. He made very little effort of any kind. His industry was measurably constant, but rather of the routine order. He wrote his fiction much as he wrote his interminable note-books, without exaltation, without heat, without noteworthy struggle. He took great pains but with great placidity. It is significant that the only exception is the writing of his only *chef-d'œuvre*. When he wrote "The Scarlet Letter" he shut himself up and wrestled continuously with the angel of his inspiration till he had conquered. Whereupon, somewhat relieved, no doubt, he resumed his habitual serenity and comfortably relaxed into the more congenial function of characterizing the types and curios of his custom-house experience. Tension was as foreign to him as expansion. In the prologue he seems to have returned from an excursion into the realm of energy and effort, of artistic endeavor, and to have settled down once more in the region of old manses and twice-told tales where he was completely, even radiantly, domesticated.

It is in a sense tragic that he should have had so little vocation. Emerson makes the same complaint of Thoreau—content, he deplores, to be the captain of a huckleberry party.[4] All one can say is that with more vocation Hawthorne would not have been Hawthorne, who is as indisputably the author of his other works as of "The Scarlet Letter." The preface to the "Twice-Told Tales," in which and in the "Mosses from an Old Manse" he felt his way to his larger fiction, is, in the main, an admirable piece of self-characterization, much of it as applicable to his entire work as to these unpretending stories. It contains three especially significant sentences. "The sketches are not," he says, "it is hardly necessary to say, profound, but it is rather more remarkable that they so seldom, if ever, show any design on the writer's part to make them so." Again, they "are not the talk of a secluded man with his own mind and heart (had it been so they could hardly have failed to be more deeply and permanently valuable), but his attempts, and very imperfectly successful ones, to open an intercourse with the world." And, finally, in words that go to the root of the matter: "Whether from lack of power, or an unconquerable reserve, the Author's touches have often an effect of tameness."[5]

Now it is evident that intercourse with the world is not opened on these terms. The world assumes that the recluse issuing from his seclusion should bring with him his warrant for dwelling in it, should communicate the result of communing with his own mind and heart. If this result is not profound or deeply and permanently valuable, it is asking too much of the heedless world to ask it to accept unconquerable reserve as the reason. The world is bound to esteem this the best you can do and refuses to ascribe its lack of profundity merely to the—truly remarkable, as you say—absence of any design on your part to make it more worth while. It may, of course, be said that a recluse is as much entitled to claim attention for trifles as any one else. Only, in that case his status of recluse is immaterial. And, plainly, Hawthorne was not at all disposed to consider it immaterial. He thought it, as others have done, the most material fact about both him and his work, as is plain from his calling his reserve "unconquerable." So that it is impossible to share his uncertainty as to whether the tameness of his touches proceeds from this reserve or from lack of power. The answer clearly is: both. And to go a step further, and as I say to the root of the matter, his unconquerable reserve proceeds in all probability from his lack of power—at least of anything like sustained, unintermittent power that can be relied upon and evoked at will by its possessor.

Power at all events is precisely the element most conspicuously lacking in the normal working of this imagination which to Lowell recalls Shakespeare's. Repeatedly he seems to be on the point of exhibiting power, of moving us, that is to say; but, except, I think, in "The Scarlet Letter," he never quite does so. His unconquerable reserve steps in and turns him aside. He never crosses the line, never makes the attempt. He is too fastidious to attempt vigor and fail. His intellectual sensitiveness, to which failure in such an endeavor would be acutely palpable, prevents the essay. In the instance of "The Scarlet Letter," where he does achieve it, he does so as it were in spite of himself, and it is curious that he instinctively re-establishes his normal equilibrium by failing to appreciate his achievement. At least he prefers to it his "House of the Seven Gables." He is much more at home in amusing himself than in creating something. "I have sometimes," he says, "produced a singular and not unpleasing effect, so far as my own mind was concerned, by imagining a train of incidents in which the spirit and mechanism of the fairy legend should be combined with the characters and manners of familiar life." [6] He was content if his effect was pleasing so far as his own mind was concerned. And his own mind was easily pleased with the kind of process he describes. That is, he follows his temperamental bent with tranquil docility instead of compelling it to serve him in the construction of some fabric of importance. The latter business demands energy and effort. And if he made so little effort it is undoubtedly because he had so little energy. His genius was a reflective one. He loved to muse. Reverie was a state of mind which he both indulged and applauded, and there can hardly be a more barren one for the production of anything more significant than conceits and fancies. Reality repelled him. What attracted him was mirage. Mirage is his specific aim, the explicit goal of his art—which thus becomes inevitably rather artistry than art. His practice is sustained by his theory. Speaking of a scene mirrored in a river he exclaims, "Which, after all, was the most real—the picture or the original? —the objects palpable to our grosser senses, or their apotheosis in the stream beneath? Surely the disembodied images stand in closer relation to the soul." [7] If this were a figure expressive of the mirroring of nature by art it would be a happy one, though not convincing to those who believe that the artistic synthesis of nature should be more rather than less definite than its material. But it is not a figure. It is a statement of Hawthorne's preference for the vague and the undefined in nature itself as nearer to the soul. Nearer to the soul of the poet it may be, not to that of the artist. The most idealizing artist can count on enough vagueness of his own—whether it handicap his effort or illumine his result in dealing with his material. And it is not near to the soul of the poet endowed with the architectonic faculty—the poet in the Greek sense, the maker. It is the congenial content of contemplation indeterminate and undirected.

The contemplative mind, the contemplative mood, are above all hospitable to fancy, and in fancy Hawthorne's mind and mood were wonderfully rich. He had but to follow its beckoning and intrust himself to its guidance to make a pretty satisfactory journey, at least so far as his own mind was concerned. He speaks, to be sure, of "setting fancy resolutely to work," [8] but I think he must have referred to continued rather than to arduous labor. A certain degree of indolence must have been allied with his indifference, as the beginnings of his career, somewhat hesitant and tentative, indicate. Once started, however, most of the undertakings that mark it must have proceeded with the same absence of friction as his career itself. Those occasions on which his fancy may be said to have worked resolutely are probably those in which it functioned regularly and in somewhat routine fashion, as, for example, those "compositions," as they may be called in quite the school-boy sense, in which he seemed to give himself a theme and proceed to set down all he could "think up" about it—"Sights from a Steeple," "A Rill from the Town Pump," "Little Annie's Ramble," and a number of similar sketches consonant with the "in lighter vein" text of school "readers," and very popular in their day. In general, one imagines he did not have to set fancy resolutely to work, but merely to give it free play. The result was amazingly productive. How many "Mosses" and "Twice-Told Tales" are there? Certainly a prodigious number when one considers the narrowness of their range and their extraordinary variety within it. Their quality is singularly even, I think. Some of them—a few—are better than others, but mainly in more successfully illustrating their common quality. What this is Hawthorne himself sufficiently indicates in saying, "Instead of passion there is sentiment; and even in what purport to be pictures of actual life we have allegory." [9] But his consciousness of his limitations does not exorcise them, though his candor, which is charming, wins our appreciation for their corresponding excellences.

Or, rather, no. It is so absolute as to make us feel a little ungracious at our inability to take quite his view after all. After all, it is plain that he has a paternal feeling for them that it is a little difficult to share. Sentiment replaces passion, it is true. But the sentiment is pale for sentiment. It is sentiment insufficiently *senti*. Allegory, it is true, replaces reality, but the allegory itself is insufficiently real. The tales are not merely in a less effective, less robust, less substantial category than that which includes passion and actual life, but within their own category they are— most of them—unaccented and inconclusive. They are too faint in color and too frail in construction quite to merit the inference of Hawthorne's pretty deprecation. They have not "the pale tint of flowers that blossomed in too retired a shade." They are hardly flowers at all, but grasses and ferns. And while he exaggerates in saying that "if opened in the sunshine" they are "apt to look exceedingly like a volume of blank pages," he is distinctly optimistic in thinking that they would gain greatly by being read "in the clear, brown, twilight atmosphere" in which they were written, and that they cannot always "be taken into the reader's mind without a shiver." [10] They can—always. There is not a shiver in them. Their tone is lukewarm and their temper Laodicean. Witchery is precisely the quality they suggest but do not possess. Their atmosphere is not that of the clear brown twilight in which familiar objects are poetized, but that of the gray day in which they acquire monotone. The twilight and moonlight, so often figuratively ascribed to Hawthorne's genius, are in fact a superstition. There is nothing eerie or elfin about his genius. He is too much the master of it and directs it with a too voluntary control. Fertile as it is, its multifarious conceits and caprices are harnessed and handled with the light, firm hand of perfect precision and guided along a level course of extremely unbroken country. There is no greater sanity to be met with in literature than Hawthorne's. The wholesome constitution of his mind is inveterate and presides with unintermittent constancy in his prose. Now caprice, conducted by reason, infallibly incurs the peril of insipidity, and it is not to be denied that many of the tales settle comfortably into the category of the prosaic.

Why, then, have they their reputation, and why does one feel a little awkward and unsympathetic in confessing that he finds them dull? In the first place the fondness of the public for them has been, in strict history, an acquired taste. They met with very little favor at first. The genial Longfellow praised them to deaf ears.[11] After the appearance of "The Scarlet Letter" readers turned back to them in appreciative disposition and, as is usually the case under such circumstances, found or fancied in them what they looked for. But mainly they won and have kept their classic position, it is not to be doubted, because of their originality, their refinement, and their elevation. There is certainly nothing else like them; their taste is perfect; and, in general, they deal with some phase of the soul, some aspect or quality or transaction of the spiritual life. They are the echoes of no literary precedent, but as much Hawthorne's own as his physiognomy.

They exhibit a literary fastidiousness not so much free from as absolutely dead to the manifold seductions of the meretricious, a literary breeding so admirable as to seem unconscious of the existence of vulgar expedients. And their informing purpose lies quite outside the material world and its sublunary phenomena. No small portion of their originality consists, indeed, in the association of their refinement and elevation with what we can now see is their mediocrity. Elsewhere in the world of fiction mediocrity is associated with anything but fineness of fibre and spirituality. The novelty of the combination in Hawthorne's case was disconcerting, and it is small wonder that for a time at least —for a generation, no doubt, so gradual is the readjustment of popular esteem of the unpopular—the importance of the "Twice-Told Tales" and the "Mosses" was argued from their distinction. Finally, some of them—too few assuredly—are good stories.

III

The rest are sterilized by the evil eye of Allegory under whose baleful spell for some reason or other he early fell. Neither the culture nor the criticism of his environment, from which besides he had as much as possible separated himself, was sufficient to rectify the individual whim by the general consensus; and in any case conformity to aught but his own traditions, which were conventional enough essentially, was as foreign to him as was the eccentricity that surrounded him. Having elected the service of this insipid sprite, there was no influence to turn him from it, and he persisted with the overweening obstinacy of the invincibly modest. Probably his ancestral strain had much to do with this addiction. It was, perhaps, a compromise on his part between his imagination and his inheritance. His imagination impelled him to the production of fiction, his Puritanism restrained his fiction within the confines of the didactic. At any rate, he took his bent, his *pli*, at the outset and rejoiced calmly and temperately in the practice of this hybrid and artificial *genre*. It is not to be denied that he had an aptitude for it. But his aptitude is less than his affection, and his devotion has something exasperating about it—the exasperation always aroused by the consecration of high powers to comparatively trivial ends.

Allegory justifies itself when the fiction is the fact and the moral the induction. "Gulliver" and "The Pilgrim's Progress," for example. Bunyan's imagination created a world of types so vividly presented as to have the force of individuals, provided them with adventures as animating as the incidents of romance, and enforced his moral by giving an independent and ideal verisimilitude to its innocent and unconscious exponents. "The Pilgrim's Progress" is undoubtedly a tract, but if it had been only a tract it would never have achieved universal canonization. It is the splendid panoramic construction of a great imagination inspired by the experience of the soul in the struggle with sin. It is, in a word, a work of art in itself, leaning lightly—though, of course, to all the more purpose—on its moral, as lightly as a dream on its interpretation or a vision on the conscious concentration of the seer. Most persons probably read "Gulliver" for the story and miss the satire. The "Divine Comedy" and "Don Quixote" and "Paradise Lost" are allegories; Æsop's "Fables," even "Plutarch's Lives," are allegories; history, conceived as philosophy teaching by example, is an allegory. So, in a sense, is all art. But allegory is art only when its representation is as imaginatively real as its meaning. The mass of allegory—allegory strictly devoted to exposition and dependent upon exegesis, allegory explicitly so called—is only incidentally art at all.

Hawthorne's is of this order. His subject is always something other than its substance. Everything means something else. Dealing with the outer world solely for the sake of the inner, he is careless of its character and often loses its significance in mere suggestiveness. His meaning is the burden of his story, not the automatic moral complement of its vivid and actual reality. Hence the sense of reality is absent from it, and for this nothing will atone in any form of art where the sense of unreality is not sought instead. It is rather singular that this latter effect is one he never sought. He never entered fairy-land—except to retell its classic tales in his manuals, "The Wonder Book" and "Tanglewood Tales," which have only a juvenile appeal and where he was not at his happiest, I think, though the volumes have his usual distinction and, measured by the "journeyman-work" standard, have unquestionably titular rank. His occasional effort for a slightly triturate effect of reality is witnessed in the introduction to "The Threefold Destiny," in which he says: "Rather than a story of events claiming to be real, it may be considered as an allegory, such as the writers of the last century would have expressed in the shape of an Eastern tale, but to which I have endeavored to give a more life-like warmth than could be infused into those fanciful productions." [12] The endeavor can hardly be called fatuous considering the comparisons it emulates, but the result, though more concrete than usual with him, is as usual less life-like in its warmth than ingenious in its illustration of its moral theme. In general, however, his disposition is disclosed by such a sentence as this in the "Sketches from Memory": "On this theme"—namely "the vain search for an unearthly treasure"— "methinks I could frame a tale with a deep moral." [13] He did frame such a tale—"The Great Carbuncle"—whose moral is doubtless deep to those to whom all morals are so, and of which, at any rate, in accordance with his practice the moral, not the tale, is the thing.

His faculty of discovering morals on which tales could be framed is prodigious. It rises to the distinction of a special capacity of the mind, like the gift for languages or a genius for chess. It is, as one may say, a by-product of the Puritan pre-occupation. He did not find sermons in stones.[14] He had the sermons already; his task was to find the stones to fit them. And these his fancy furnished him with a fertility paralleling his use for them. But his interest in shaping these was concentrated on their illustrative and not on their real qualities. Instead of realizing vividly and presenting concretely the elements of his allegory, he contented himself with their plausibility as symbols. On this he always insisted and to compass it he expended much ingenuity. His fancy was of the kind that never completely loses its hold of the actual. His literary taste was too serious to content itself with pure mystification. The insubstantiality he sought was to consist in the envelope, not in the object. He desired to dissemble, not to abjure reality. But the sense of reality even as a substructure for fancifulness is not to be obtained merely by the ingenuity which finds a possible scientific basis for what performs its sole service as apparently imaginary.

To take a crude instance of this oftenest subtle practice: "Egotism, or the Bosom Serpent" is not, artistically speaking,

made more real by the foot-note that explains the actual occurrence of the physical fact in several cases. The story *as a
story* stands or falls by the reality with which the man with the
snake in his bosom is presented. In the course of this presentation
the victim exclaims, "It gnaws me! It gnaws me." "And then," the
narrator says, "there was an audible hiss, but whether it came
from the apparent lunatic's own lips, or was the real hiss of a
serpent, might admit of discussion." [15] We are, of course, spared
the discussion, which might easily fail to interest us, but the
point is that the suggestion of it is precisely one of those touches
which diminish the sense of reality in the presentation, and of
which Hawthorne is so inordinately fond. Here it is of small
comparative importance. The same thing is even charming, I
think, in the author's speculation about Donatello's possibly
pointed ears in "The Marble Faun," though I think also that he
greatly overworks the faun-like resemblance, which apparently
he cannot convince himself he has made sufficiently clear, and
follows to ridiculous lengths in Donatello's skippings and capri-
olings, as well as in his conformation and character. But oftenest
his intrusion of symbolism, that parasite on allegory itself, is
a crying abuse of a perfectly superficial and trivial expedient.
He was, in fact, allegory-mad. Allegory was his obsession. Consequently, he not only fails to handle the form in the minimizing
manner of the masters, but often fails in effectiveness on the
lower plane where the moral occupies the foreground. "The
Birthmark" is an instance. Nothing could be finer than the moral
of this tale, which inculcates the fatal error of insisting on absolute perfection in what one loves most absolutely. But it is
a moral even more obscurely brought out than it is fantastically
symbolized. In the same way, the moral of "Rappacini's Daugh-
ter," distinctly the richest and warmest of Hawthorne's productions, is still less effectively enforced. It is quite lost sight of in
the development of the narrative, which is given an importance
altogether disproportionate to the moral, and which yet is altogether dependent upon the moral for significance—sustained
as it is, and attractive, as it might have been, had it been taken
as a fairy tale frankly from the first.

In consequence, too, of this obsession by allegory, the tales
in which he leaves it alone altogether or at all events does not

lean upon it, are the best, I think. His excellent faculty is released
for freer play in such tales as "The Gentle Boy," in which if he is
less original, he is more human, and takes his place and holds his
own in the lists of literature—instead of standing apart in the
brown twilight and indulging his fancy in framing insubstantial
fictions for the illustration of moral truths, not always of much
moment. But the tendency grew upon him and developed into
a fondness for almost pure symbolism, symbolism in which
paradoxically the allegorizing element itself becomes attenuated
and no truths at all are illustrated—the result being simply one
thing told in terms of another. In 1858—that is, at the age of
fifty-four—this is what attracts his mature powers and ripened
mind, as recorded in the "Italian Note-Books": Apropos of a
newspaper paragraph respecting a ring worn by a widower and
containing a stone into which his wife's body had been "chem-
ically resolved," he says, "I think I could make a story on this
idea," and proceeds to sketch it. "The ring should be one of the
widower's bridal gifts to a second wife; and, of course, it should
have wondrous and terrible qualities, symbolizing all that dis-
turbs the quiet of a second marriage," and so on, in enumeration
of this disturbing detail. The "story" [16] could hardly have been
remarkable, but, assuming that it had to be built on the "idea,"
it would clearly be better for the story, once built, to take the
"idea" out of it afterward. A great deal of Hawthorne would be
the better for the extraction of the allegorical and symbolic elements combined with it and constituting in its author's view its
raison d'être. Very certainly it would be if upon the rest he had
seriously exercised his imagination, instead of so completely sur-
rendering to his fancy, content to depreciate complete irresponsibility by the counterpoise of his disillusioning good sense—
which was remarkable, but the intrusion of which leaves his
story often still more "in the air."

IV

For the real misfortune of Hawthorne—and ours—was the
misconception of his talent, resulting in this cultivation of his
fancy to the neglect of his imagination. Issuing from the curious
by-paths of literature into which this led him—a seclusion that

quite matched the seclusion of his life—and engaging in the general literary competition on the immemorial terms for the exercise of the imagination, it is not to be doubted that he would have produced works far otherwise important than those which in the main he wrote. "The Scarlet Letter" is there to prove it. His imagination was a puissant one—or "beautiful and light," as Mr. James says: the distinction is not important analytically, since in the case of the imagination power is a prerequisite to its beautiful and light as well as to its robust exercise, just as force is essential to the most sensitive precision; it is the effects that are beautiful and light, not their agent. And such effects—which I should, rather, incline to call inconclusive and faint—Hawthorne produced, by following the line of least resistance, not by effort and concentration. Instead of giving a tale more substance he wrote another equally slight. And he neglected his imagination because he shrank from reality. Now, reality is precisely the province, the only province, the only concern, the only material of this noblest of faculties. It is, of course, as varied as the universe of which it is composed. There is the reality of "Tom Jones" and the reality of "Lear," for example; the reality of the ideal, indeed, as well as that of the phenomenal—its opposite being not the ideal but the fanciful. And Hawthorne coquetted and sported with it and made mirage of it. Instead of accepting it as the field of his imagination he made it the playground of his fancy.

Imagination and fancy differ, according to the old metaphysic, in that, both transcending experience, one observes and the other transgresses law. Every one thus discriminates, at all events, between the imaginative and the fanciful. No writer ever had a deeper sense, or at least a firmer conviction, of the august immutability of law—those ordaining principles of the universe unbegotten by the race of mortal men and forever immune from the sleep of oblivion itself—to paraphrase the classic panegyric. His frequent theme—the soul and the conscience—absolutely implies the recognition of law and involves its acceptance. And philosophically his conception of his theme fundamentally, even fatalistically, insists on it. Three of the four novels embody its predetermination. But too often in his treatment of his theme its basis crumbles. The centre of gravity too often falls outside of it—falls outside of law as well as of experience—because reality impresses and appeals to him so little, because his necessity for dissolving it into the insubstantial is so imperative, that the theme itself is frittered away in the course of its exposition. The law, the moral truth, which is the point of departure, or, as I say, the foundation of his more serious work, is not only not enforced but positively enervated. At every turn the characters and events might, one feels, evade its constraint, so wholly does the unreal and the fantastic predominate in both their constitution and their evolution. Beings so insubstantial and transactions so fantastic (one or both elements are generally present) can but fitfully and feebly illustrate anything so solid and stable as the moral principles upon which the real universe is conducted.

On the other hand, as I have already noted, when his theme is purely fanciful it frequently does not receive a frankly fantastic treatment. He seems to shrink from anything so inelastic as the careful preservation of its proper character and is, in a word, so enamored of mirage that he even seems bent on blurring his illusion, and if it seems to be acquiring a consistency of its own introduces some element of reality for its resolution. This practice, to be sure, has small comparative importance, save as illustrating the inveteracy of his bias. It has spoiled far less literature than his fanciful perversion of the imagination, which has had serious results. I do not suppose anything could have been made of "Septimius Felton, or the Elixir of Life" in any case, except under the happiest circumstances and with the nicest art. But it is a capital instance of what Hawthorne's fancy can do with a theme of some suggestiveness in the way of emptying it of all significance. Contrast his performance for a moment with the treatment of the same theme by unmixed imaginative genius— Swift's account of his Struldbrugs.[17] The mere material of this vision of earthly immortality, without the addition of any further detail, felicitously moulded into the form of a romance, would make one of the masterpieces of literature. For its profound and sombre power resides in its appalling reality. *This* is what a draught of the Elixir of Life would produce if the puerile decoction over which Septimius Felton labors through so many wearisome pages had crowned his hopes—this, and not the insipid experiences foreshadowed in the vaporings of his infatuated fancy.

But "Septimius Felton" is a posthumous production and one of Hawthorne's failures. Consider a work of far more serious ambition if not in all respects of more representative character—"The Marble Faun." There is the same *kind* of ineffectiveness and for the same reason, the frivolity of fancy. The theme of "The Marble Faun," the irretrievableness of evil conjoined with its curious transforming power—the theme in short of that profoundly imaginative masterpiece, the myth of the Fall of Man—is rather stated than exemplified in the story, overlaid as this is with its reticulation of fantastic unreality. Its elaboration, its art, tends to enfeeble its conception; its substance extenuates its subject. It has had an extraordinary vogue. In Rome for thousands of Americans "Hilda's tower" [18] probably still divides interest with the Sistine Chapel and the Vatican Stanze. Dean Stanley said he had read it seven times and meant to continue.[19] But though its central conception is one of the noblest in literature, and though there are charming and truly characteristic touches in it—for instance the effect on innocence of the mere consciousness of evil as shown in Hilda, the admirable little icicle existing for this express purpose—its significance is entombed rather than exhibited in its treatment. Probably its admirers considered that the treatment poetized the moral. That is clearly the author's intention. But a truth is not poetized by being devitalized, and certainly the consequences of sin and the inexorableness of expiation are inadequately presented in a tale padded out of all proportion by material alien in its nature, however "artistic" in its atmosphere and constituting half its volume, and a tale moreover obliged to make its moral plain in a formal statement, and to rectify its inconclusiveness in a postscript. The lack of construction, of orderly evolution, in the book is an obvious misfortune and shows very clearly Hawthorne's artistic weakness, whatever his poetic force. But its essential defect is its lack of the sense of reality, to secure which is the function of the imagination, and through which alone the truth of the fundamental conception can flower into effective exposition.

Though what I have called its alien constituent is real enough —ruins, studios, the campagna, the carnival, etc.—the material of "The Marble Faun" is perhaps too miscellaneous and unrelated for Hawthorne's imagination to unify into a solid support of his moral theme, even if it had not, after its habitual fashion, relaxed into the fantasticality of fancy in the detail. But certainly his imaginative success varies directly as the density of his material. This is greatest in "The Scarlet Letter," for instance; least in "Septimius Felton" among the longer productions. In "The House of the Seven Gables" there is detail enough, but of singular thinness and an almost gaseous expansion. The interest of "The Blithedale Romance," the most artistically articulated as well as the most naturalistic of his novels, resides almost altogether in the part suggested directly by Hawthorne's Brook Farm experience. "Everything, you know," he says or makes Sybil Darcy [20] say, "has its spiritual meaning, which is to the literal meaning what the soul is to the body." This unfortunate doctrine is the only thing that Hawthorne ever appears to have taken literally. But even this doctrine, taken literally, recognizes the literal meaning and the body as media for the manifestation of the spiritual meaning and the soul. Hawthorne's distinction assuredly lay in his treatment of the soul, yet since he was in no danger at all from materialistic excess or emphasis but quite the contrary, his treatment of the soul is most successful when he is least neglectful of the body.

It is indeed generally true that even the magical and the miraculous gain rather than lose from the emphasized reality of their setting; it is even true that some of the most noteworthy works of the imagination containing this element have depended for their abiding interest on this setting even more than on their miracles and magic. It requires no realistic pedantry to perceive that even such a work as "The Arabian Nights"—to take a crucial instance—exerts its permanent charm largely in virtue of its splendid portrayal of an entire civilization, whose manners, personages, institutions, and happenings are so solidly depicted as to anchor in reality the dreams in which they figure. Quite aside from the historical value of the "Nights'" indirect account of an extraordinary society in decadence—though it is not to belittle but to magnify fiction to recognize this service as within its province, however ponderous such a view would have seemed to Hawthorne—quite independently of the value of their "criticism of life" in itself, that is to say, it is directly because of this very element that their magic element is given a body and substance without which its appeal to the imagination would be slender and insipid. The magic is a convention—like the conventions of the stage. Its interest is in its assumed reality. If Scheherazade had constantly called Schariar's [21] attention to the fact of its assumption, as Hawthorne does with his readers, we may be sure that her career would have been brief. On the contrary, she makes the unreal seem real by the surrounding pressure of the indubitably real—just as the stage does. In other words the fanciful element of fiction must be given the appearance of reality, and there is no other way to do this than by providing at least an atmosphere of indisputable reality. The borderland between the two is an arid marsh. Either reality or the sense of it is necessary to the seriousness of any composition—except, apparently, allegory of the Hawthorne type. This is why the perennial discussion of classicism, romanticism, realism, is so barren and has come to seem so jejune. The names indicate phases of taste rather than principles of art. What abides as the necessary element of all *genres* of fiction is reality, or the sense of it, conventionally or otherwise secured. And without dealing with its elements, how is its effect to be obtained? The end of art, in brief, is illusion, but the illusion of reality. Hawthorne may be said to have conceived it as hallucination—in which, according to the medical definition, "there are no external stimuli."

Now, however his divorce from reality and consecration to the fanciful may have succeeded in giving him a unique position and demonstrating his originality—however successful he may have been, that is to say, from his own point of view—there is one vital respect, at all events, in which he almost drops out of the novelist's category. There is no element in fiction at all comparable in importance with its portrayal of human character and its picture of human life. Fiction is the genre-painting of literature as its decorative painting is poetry. But Hawthorne cared nothing for people in life and made extraordinarily little of them in his books. In no other fiction are the characters so little characterized as in his, where in general their *raison d'être* is what they illustrate, not what they are. In none other are they so airily conceived, so slightly sketched, so imperfectly defined. Mr. James points out, I think justly, that with the partial exception of Donatello in "The Marble Faun" there are no types among them. Elsewhere, to be sure, he complains that "Holgrave is not sharply enough characterized" and "is not an individual but a type." [22] The inconsistency is natural, because it is natural to think of a character in fiction as either a type or an individual, and when you are considering one of Hawthorne's as either, you think he must be the other, the truth being that he is neither. He has not enough features for an individual and he has not enough representative traits for a type. His creator evokes him in pseudo-Frankenstein fashion for some purpose, symbolical, allegorical, or otherwise illustrative, and has no concern for his character, apart from this function of it, either for its typical value or its individual interest. He cares nothing for his personality; the more real he made it the more superfluous it would seem to him, since, though it is a prime necessity to establish it first of all if its associated actions are to have the effect of reality, the effect of reality is precisely what he does not desire to secure. Consequently his dramas have the air of being conducted by marionettes. This is less important in the short stories, of course. It may be said that of such a character as the minister in "The Black Veil" the reader needs to be told nothing, that his character is easily inferred and, anyhow, is not the point, that the point is his wearing the veil and thereby presenting a rueful picture illustrative of our uncleansed condition from secret faults. In that case the idea is enough, and a hortatory paragraph would have sufficed for it. And in any case it is easy to see how immensely the idea would have gained in effectiveness, in cogency, if the minister had been characterized into reality—if he had been characterized, say, by the author of the "Vénus d'Ille," [23] a story that makes an abiding impression on readers whom its significance, if it have any, wholly escapes. But in sustained fiction, in novels, to neglect the personality of the personages is to invite failure.

Few novelists probably realize their characters sufficiently to be able to say, with Thackeray, that they "know the sound of their voices." But most of them doubtless would like to. The origin of most characters, indeed, in fiction of any moment is well known to be such as Thackeray himself has described in speaking of "a certain Costigan whom I had invented (as I suppose authors invent their personages) out of scraps, heel-taps, odds and ends of character." [24] Hawthorne's, it is needless to say, were not thus conceived. When he needed a character to illustrate one of his deeply meditated truths or one of his fanciful conceits, he invented it *ad hoc*. His characters, indeed, are not creations, but expedients. Roger Chillingworth is an expedient—and as such the only flaw in "The Scarlet Letter," whose impressive theme absorbed its author out of abstractions, as I have heretofore intimated, and compelled him, except in the case of Chillingworth, to create the only real people of his imaginary world. In creating Dimmesdale and Hester—and I am quite sure Pearl, also—Nature herself, as Arnold says of Wordsworth, "seems to take the pen out of his hand and write for him." [25] Even here, one is bound to add, the portraits lack the loving touch. Hawthorne seems himself to care quite as much for Feathertop as for Hester Prynne. In fact, he is rather partial to Feathertop—a circumstance which a reader similarly disposed to the symbolical might feel justified in considering significant. He has perhaps a weakness for such characters as Phœbe in "The House of the Seven Gables" and Hilda in "The Marble Faun." But no one would pretend to say they were realized with any definition. They are such generalized portraits as the fancy might paint of youth and innocence in a sunbonnet or a Leghorn hat passing its window in a quiet street of Concord or Salem. Kenyon is certainly *sculpté en bois;* considering the state of the art among his compatriots then in Rome it was perhaps a happy stroke to give him his particular profession. Hollingsworth is a caricature—etched with unaccountable acidity for philanthropism, than which, at least in its less odious forms, one would say there were worse things. Zenobia, Miriam, linger in one's memory rather as brunettes than as women. Coverdale is quite as anemic a character as Priscilla is in the physique given her largely for mesmeric reasons, and the concluding announcement that he is in love with her is probably an idle boast. Hawthorne particularly enjoyed Trollope, and he had a shrewd observation for casual types in actual life. One would hardly infer it from his own personages and is inclined to find in the inconsistency not, or not only, the frequent contrast between actual taste and artistic practice, but additional evidence of his curious conception of and respect for his peculiar and original "genius."

The result was that his genius took him out of the novelist's field altogether. His novels are not novels. They have not the reality of novels. And they elude it not only in their personages but in their picture of life in general. "The Scarlet Letter" itself is the postlude of a passion. Just so much of the general Salem scene as is necessary for the setting of the extremely concentrated drama is presented and no more. Nowhere else is the scene treated otherwise than atmospherically, so to speak. It does not constitute a medium or even background, but penumbra. The social picture does not exist. The quiet Salem streets of "The House of the Seven Gables," the community life of Blithedale, the village houses and hillocks and gossip and happenings of "Septimius Felton," though the War of Independence is in progress and Concord fight is actually an incident, contribute color, not substance, to the story. The Roman ruins and churches, and studios and museums, the campagna landscape and the Italian towns and country, contribute even less to the drama of "The Marble Faun," being distractions and digressions in large part, and so not only not an integral part of it but even applied rather than integumental embroidery of it. The action is always a skeleton. Its direct illustrative function is exclusively considered. It receives no aid from anything incidental or indirect, anything superfluous or subsidiary, which in a certain degree is absolutely necessary if the theme is to be presented with the fulness and concreteness of a picture. It is presented, on the contrary, with the lean explicitness of the diagram. One "gets the idea"—a *sine qua non*, to be sure, of a serious fiction that is designed like Hawthorne's to enforce some particular truth—but the sensuously (and logically) inclined must ruefully reflect that if this is all that is to be had, it could be had at even less expense; a statement would serve as well as a story. It is like a building in which the supports and buttresses should exactly, instead of superabundantly, counterbalance the weights and thrusts. The insubstantial effect so much admired in Hawthorne would be secured, but it would hardly be satisfactory to the eye or the mind, which are adjusted to the sense of substance in the embodiment of even the ethereal.

Not that the novels have any effect of succinctness corresponding to their slenderness, or of pith matching their lack of luxuriance. On the contrary, at least three of them are distinctly too long. But this is simply, to put it brutally, because they are spun out. "The Scarlet Letter" he, perhaps unfortunately, conceived as a short story and, beyond doubt unfortunately, pieced out with an incongruous portal. The episodical form of "The Blithedale Romance" injures its evolution, which, however, its interest would hardly have justified prolonging. But, if in these two works he did not very well know how to continue, in "The House of the Seven Gables," "The Marble Faun," and "Septimius Felton" he did not at all know how to stop. The first is swamped in detail over which the author lingers as if mesmerized by his own daguerrotypist, and unable to awake from his dream of rendering it intangible by endless retouching. In "The Marble Faun" not only is the action retarded by frequent breaks, but the narrative is greatly expanded by what, as I have said, is not *remplissage* but incrustation. In "Septimius Felton" bulk is achieved by the primitive expedient of pure redundancy. Its redundancy passes the prolixity of Cooper in his most complacent moods, and is the plain witness, the unmistakable symptom, of a sterility in the subject that illusion itself could only hope to fertilize by indefatigable persistence.

The incompleteness of Hawthorne's characters, the inadequacy of his social picture, the lack of romantic richness in his work, have, to be sure, been attributed largely to the romantic poverty of his material—his environment. The leanness of this social world has been summed up from the romancer's point of view with the explicitness of the dilettante dwelling on the disagreeable:

No State in the European sense of the word, and indeed barely a specific national name. No sovereign, no court, no personal loyalty, no aristocracy, no church, no clergy, no army, no diplomatic service, no country gentlemen, no palaces, no castles, nor manors, nor old country houses, nor parsonages, nor thatched houses, nor ivied ruins; no cathedrals, nor abbeys, nor little Norman churches; no great universities nor public schools—no Oxford, nor Eton, nor Harrow; no literature, no novels, no museums, no pictures, no political society, no sporting class—no Epsom nor Ascot.

The dirge is Mr. James's—not Ouida's.[26] It is in a familiar key. Nothing is more common than to hear it echoed by our practitioners in all the arts. Yet, however just his complaint of the lack of an atmosphere to stimulate his initiative, develop his talent, and train his taste, the artist's complaint of the meagreness of his material is, speaking strictly, a loose one, for the reason that art does not reside in material but in treatment. All that "Alexandre the Great," [27] as Thackeray calls him, needed was, he said, "four boards, two actors, and a passion." Indeed, richness of material may be as much of a handicap as a help to the artist. If, as Taine says, "the ugly is beautiful, but the beautiful is still more beautiful," the artist who deals with it, being under bonds to make it serve and not master his art, must proportionally make his art still more effective. His failure to do so is the cause of the inanities which strew the path of so-called academic art. But for their material, these might, it is true, be positive instead of negative failures, but it is only mediocrity that can really profit by the adventitious. So far as regards his material, the true artist's concern is not with his star but with himself. Rembrandt would have found no advantage in Veronese's material, and Veronese himself would interest us more deeply if, like Titian and Tintoretto, he had possessed the personal force to answer to the artistic demand that the sumptuousness and splendor of his material made more rather than less exigent. On the other hand, one may well doubt if Ibsen, for example, would ever have suggested Shakespeare, even to the order of appreciation to which he does suggest Shakespeare, if he had had to deal with a world remotely approaching Shakespeare's in richness of material. But as to Hawthorne there is no possible question. His environment furnished him material exactly, exquisitely, suited to his genius. His subject was the soul, and for the enactment of the dramas of the soul Salem was as apt a stage as Thebes. The New England of Hawthorne's time certainly cannot be considered as a possible theatre for the *comédie humaine*, but Hawthorne has himself demonstrated that the New England of an even blanker and bleaker period was a fit theatre for the human tragedy. "The Scarlet Letter" is so exclusively a drama of the soul as to be measurably independent of an elaborate setting in a social picture. But if Hawthorne's other works were as well placed, as firmly established, as deeply rooted in their environment, they would be works of very different value. That they are not is not the fault of their *milieu*, but of their author.

V

Something seems distinctly left out of his organization—that particular faculty whose function it is to make the most of its fellows. In default of it he took apparently the same serenely fatalistic view of himself, of his own genius, that he did of life in his books. This is a familiar phenomenon in the sphere of character and morals. We are all acquainted with the morally fatalistic character. It is almost invariably of a high type; otherwise it could not get along at all, since its peculiarity is that it dispenses with effort. This nature, with its acceptance of its own constitution as unalterable, experiencing satisfaction without elation, and meeting discouragement without thought of amendment, self-centred and independent, without alien support or altruistic endeavor, never dreaming of regeneration or submissive to discipline, conceiving its constitution as a given and constant quantity that may mould its environment so far as it must meet it, but never be subdued to what it works in, and, above all, sceptical of climbing on stepping-stones of its dead self to higher things—this morally fatalistic temperament, which, as I say, is not unfamiliar, Hawthorne undoubtedly possessed. But what is more remarkable is that he possessed the mental organization to match it. Back of both lay the feeling of reasonable self-satisfaction—the self-satisfaction which the instinct of self-preservation makes an indispensable postulate of fatalism. Though they have depressed moods, as Hawthorne certainly did, few Calvinists doubt their own election. It is almost amusing to note the old Pagan pride, having in due course of evolution passed through the phase of the Christian *humilitas*—the great mediæval virtue—partially reverting to type in the self-satisfaction of the Puritans, of whom Hawthorne was a very genuine son.

Hence, no doubt, in considerable measure, his bland acceptance of his genius as something fixed rather than potential, and his diversion into its particular channels of the material he might otherwise, by energy and effort, by study and application, have dealt with on a larger scale, to profounder purpose and with more substantial results. "The Scarlet Letter" is an eloquent and convincing witness against his comfortable and unfortunate illusion. Yet he seems to see only its leaden casket,[28] and calls its negligible successor "more characteristic of my mind and more proper and natural for me to write." "In the name of the Muses, then," one feels like exclaiming, "bring some pressure to bear on this sacrosanct mind, and, with less regard for what is proper and natural to its preferences, demonstrate by another masterpiece, and still another, that its constitution is not so immutable as you conceive it."

Descend into the arena, however, and contend for the world's prizes in the recognized lists of literature, Hawthorne could not. Of the mental constitution and capacities which heredity disposed him to look upon as final, environment, too, restricted the development. He was, to be sure, quite out of sympathy with his time and its tendencies. But New England transcendentalism was too universal a movement for any one wholly to escape its influences. Hawthorne's aloofness did not secure his immunity. It was indeed a gospel expressly designed for the isolated. Thoreau at Walden was its archetype. And, though Hawthorne's solitude was less express and voluntary and certainly not of an explicit transcendental sanction, but rather due to temperament and mood, it nevertheless fostered his preoccupation with the soul rather than with the mind or the senses. He could think out his allegories and polish up their articulation with the actual more unremittingly by himself than by talking them over with Alcott. But transcendentalism was in the very air he breathed, and though he had little joy in the company of its votaries, he hardly changed his moral atmosphere in sequestrating himself from their society.

Transcendentalism was the sublimation of the gospel of individuality, and may be summed up in Carlyle's pronouncement that the light of one's own mind is "the direct inspiration of the Almighty." [29] Hawthorne could not only perceive but satirize the eccentricities derived from a literal subscription to this doctrine. But the contemplation of these increased his self-concentration, and the doctrine itself was as much his own as it was that of the most fantastic speculators around him. And as a corollary of this universal belief in individual inspiration the belief in the prevalence of genius was general. There has never, probably, before or since, been so much "genius" abroad. The word talent does not

exist in the transcendental vocabulary. The profession of literature presupposed genius. Every one who wrote had it. Channing,
Everett, even Alcott had it.[30] Hawthorne was singularly modest.
His belief in his genius, its peculiar character, and the propriety
of considering this in his writings was not in the least vain-
glorious. His serene satisfaction with what he conceived to be its
limitations, as inevitable, as immitigable, led him in fact to exaggerate them. Thus both his ancestral fatalism and his transcendental environment obscured for him the fact that he had an
extraordinary amount of talent which it behooved him to cultivate, and magnified his consciousness of having a particular kind
of talent which it amused him to exercise. And thus he made
what seems to me, as I have said, the cardinal error of his career
—an error of tragic import to American literature—by indulging
his fancy in lieu of developing his imagination.

For the development of his imagination, too, his own temperament was too little enthusiastic. He was eminently a man of
sound sense—distinctly the most hard-headed of our men of
genius. Beyond thinking the vague and the mysterious nearer
the soul and real truth than the definite and the explicit, and
consequently the proper content of literature, he did not go. He
never systematized in the least nor even speculated. There is no
mysticism in his philosophy. He had not in fact any particular
spiritual adventurousness. His entire body of doctrine is traditional. What interested him in the speculative sphere is to be
found in the theology in which he had been brought up—the
irreparableness of sin, the necessity of expiation, the allegory of
the Fall, and its fast anchorage in human nature, the suffering of
the innocent through the guilty. The emancipation of transcendentalism was as much moonshine to him as was the materializa-
tion of dogma and doctrine. His clear-seeing mind robbed revelation of its sanctions, without in the least reconstructing its fundamental data. He was not only hard-headed, he was distinctly
unsentimental, if the epithet may be applied to a nature just,
kind, and devoted in the family relations and domestic life. He
was particularly insensitive to exterior personal influences. All
the enthusiasm for reform with which the middle decades of his
century echoed left him cold. He was unmoved by their numerous agitations, from questions of diet to those of philosophy, from

reform of attire to negro emancipation. Philanthropy in general he thoroughly disbelieved in. He ridicules it throughout the whole course of one of his few novels, and tries hard to prove there is something sinister in it, his imagination having discovered a veritable mare's nest, apparently, in pondering in his seclusion the adage that "Charity begins at home." He says expressly, and to considerably more purpose, in a letter to his sister-in-law, "The good of others, like our own happiness, is not to be attained by direct effort, but incidentally"; [31] which statement is nevertheless singularly free from the ardor of illusion. But the ardor of illusion is exactly what he never had. This is why a discerning French critic, Emile Montégut, describes him as a "romancier pessimiste" [32]—a pessimist being precisely a nature without illusions. He had even less ardor than he had illusion. During what is usually, even for the unusually self-possessed, a period of fervor he writes to his affianced: "Our souls are in happiest unison, but we must not disquiet ourselves if every tone be not re-echoed from one to the other—if every shade be not reflected in the alternate mirror. Our broad and general sympathy is enough to secure our bliss, without our following it into minute details." [33]

His nature clearly was self-sustaining. He never felt the need of the support that in the realm of the affections is the reward of self-surrender. He had no doubt an ideal family life—that is to say, ideal in a particular way, for he had it on rather particular terms, one suspects. These were, in brief, his own terms. He was worshipped, idolized, canonized, and on his side it probably required small effort worthily to fill the rôle a more ardent nature would have either merited less or found more irksome. He responded at any rate with absolute devotion. His domestic periphery bounded his vital interests. He had a few early friends, such as youth that is not abnormal or eccentric, and Hawthorne certainly was neither, cannot fail to make, and these he kept throughout life with admirable loyalty, but without adding to their number. Loyalty itself is of quite a different fibre from warm-heartedness. It has often less than nothing to do with susceptibility to the attractiveness of others. Hawthorne's loyalty to Pierce [34] was more than honorable to him, it was in every way admirable, the trait of a man instinctively convinced that there is nothing in the changes of circumstance, or even of character this side of grave deterioration, to make a change of real feeling in a friendship more important than its conservation. With Hawthorne opinion had certainly no more than its just weight, and differences in it were of small account compared with fundamental agreement of feeling. Of course, too, he never differed greatly with Pierce in opinion. He was, after all, a Democrat, though he was for his day extraordinarily non-partisan. Non-partisanship, however, *inter arma,* is itself a proof of a cool temperament when it is not itself of an ardent nature, as Hawthorne's was not. He was thoroughly patriotic in his sympathies, rejoiced at Northern victory and despaired at Northern defeat; but he stood rather aloof from the struggle, not so much because he saw both sides so sympathetically as because *Schwärmerei* in any degree was foreign to him.

He met and conversed with Lincoln, but quite missed his personality, which was curious considering his eye for character. For character he had the observer's, not the divining eye. He was eminently an observer—lynx-like on occasion. He made little or no use of his faculty of observation in his novels. But his notebooks testify to an almost microscopic exercise of it. He notes everything; far beyond the confines of the significant he is still scrutinizing. And the "Tales" and "Mosses" here and there witness a searching notation of the "types" of his environment, from the old apple-man to the parson, from the custom-house lounger to the sequestered spinster, their various characteristic traits, and the various suggestions of these as they appealed to his indefatigable but otiose fancy. Yet his study of traits never led him to create a character, nor his reflection on character to illustrate a moral truth with one—save in the exotic instance of Donatello, whose abundantly described faun-like *nature* is "transformed" into rather characterless character. His manifest preferences for Phœbe, Priscilla, Hilda, Pearl, among his personages accord with his predilection for the undeveloped. He observed too coolly. He lacked the ardor in which the data he accumulated should fuse into some general imaginative conception of real significance and substantial proportions. His humor lacks mirth. He has less sentiment than Irving—far less. His stories do not touch him. An occasional note like that of "The Gentle Boy" sounds rather plaintive than pathetic, and hardly moves us as the franker feeling of

Irving's "Rural Funerals," [35] for example. He is not moved himself. He preserves his equilibrium a little too admirably. The subject does not call for reserve; it is too slight. Considered as a creative artist he writes too much like a critic. His detachment is too great.

With such a character—so eminent for good sense, so unsentimental—his much-talked-of shyness needs qualification. One of those friends from whom nothing saves the shyest, Dr. Loring, his fellow townsman, says: "The working of his mind was so sacred and mysterious to him that he was impatient of any attempt at familiarity or even intimacy with the divine power within him. . . . The sacredness of his genius was to him like the sacredness of his love." [36] But this may easily be the transcendental way of recording an occasion on which when engaged in composition he was unwilling to be disturbed, even by Loring. He was less shy, perhaps, than taciturn—his own epithet. "Hawthorne was among the most enterprising of the merry-makers," says Fields of a picnic occasion. In England he turned out a ready and apt after-dinner orator—an impossibility for a thoroughly shy man. He apologizes in "The Scarlet Letter" prologue for his tendency to talk about himself to his readers and, as I have said, this tendency was marked. He writes to Longfellow, a dozen years after leaving college: "By some witchcraft or other—for I cannot really assign any reasonable why or wherefore—I have been carried apart from the main current of life. . . . I have secluded myself from society; and yet I never meant any such thing." That is Hawthorne's weakness. In a sense he never meant anything. He drifted. In his own words: "An influence beyond our control lays its strong hand on everything we do and weaves its consequences into an iron tissue of necessity." [37] He was, in fact, a fatalist. No wonder that his ideality was fanciful and insubstantial, and that its glimpses of real and vital truth are less frequent than they are sombre and profound.

VI

Thus predisposed by heredity, by environment, and by constitution to work what he conceived to be his own peculiar vein, and what every one around him agreed was his rare and original genius, Hawthorne, for the most part, as I say, supinely suffered his real gift to lie fallow. What it needed was development, and for development it needed not only exercise but nurture. With its moral austerity it would have responded beautifully to the influences of culture. And from such influences he protected himself with signal perversity and success. His imagination was not nurtured because his mind was not enriched. His mind, in fact, contained much less furniture than that usually possessed by writers who are ever called great. He had no particular amount of reading—beyond that current at the time among all so-called educated people: Dr. Johnson, Scott, Byron, Tom Moore, the belles-lettres of the period then closing. Instead of reading he reflected—"brooded," perhaps, in his pythian character. But he had very little to brood over. Hence the insubstantial nature of his fanciful progeny. Hence his fondness for mirage. Familiarity with the best that has been thought and said—and done—in the world [38] would have diverted him from his irresponsibility and not only stimulated his imagination by enlarging its horizon but provided it with material—dispensed him from the necessity, however dissembled as his true and native function, of spinning his web of fantasticality from his own substance. Not only was his imagination of just the quality to react admirably under such stimulus and deal admirably with extended material, but his temperament was of just the order to be developed instead of paralyzed by external agencies. What drove it in upon itself was not sensitiveness but non-receptivity. He had the good sense, the lack of enthusiasm, the disillusioned pessimism of the man of the world. Only, his world was Salem and Concord when it was not, indeed, the still narrower confines of the custom-house and the old manse.

The real world was to him *terra incognita,* or at least negligible. Europe, especially, was but a museum to him. Nothing could show more levity than the detached and essentially supercilious attitude betrayed in his account of it. England, France, Italy all rubbed him the wrong way. Yet he never had any suspicion that the fact might be his fault. His candor is delightful; his conviction that candor is the one virtue of criticism, that it "lets him out," so to speak, still more so; his loyalty to his crudest conclusions, most of all. English readers find him ungallant in recording his view of the British matron as compound of steaks and sirloins.[39] His answer is that he loves Englishmen as much as his own country-men, but that the passage must stand because the view is correct. He *was* beautifully honest—always. No doubt he would have been if he had appreciated how it made him appear, if he had realized that one opinion is not as good as another; but as a sensi-tive plant he is surely a superstition. He travelled all over Eng-land, and chronicled his journeys and reflections with the assidu-ous minuteness—and somewhat the interest—of Irving's account of Columbus's voyages.[40] But he never became familiar with English life and rarely met any representative Englishmen. Those of his own profession he avoided with marked success. He never met Thackeray, or Dickens, or Bulwer, or Disraeli. George Eliot he would not go to see because there was another Mrs. Lewes.[41] He seems to have had no curiosity—which, of course, is the *pri-mum mobile* of culture. His substitute for it is the most singular interest in the world—peculiar probably to American psychology —namely, that of travelling around the great world and applying one's own yard-stick to the phenomena it presents to one's virgin view. The English are more unmoved, more listless in their con-templation of what the world has to offer. I remember in Athens, once, a party of Nonconformists returning from Palestine and delayed a few hours by the necessity of changing steamers at the Piræus. They were sitting around the palace square. I asked their "personal conductor" why he didn't take them up to the Acropo-lis. "I tried to," he replied, "but they said they had 'seen ruins enough.'" Analogous Americans would have gone up, but would not have been unduly impressed.

Art occupied a good deal of Hawthorne's thoughts while he was in Italy, but it certainly did not unduly impress him. He never found out what it was. The fact is not so remarkable as it may seem at the present time. In his day most Americans, edu-cated or not, were in his case. That art had a particular province, language, and sanction of its own was not widely understood. But then it was, in general, almost wholly neglected. There was, however, a colony of American artists in Rome and Hawthorne saw a good deal of these, and naturally came to consider the sub-ject a good deal and with his usual candor. The amount of atten-tion he paid it, yes and the exceptional ill luck he had with it,

make him exceptional among his contemporary countrymen—
who, besides, were not great writers. Moreover, he made it a distinct feature of "The Marble Faun." He seems to have thought it
was chiefly sculpture, partly perhaps because Story [42] was a
sculptor, and Hawthorne was very loyal to his friends; having in
the case of Pierce got around the question of slavery, he would
naturally not let a bagatelle like art handicap his good-will. He
was undoubtedly perfectly sincere in either instance, and the latter at all events shows how lightly, morals aside, he took the
world which he had so long made the sport of his fancy. He cannot say enough about Story's "Cleopatra." She is "a terrible, dan-
gerous woman, quiet enough for the moment, but very likely to
spring upon you like a tigress." [43] Her Coptic cast of countenance
also illustrates Story's historical accuracy—in modelling a Greek.
It is impossible to defend him from the late R. H. Hutton's charge
of sprinkling "The Marble Faun" with "puffs of American sculpture," [44] which shows, too, how lightly he took literature also, or,
at least, his own contributions to it. For painting he did not
greatly care. He admitted Claude, but he preferred Brown—preferred Brown indeed to any one, except possibly Thompson.[45]
Furthermore, he seems to have looked upon sculpture as essentially marble, whose "purity" and transparency afforded him positive sensations of pleasure. Bronze left him cold and he would
not have subscribed to its current aggrandizement. Perhaps he
unconsciously transferred to marble some of the pleasure he took
in the moral spotlessness of such characters as Hilda and Phœbe.

His interest in all art was indeed a specifically moral, not an
æsthetic one. He takes the "literary view" with a vengeance. He
terms the so-called "Beatrice Cenci" [46] the greatest picture in the
world, apparently forgetting that he has not seen all its rivals for
such pre-eminence, and finds its neighbor, the so-called "Forna-
rina," repulsive—because the one portrait makes him think of a
pitiful tragedy and the other recalls the fact that the painter to
whom it was then ascribed had a mistress. The so-called question
of "the nude in art"—which, so far as it is a question, certainly
belongs rather to the police than to general criticism—troubled
him a good deal. Mr. James finds his objection to the nude indicative of his lack of the plastic sense,[47] which is surely to consider
it as a superfluity. However, another biographer, Mr. Moncure

Conway, says he was converted from a position savoring of intolerance so far as to declare his first views only through one of his characters [48]—rather fatuously, I should say, selecting Miriam for the purpose—and that the honor of this partial conversion is due to Mrs. Jameson,[49] whom doubtless he felt he could trust. The choice he offers among the many evidences of his æsthetic innocence is bewildering, but without being quite sure I am inclined to fix on the gift with which he endows Hilda as the one that demonstrates it most absolutely. Hilda's peculiar talent, it will be remembered, consisted in a faculty of copying the masterpieces of art with such penetration as to bring out beauties in them unsuspected by the masters themselves. It is needless to add that this power was accompanied by a complete inaptitude for original work. Hawthorne's fancy is here at its most characteristic. Providing Hilda with an exclusively sympathetic nature, he deduces from it a faculty incapable of self-expression, but able to divine what the greatest artists were groping for in their approximate productions. This puerile degradation of art in the interest of irresponsible fancy is, at all events, both a striking illustration of what Hawthorne perversely preferred to the exercise of a noble imagination, and a striking witness of the insufficiency of his culture to save his intellectual levity from reduction to the absurd.

With another great factor of civilization and consequently a quintessential of culture, history, namely, his acquaintance was even slighter than his familiarity with plastic art. The Parthenon's reputation might have drawn him to the Athenian Acropolis, but that of Pericles would hardly have stirred him from the palace square. Prattling pleasantly of the Concord battleground, he says with that candor which so frequently fringes fatuity, quite in the conventional manner of pride aping humility: "For my own part, I have never found my imagination much excited by this or any other scene of historic celebrity." [50] "Septimius Felton" is a tale of the Revolution, but its references to it are casual and reluctant. "Our story," says Hawthorne, "is an internal one, dealing as little as possible with outward events, and taking hold of these only where it cannot be helped." [51] In Rome itself he is quite imperturbable and detached. The perpetual pageant passing before the cultivated imagination hardly wins a glance from him. "It is a singular fascination that Rome exercises upon artists. There is clay elsewhere, and marble enough, and heads to model," he exclaims, identifying, as usual, art with sculpture and sculpture with marble.[52] Beside his "Note-Books" Baedeker reads like Gibbon. His own experiences amid the paraphernalia of the past largely preoccupy his pen. In the Louvre, for example, he encountered Catherine de' Medici's dressing-glass, "in which," he records, "I saw my own face where hers had been." [53] Profound thought, no doubt, to one, part of whose originality consists in the independence that can cherish the banal as well as the recondite, but devoid of historic sentiment. He would, however, have done better to confine himself to such reflections than to record such historic sentiment as he had. On the latter occasions he is apt, in familiar phrase, to "get it all wrong." The remains of the Forum, for example, he says, "do not make that impression of antiquity upon me which Gothic ruins do." They certainly should, since they *are* antique ruins and Gothic ruins are not. What, however, he means by antiquity is the sense of remoteness, and it is true that classic remains seem nearer to us than mediæval. But his reason for it is "because they belong to quite another system of society and epoch of time, and in view of them we forget all that has intervened betwixt them and us; being morally unlike and disconnected with them, and not belonging to the same train of thought; so that we look across a gulf to the Roman ages and do not realize how wide the gulf is." [54] The nearness of antiquity to our sense being due precisely to our "belonging to the same train of thought," nothing could be more "mixed" than this— except (as Macaulay would say) the passage following, apropos of the Cathedral of Amiens:

It is perhaps a mark of difference between French and English character, that the Revolution in the former country . . . does not seem to have caused such violence to ecclesiastical monuments as the Reformation and the reign of Puritanism in the latter. I did not see a mutilated shrine, or even a broken-nosed image in the whole Cathedral. But, probably, the very rage of the English fanatics against idolatrous tokens, and their smashing blows at them, were symptoms of sincerer religious faith than the French were capable of. These last did not care enough about their Saviour to beat down his crucified image.[55]

Of the copious comment that each of these sentences almost automatically suggests, the most pertinent would, perhaps, note the singularity that such a Puritan as Hawthorne should have never heard of the Huguenots, however he might be at sea about the comparability of the English Revolution in the seventeenth century with that of the French in the eighteenth. However, it is not his speculation about, but his neglect of, history that betrays a signal defect in Hawthorne's culture. If he withdrew from the world around him it was not into the past that he retired. He had no more the historic sense than he had an ear for music or an eye for beauty—save in landscape of an idyllic character—or an appreciation of art, or a love of poetry. At least, if he had them he had them in the germ. And he never cultivated the germ. His books contain no evidence of an interest in either science or philosophy. As he lacked the curiosity, he lacked also the enthusiasm that is also a prerequisite of culture. He visits Shakespeare's house unconscious, he says, of "the slightest emotion while viewing it, nor any quickening of the imagination." "It is pleasant, nevertheless," he admits, "to think that I have seen the place." It helps him to visualize Shakespeare. Still he has misgivings. He is "not quite certain that this power of realization is altogether desirable in reference to a great poet." [56] And he proceeds to sketch the seamy side of Shakespeare in quite otherwise dark colors than Mr. Sidney Lee would countenance, concluding illogically with the moral that such things as he has just recorded anew had better not have been discovered.[57] One misses the "note" of culture in his dispraise of Shakespeare as one misses it in his eulogy of Pierce. Pierce, indeed, enjoyed a monopoly of his enthusiasm, and, perhaps, because among our public men he was rather noteworthy for evoking none of it in any one else.

One field of history, however, he knew, and knew thoroughly. The New England of the early Puritans he had studied, if not systematically, at any rate to repletion. He had made it his own. He understood it as a phase of civilization, an epoch, an era, in the community life of the American people. And if any one contests the value of culture, even to a writer of pure romance, a complete answer is to be found in the fact that Hawthorne succeeded in the main when he dealt with the Puritans and almost invariably failed when he did not. There, he had a background, material, and a subject of substance.

VII

"The Scarlet Letter" is not merely a masterpiece, it is a unique book. It does not belong in the populous category with which its title superficially associates it, and the way in which Hawthorne lifts it out of this and—without losing his hold of a theme that from the beginnings of literature has, in the work of the greatest masters as well as in that of the most sordid practitioners, demonstrated its vitality and significance—nevertheless, conducts its development in a perfectly original way, is indisputable witness of the imaginative power he possessed but so rarely exercised. So multifariously has the general theme that the scarlet letter symbolizes been treated in all literatures and by all "schools" from the earliest to the latest, that however its inexhaustibility may be thus attested—an inexhaustibility paralleled by that of the perennial instinct with which it deals—any further treatment of it must forego, one would have said, the element of novelty, at least. Hawthorne's genius is thus to be credited even in this respect with a remarkable triumph. But that it should not only have thus won a triumph of originality by eluding instead of conquering the banality of the theme—by taking it in a wholly novel way, that is to say—but have produced, in its new departure, a masterpiece of beauty and power, is an accomplishment of accumulated distinction. "The Scarlet Letter," in short, is not only an original work in a field where originality is the next thing to a miracle, but a work whose originality is in no wise more marked than its intrinsic substance.

It is not a story of adultery. The word does not, I think, occur in the book—a circumstance in itself typifying the detachment of the conception and the delicate art of its execution. But in spite of its detachment and delicacy, the inherent energy of the theme takes possession of the author's imagination and warms it into exalted exercise, making it in consequence at once the most real and the most imaginative of his works. It is essentially a story neither of the sin nor of the situation of illicit love—presents neither its psychology nor its social effects; neither excuses nor condemns nor even depicts, from this specific point of view. The love of Hester and Dimmesdale is a postulate, not a presentment. Incidentally, of course, the sin colors the narrative, and the situation is its particular result. But, essentially, the book is a story of concealment. Its psychology is that of the concealment of sin amid circumstances that make a sin of concealment itself. The sin itself might, one may almost say, be almost any other. And this constitutes no small part of the book's formal originality. To fail to perceive this is quite to misconceive it. As a story of illicit love its omissions are too great, its significance is not definite enough, its detail has not enough richness, the successive scenes of which it is composed have not an effective enough cohesion. From this point of view, but for the sacred profession of the minister and the conduct this imposes, it would be neither moving nor profound. Its moral would not be convincing. Above all, Chillingworth is a mistake, or at most a wasted opportunity. For he is specialized into a mere function of malignity, and withdrawn from the reader's sympathies, whereas what completes, if it does not constitute, the tragedy of adultery, is the sharing by the innocent of the punishment of the guilty. This inherent element of the situation, absolutely necessary to a complete presentment of it, the crumbling of the innocent person's inner existence, is absolutely neglected in "The Scarlet Letter," and the element of a malevolent persecution of the culpable substituted for it. The innocent person thereby becomes, as I have already said, a device, and though in this way Hawthorne is enabled to vivify the effect of remorse upon the minister by personifying its furies, in this way, too, he sacrifices at once the completeness of his picture and its depth of truth by disregarding one of its most important elements.

He atones for this by concentration on the culpable. It is *their* psychology alone that he exhibits. And though in this way he has necessarily failed to write the *chef-d'œuvre* of the general subject that in the field of art has been classic since monogamy established itself in society, he has produced a perfect masterpiece in the more detached and withdrawn sphere more in harmony with his genius. In narrowing his range and observing its limits he has perhaps even increased the poignancy of his effect. And his effect *is* poignant and true as reality itself. In confining himself to the concealment of sin rather than depicting its phenomena and its results, he has indeed brought out, as has never been done elsewhere, the importance of this fatal increment of falsity among the factors of the whole chaotic and unstable moral equilibrium. Concealment in "The Scarlet Letter," to be sure, is painted in very dark colors. In similar cases it may be a duty, and is, at all events, the mere working of a natural instinct—at worst a choice of the lesser evil. But surely there is no exaggeration or essential loss of truth in the suggestion of its potentialities for torture conveyed by the agony of the preacher's double life. It is true his concealment condemned another to solitary obloquy. But if that be untypically infrequent and also not inherent in the situation as such, it is fairly counterbalanced by consolatory thought of the exceptional havoc confession would have wrought in his case. That is to say, if his remorse is exceptionally acute it is also exceptionally alleviated. On the whole the potential torture of remorse for a life that is flagrantly an acted lie is not misrepresented, either in truth or art, by the fate of Dimmesdale, though it is treated in the heightened way appropriate to the typical.

Concentration upon concealment further contributes to the originality and the perfection of "The Scarlet Letter" by eliminating passion. The sensuous element which might have served to extenuate the offence—since it is of its tragic essence that nothing can excuse it in anything like normal conditions—or if not that to render the story attractive and affecting, is rigidly excluded. There is more sensuousness sighed forth by the unhappy pair [58] of the famous fifth canto of the "Inferno" than in the whole volume. There is but a single reference to the days when Hester and her lover "read no further," and this, though a kindly and catholic touch, is characteristically a moral one.

With sudden and desperate tenderness she threw her arms around him and pressed his head against her bosom; little caring though his cheek rested on the scarlet letter. . . .

"Never, never," whispered she. "What we did had a consecration of its own. We felt it so! We said so to each other! Hast thou forgotten it?"

"Hush, Hester!" said Arthur Dimmesdale, rising from the ground. "No; I have not forgotten." [59]

There is no sensuous, scarcely even an emotional, digression from the steady conduct of the theme. The chill of destiny is sensible even in the chapter called almost mockingly "A Flood of Sunshine," and at the end to the dying minister only doubt redeems eternity itself from despair:

"Hush, Hester, hush!" said he, with tremulous solemnity. "The law we broke!—the sin here so awfully revealed!—let these alone be in thy thoughts! I fear! I fear! It may be that when we forgot our God—when we violated our reverence each for the other's soul—it was henceforth vain to hope that we could meet hereafter, in an everlasting and pure reunion. God knows: and He is merciful." [60]

To this New England "Faust" there is no "second part." The sombre close, the scarcely alleviated gloom of the whole story are in fit keeping with the theme,—which is the truth that, in the words of the tale itself, "an evil deed invests itself with the character of doom"—and with its development through the torture of concealment to the expiation of confession.

Here, for once, with Hawthorne we have allegory richly justifying itself, the allegory of literature not that of didacticism, of the imagination not of the fancy, allegory neither vitiated by caprice nor sterilized by moralizing, but firmly grounded in reality and nature. Note how, accordingly, even the ways of the wicked fairy that obsessed him are made to serve him, for even the mirage and symbolism so dear to his mind and so inveterate in his practice, blend legitimately with the pattern of his thoroughly naturalistic fabric. The fanciful element is, at least, so imaginatively treated as to seem, exceptionally, to "belong." Hawthorne seems to have been so "possessed" by his story as to have conducted the development of its formal theme for once subconsciously, so to speak, and with the result of decorating rather than disintegrating reality in its exposition. At all events, to this "possession" (how complete it was in material fact all his biographers attest) two notable and wholly exceptional results are due. In the first place he *felt* his theme, as he never felt it elsewhere, and consequently presented it with an artistic cogency he never elsewhere attained. The story, in other words, is real and true. If it is thought to show a bias in pushing too far the doom of evil, to ignore the whole New Testament point of view, as it may be called, epitomized in the Master's "Go and sin no more," [61] the answer is that though in this way it may lose in typical value, it gains in imaginative realism, since it is a story of that Puritan New England where it sometimes seems as if the New Testament had been either suspect or unknown. Besides, there is enough demonstration of its text on the hither side of what it is necessary to invoke the Puritan *milieu* to justify. Every erring soul may not suffer the extremity of Dimmesdale's agony, but it suffers enough, and the inevitability of its suffering was never more convincingly exhibited than in this vivid picture, softened as it is into a subdued intensity by the artist's poetized, however predetermined, treatment. For, in the second place, it is here alone that Hawthorne seems to have felt his *characters* enough to feel them sympathetically and so to realize them to the full. They are very real and very human. What the imagination of a recluse, even, can do to this end when held to its own inspiration and not seduced into the realm of the fantastic, may be seen in the passage where Hester pleads for the continued custody of her child. Pearl herself is a jewel of romance. Nothing more imaginatively real than this sprite-like and perverse incarnation of the moral as well as physical sequence of her parents' sin exists in romance. Her individuality is an inspiration deduced with the logic of nature and with such happy art that her symbolic quality is as incidental in appearance as it is seen to be inherent on reflection. Mr. James, who objects to the symbolism of "The Scarlet Letter," [62] nevertheless found her substantial enough to echo in the charming but far less vivid Pansy of his "Portrait of a Lady." Chillingworth, the other symbolic character, is in contrast an embodied abstraction —the one piece of machinery of the book. But it cannot be denied that he performs a needful function and, artistically, is abundantly justified. As a Puritan parallel of Mephistopheles he is very well handled. "The Scarlet Letter" is, in fact, the Puritan "Faust," and its symbolic and allegorical element, only obtrusive in a detail here and there at most, lifts it out of the ordinary category of realistic romance without—*since nothing of importance is sacrificed to it*—enfeebling its imaginative reality. The beautiful and profound story is our chief prose masterpiece and it is as difficult to overpraise it as it is to avoid poignantly regretting that Hawthorne failed to recognize its value and learn the lesson it might have taught him.

VIII

Hawthorne's style, doubtless less original than his substance, is nevertheless indubitably his own. It is far more the general cultivated medium of writing than his works are within the general lines of romance, but it is that medium colored and modelled —or, perhaps, one should rather say, tinted and traced—by his own idiosyncrasy. This indeed is its importance. As style it has no other. Its hue and figure are of interest as their faintness and evenness mirror his personal traits. These are, however, very crisply reflected by it, and a study of it is useful as certifying the impressions made by its substance. It is, to begin with, difficult to define, and its lack of positive qualities quite exactly parallels the insubstantiality of its subject-matter. Only by a miracle, one reflects, could subject-matter of much vital importance be thus habited—so plainly, placidly, unpretendingly presented, though in such an exceptional instance as "The Scarlet Letter" the latent intensity of the theme is doubtless set off by the sobriety of its garb, to which also it gives a deepened tone. But the harmonious, rather than contrasting, services of such a style as Hawthorne's in general, could be useful only for the direct expression of something bordering on informing insipidity. It is above all a neat style. It wears no gewgaws of rhetoric and owes little or nothing to the figures of speech. It is saved from the conventional mainly by the author's own interest in its substance, and would be prim if it were not personal. But it is too sincere for any, even Puritan, affectation. Its neatness is a native, not a cultivated quality. It is the neatness of innocence, not of virtue. It has never been assailed by the temptations of the meretricious, and its avoidance of ornament is preference for the plain, not distaste for the rococo. It views the purple patch with the unmoved placidity of the color-blind, and the staidness of its expression corresponds to the propriety of its thought, whose wildest antics are decorous with the consciousness that it is "all pretend." Nothing shows more clearly the dilettante character of Hawthorne's exercise of his fancy than this neatness, which is never discomposed by fervor or thrown into disarray by heat.

It is in fact the antithesis of heat, and the absence of heat in

Hawthorne's genius appears nowhere so markedly as in his style. His writings from beginning to end do not contain an ardent, or even a fervent passage. They are as empty of exaltation as of exhilaration. Here, for example, is a single sentence by a fellow-townsman of his descriptive of one of nature's daily phenomena: "In deep ravines, under the eastern sides of cliffs, Night forwardly plants her foot even at noonday, and, as Day retreats, she steps into his trenches, skulking from tree to tree, from fence to fence, until at last she sits in his citadel and draws out her forces into the plain." No one can read that without recognizing its almost incandescent quality, or compare it with the most glowing period to be found in Hawthorne, without distinguishing between the imaginative flame that burned in Thoreau's Walden cabin and the flicker of fancy that played over the embers of the Old Manse hearth. Or take a few phrases inspired by the little convent cemetery at Brussels, the writer of which

came to this spot one summer evening of spring and saw among a thousand black crosses casting their shadows across the grassy slope that particular one which marked his mother's resting-place. . . . A thousand such hillocks lay round about, the gentle daisies springing out of the grass over them, and each bearing its cross and requiescat. A nun, veiled in black, was kneeling hard by at a sleeping sister's bed-side (so fresh-made that the spring had scarce had time to spin a coverlid for it); beyond the cemetery walls you had glimpses of life and the world and the spires and gables of the city. A bird came down from a roof opposite, and lit first on a cross and then on the grass below it, whence it flew away presently with a leaf in its mouth: then came a sound as of chanting, from the chapel of the sisters hard by. . . . Might she sleep in peace—might she sleep in peace; and we, too, when our struggles and pains are over! But the earth is the Lord's as the heaven is; we are alike his creatures here and yonder. I took a little flower off the hillock and kissed it, and went my way, like the bird that had just lighted on the cross by me, back into the world again. Silent receptacle of death, tranquil depth of calm, out of reach of tempest and trouble! I felt as one who had been walking below the sea, and treading amid the bones of shipwrecks.[63]

To curtail this passage of perhaps the foremost master of English prose is to mutilate it, but I have transcribed enough of it to exemplify precisely the quality that Hawthorne's style most conspicuously and most characteristically lacks. It exemplifies perfectly the exaltation of an ardent imagination constrained and modulated by instinctive artistic reserve. It is as far removed from the purple splendors of rhetoric as Hawthorne at his simplest, but it is simplicity sublimated by feeling, not expressed with placid adequacy. Imagine "the rarest imagination since Shakespeare" exclaiming, "The earth is the Lord's!" [64] He has not the authority requisite for such an utterance. He writes as the scribes, and lacks the conviction, the assurance of his vocation, the authentic literary and artistic commission for exclamation or utterance with any fire or particular fervor. It is simply extraordinary that so voluminous a writer should care so little for writing as an art of effective expression, should practise it so exclusively as an exercise—as mere record and statement. In "The Scarlet Letter," as I have intimated, the style to a certain extent reflects the greater depth and richness of the substance. But compare its most moving passage with the sentences just cited from Thackeray:

They sat down again side by side and hand clasped in hand on the mossy trunk of the fallen tree. Life had never brought them a gloomier hour; it was the point whither their pathway had so long been tending, and darkening ever as it stole along;—and yet it enclosed a charm that made them linger upon it, and claim another, and another and, after all, another moment. The forest was obscure around them and creaked with a blast that was passing through it. The boughs were tossing heavily above their heads; while one solemn old tree groaned dolefully to another, as if telling the sad story of the pair that sat beneath, or constrained to forebode evil to come.[65]

The drop—in tone, in spirit and in rhythm—from real elevation to that "one solemn old tree" groaning "dolefully" and the perpetual symbolism, is characteristic. It is just what the instinct for style would save a writer from. And it is but a partial explanation to attribute Hawthorne's lack of this instinct to his lack of plastic sense. It is explained ultimately by his lack of real energy, to which no doubt his lack of plastic sense is itself due; though it may be said that his imagination, cool enough in his view of life, content to contemplate instead of construct, seems to lose still more heat in his expression, and his style to have even less warmth than his conceptions. Evidently, though these amuse, they do not impose upon him, and his extremely detached treatment of them is the most convincing impeachment

of his "high seriousness" [66] as a writer, however sombre, even,
his philosophy of life.

And though it is only superficially strange, it is at least superficially piquant, that his style should disclose his lack of ardor
by its absence of restraint as well as by poverty of feeling. Never
was such copiousness associated with so little exuberance, or at
any rate exuberance with so little enthusiasm. His simplicity
appears thus as the expression not of contained but of uncom-
plicated substance. Simple as his style is it is never severe and
its quietness is not the result of reserve. Just as its purity is due
to the absence of sensuousness rather than to spiritual elevation,
its simplicity is that of a map rather than that of a picture. The
fertility of his fancy is not matched by the subtlety of its expression. He does not deal in *nuances,* but accumulates detail.
No writer was ever fonder of detail. The flood of it drowns his
descriptions. One cannot trace the general skeleton, the grand
construction. He does not even subordinate the trivial, but
chronicles everything that occurs to him with an amused and
sportive assiduity. His personal taciturnity disappears as he
contemplates his subject and he abandons himself, with more
zest than he ever otherwise betrays, to a kind of quaintly otiose
but unmistakable garrulity. In this respect not his first but his
very last story—written after a lifetime of professional practice
—gives a very striking impression of the amateur with a pen in
his hand and endless leisure before him. Our peculiar Anglo-
Saxon delusion of arguing inner intensity from outward composure can find no support in Hawthorne's style for ascribing to
him any elements of energy that are indicated by restraint in
their expression. What his extreme copiousness witnesses is the
diffusion instead of the concentration of his interest. His interest
is extraordinarily spread out over the rather narrow field that
awakens it at all and perhaps could not be so inclusive if it
centred around any cardinal foci to the disparagement of the
apparently negligible.

Such copiousness is, naturally, inconsistent with any effective
ordering of the elements of style, and Hawthorne's is as unaccented periodically as it is monotonous in color. But it has the
great merit of ease, conjoined with exactness. One without the
other is not uncommon, but the combination is rare. The kind

of care that goes with deliberateness he undoubtedly took, though he certainly took none that demanded strenuous and scrupulous effort, or his result would have been more distinguished instead of being purely satisfactory—markedly felicitous as well as adequate and correct. But his ease, thus untinctured by either study or sloth, and marking the free movement of a style that is not only flexible but correct, was undoubtedly a natural gift. He had it in the form that is both academic and elastic. Hence his style has in some degree the classic note. As free from eccentricity or excess as from any particular pungency or color it is eminently the style of literary good-breeding and images its author's personal fastidiousness. Its vocabulary is that of cultivated English. It is as free from the crude as from the far-fetched. And though often as familiar in tone as it is simple in diction its smoothness never lacks dignity and often attains grace. Why has it not in greater degree the truly classic note? Why is it that after all—perfectly adapted as it is to the expression of its substance, to the purpose of its author—it lacks quality and physiognomy? Or at all events why is its quality not more marked, more salient? Because it *is* such an adequate medium for its content, for the expression of a nature without enthusiasm, a mind unenriched by acquisition and an imagination that is in general the prey of fancy rather than the servant of the will. Hawthorne should have taken himself more seriously at the outset—in his formative period—and less so in the maturity of powers whose development would have produced far more important results than those achieved by their leisurely exercise in tranquil neglect of their evolution.

EMERSON

EMERSON

I

The perspective of time, doubtless for the most part in substantial alliance with equity, diminishes many imposing literary
figures, but it has already enlarged Emerson's. His fame grows.
More and more generally, and more and more distinctly, it is
discerned as our answer to the literary challenge of the world.
Emerson is of the company of Plato and Pascal, of Shakespeare
and Goethe, emulating easily their cosmic inclusiveness. And
he is ours—absolutely and altogether our own. If he is not typi-
cally, he is peculiarly, American. No other country could have
produced him. And his own may take a legitimate satisfaction
in the consciousness that its greatest is also one of its most
characteristic minds. Especially may the American lover of
literature joy in finding this intellectual pre-eminence illuminating
the firmament of letters, rather than arising in some field of
activity more commonly associated with our character and
achievements.

II

Except a childhood recollection of Lincoln speaking from a
hotel balcony on his way to his first inauguration—of his tower-
ing size, his energy in gesture and emphasis, his extraordinary
blackness, his angularity of action, and a certain imposing
sincerity of assertion, the last very likely an imputation of later
years—I have no memory of any of our public men more vivid
than that of hearing in early youth a lecture by Emerson. Surely
when Lowell called Lincoln "the first American" [1] he forgot
Emerson. Or he was thinking of Lincoln's representative character in, rather than of, his country. Politics is "too much with
us." [2] The first American both in chronology and in completeness
appeared in the field of letters, and—if we are, as of course

93

Lowell meant, to consider personal greatness in the comparison and thus exclude Cooper—in the efflorescence of New England culture. Naturally I do not in the least recall the topic of Emerson's lecture. I have an impression that it was not known at the time and did not appear very distinctly in the lecture itself. The public was small, attentive, even reverential. The room was as austere as the chapel of a New England Unitarian church would normally be in those days. The Unitarians were the intellectual sect of those days and, as such, suspect. Even the Unitarians, though, who were the aristocratic as well as the intellectual people of the place, found the chapel benches rather hard, I fancy, before the lecture was over, and I recall much stirring. There was, too, a decided sprinkling of scoffers among the audience, whose sentiments were disclosed during the decorous exit. Incomprehensibility, at that epoch generally, was the great offence; it was a sort of universal charge against anything uncomprehended, made in complete innocence of any obligation to comprehend. Nevertheless the small audience was manifestly more or less spellbound. Even the dissenters—as in the circumstances the orthodox of the day may be called—were impressed. It might be all over their heads, as they contemptuously acknowledged, or vague, as they charged, or disintegrating, as they —vaguely—felt. But there was before them, placidly, even benignly, uttering incendiarism, an extraordinarily interesting personality. It was evening and the reflection of two little kerosene lamps, one on either side of his lectern, illuminated softly the serenest of conceivable countenances—nobility in its every lineament and a sort of irradiating detachment about the whole presence suggestive of some new kind of saint—perhaps Unitarian. There was nothing authoritative, nothing cathedral in his delivery of his message, the character of which, therefore, as a message was distinctly minimized; and if nevertheless it was somehow clear that its being a message was its only justification, it was in virtue of its being, so to say, blandly oracular. It was to take or to leave, but its air of almost blithe aloofness in no wise implied anything speculative or uncertain in its substance—merely, perhaps, a serene equability as to *your* receptivity and its importance to *you*. Communication was manifestly the last concern of the lecturer. That was conspicuously not his affair. If, in turning over the leaves of his manuscript, he found they had been misplaced and the next page did not continue his sentence, he proceeded unmoved, after an instant's hesitation, with what it recorded. The hiatus received but the acknowledgment of a half smile—very gentle, wise, and tolerant. Nothing could better emphasize the complete absence of pretension about the entire performance, which thus reached a pitch of simplicity as effective as it was unaffected. "It makes a great difference to the force of a sentence," he says somewhere, "if there is a man behind it." [3] Such lyceum technic cannot be considered exemplary. But in this case the most obvious fact about the lecture was that there *was* a man behind it. Conventions of presentation, of delivery, of all the usually imperative arts of persuasion—even of communication, as I say—seemed to lose their significance beside the personal impressiveness of the lecturer.

This, at all events, is true of the literature he produced—of his works in both prose and poetry. His life, his character, his personality—quite apart I mean from the validity of his precepts —have the potency belonging to the personality of the founders of religions who have left no written words. All the inconsistencies, the contradictions, the paradoxes, the inconsequences, even the commonplaces of his writings are absorbed and transfigured by his personal rectitude and singleness. One feels that what he says possesses a virtue of its own in the fact of having been said by him. He has limitations but no infirmities. He is no creature of legend. From cradle to grave his life was known, intimately known, of all men. There is a wealth of recorded personal reminiscence about him and one may soberly say there has been found "no fault in him." [4] Everything testified of him explicitly attests this. "I never heard of a crime which I might not have committed," he says (or cites), in speaking of "Faust." [5] But this was the sportiveness of his obsessive intellect. As a matter of fact he never committed any—not even the most venial error. Nor was his blamelessness in the least alloyed with weakness. His energy was as marked as his rectitude. He had the dauntless courage of the positively polarized—as he might say—and in no wise illustrated the negative virtues of passivity. He is of our time, of our day, he lived and wrote but yesterday at Concord, Massachusetts, he passed through the most stirring times, he shared, with whatever spiritual aloofness, the daily life of his fellows and neighbors and was part and parcel of a modern American community for nearly four score years, and never in any respect or in the slightest degree, in any crisis or any trivial detail of humdrum existence, failed to illustrate—to incarnate— the ideal life. Introducing his lectures on "The Ideal in Art," Taine exclaims eloquently: "It seems as if the subject to which I am about to invite your attention could only be treated in poetry." [6] Similarly, one feels in approaching any consideration of Emerson that his character is such as to implicate a lyric strain. Criticism is exalted into pure appreciation. Not only is there no weakness, no lack of heroic ideality in his life and conduct, but neither is there in his writings. Not only every poem, every essay, but every sentence, one may almost say, is fairly volatile in its aspiration toward the ideal. His practical admonitions and considerations—and his works are full of these —all envisage the empyrean. His homeliest figures and allusions direct the mind to the zenith and never stop at the horizon. And this incarnation of the ideal is a Massachusetts Yankee, for he was absolutely nothing else. I know of nothing in the history of literature, or in history itself, more piquant as an indifferent, more inspiring as a patriotic, critic would say. Emerson is, as I have said, our refutation of alien criticism, grossly persuaded of our materialism and interestedness. To "mark the perfect man" [7] has been left to America and American literature.

III

Note moreover that Emerson's moral greatness—most con- spicuous of all facts about him, as I think it is—receives its essentially individual stamp, aside from its perfection, from its indissoluble marriage with intellect. When he left his church he took his pulpit with him. He preached throughout his life. And he did nothing but preach; even his poetry is preaching. Of course, his sermons are lay sermons. There is, I think, rather a marked absence of the religious element in them. But the ethical note sounds through them all. He discovers the moral in the bosom of the rose, and of art itself finds its chief value to be the teaching of history. His distinction, his true originality, is missed if this is not perceived. As a man of letters, an artist, a poet, a philosopher, a reformer, he has limitations that it is impossible to deny. As a preacher—a lay preacher—he is unsurpassed. Since the days of the Hebrew prophets, whom temperamentally he in no wise resembled, there has been no such genius devoted to the didactic. He was quite conscious of his mission. "I have my own spirits in prison," he says, "spirits in deeper prisons whom no man visits if I do not." [8] Confident in his sublimated pantheism, feeling himself an organic constituent of the universal substance, the authenticity of his didactic title was, one may almost say, more a matter of consciousness than of assumption with him. His capacity was not so much representative as original. He was not so much a delegate of the divine as a part of it, and consequently scorned credentials as he did exposition and spoke *ex proprio vigore*.

His distinction *as* a preacher, however, is not the authority with which he speaks—others have spoken as authoritatively—but that, though preaching always, his appeal is always to the mind. He never pleads, adjures, warns, only illuminates. He may talk of other gods, his Zeus is intellect. The hand may be Isaiah's, the voice is that of the intelligence.[9] "The capital secret of the preacher's profession," he says, "is to convert life into truth." [10] These five words define his own work in the world with precision. And his instrument, his alembic, for this conversion was the intellect. Treating moral questions, or questions which by extension are to be so called, almost exclusively, he treats them without reference to any criterion but that of reason. Pure intellect has never received such homage as he pays it. Its sufficiency has never seemed so absolute to any other thinker. "See that you hold yourself fast,"—by the heart, the soul, the will? No,—"by the intellect," is the climax of one of his earliest and most eloquent preachments. The strain is recurrent throughout his works. "Goethe can never be dear to men," he says, with his extraordinary penetration. "His is not even the devotion to pure truth: but to truth for the sake of culture." [11] He would have blandly scouted Lessing's famous preference for the pursuit over the possession of truth, and was far from "bowing humbly to the left hand" of the Almighty and saying, "Father, forgive: pure truth is for Thee alone." [12] He never pursued truth—or anything. He simply uttered it, with perfect modesty but also with absolute conclusiveness. He never pretended to completeness, to the possession of all truth. "Be content with a little light, so it be your own," he counsels the youthful "scholar." [13] He was imperturbably content with his; it was indubitably his own, and he trusted it implicitly. To increase one's store of light he prescribes a "position of perpetual inquiry" and commends not study but examination, exclaiming eloquently, "Explore, and explore!" What with? Under whose guidance? That of your intellect of course. He is in essential agreement with Carlyle, in calling the light of the mind "the direct inspiration of the Almighty" [14]— except that he would have substituted Nature for the Almighty, to whom his references are as few as Carlyle's are frequent.

Moreover it was the pure, as distinguished from the practical, intellect that he worshipped. Naturally, since it was this that he possessed. He himself admits, or rather proclaims, that his "reasoning faculty is proportionally weak." [15] Logic was apparently discovered by Aristotle and Emerson is a pure Platonist. He cites the Stagirite when it serves his Platonist purpose—for example, the beautifully Platonist definition of art as "the reason of things without their substance" [16]—but he has no native sympathy with him. He is in fact Plato *redivivus* in his assumption that conceptions as such justify and prove themselves; or rather, that all kinds of proof are impertinent. Logic, indeed, has been superstitiously overvalued. It has been responsible for an enormous amount of absolutely artificial error, as one need go no farther than to remember Aristotle's despotic rule during the Middle Ages—still persisting in both Roman and Protestant ecclesiasticism—to recall. At the same time, quite apart from its pretensions as a science, it has the supreme value of being the only test which we may apply to the verification of our otherwise unestablished intuitions. The rôle of verification, however, is altogether too humble to win respect from such an Olympian spirit as Emerson. He speaks always as little like the logicians as the scribes.[17] Not only his practice—which others have shared— but his theory, in which he is unique among the serious philosophers of the modern world, is quite definitely that of the seer. However blandly, however shrewdly, he unfolds his message, he has consciously and explicitly as well as inferentially the attitude of merely transmitting it. More—far more—than that, for with his inveterate didacticism he insists that this attitude be universal. Abstract yourself sufficiently, he seems to say to his audience, and let the god speak through you. Then all will be well. To what purpose? Well, to no purpose, except the end of the formulation of truth. Truth he viewed almost as a commodity. If you could but get enough life converted into truth, there would be nothing left to ask for. That would be the legitimate end and conclusion of effort, because—though of course he never stooped to assign any reason for assuming the all-sufficiency of truth—since error is blindness, once perceived it won't be followed. He is, I confess, a little exasperating in his airy avoidance of this "conclusion of the whole matter." [18] Even artistic completeness—for which, however, he had no sense— seems to require it. Logic also; axiomatically the highest good is goodness. But doubtless there are plenty of people to draw conclusions. Emerson was concerned mainly with premises—even major premises. The utilities he in general abhorred. There were in effect too many people to attend to them; to say nothing of the notorious fact that they would take care of themselves. The important thing was, as one may say, to illustrate Tennyson's exquisite image,

"Now lies the earth all Danaë to the stars," [19]

and let the divine interpenetrate and fecundate human deliverances on any subject—as little alloyed as possible with any ratiocination or other obstruction of pure transmission. In Emerson's case we know who the god was—even his name and address. His utterances are too highly differentiated for mistake. The divine voice is of course one. All things are one to Emerson. But the one in this instance seems sufficiently distinguished from its other articulatenesses to involve a polytheistic rather than a generally immanent explanation. To us the god is inescapably Emerson himself; it is at least excusable, practically, to identify what you find in no other conjunction. Naturally the inference is that we are all gods, and no doubt Emerson would willingly have adopted, with whatever modifications, the current "panentheism" [20] which unites his pantheism with theism, for though he never lost sight of the existence of the many he always saw them as ultimately resident in the one. In this case we have only to say that Emerson was a most superior kind of god, or in other words—hardly more specific perhaps, but more in accord with current parlance—that he was a man of genius. However, genius too has its privileges, whether divine in the transcendental or in the merely literary sense. And one of them is notoriously independence of logic. Of this practical privilege he took the amplest advantage. "We cannot spend the day in explanation," he says theocratically.[21] There is no syllogism in all his essays —not even, I fancy, a "therefore." There is no attempt to argue, to demonstrate even statements and positions that almost seem to cry out for such treatment. It is all distinctly facultative, but all instinct with the authority of the Hebrew prophets, the *ex cathedra* tone of the inspired or even the possessed. As I have intimated, the contrast between this tone—this assumption—and the frequently homely, workaday, Yankee expression of it is particularly picturesque. In general the prophets are in the distance—enwrapped in the mists of legend or enlarged in the mirage of remoteness.

Naturally, thus, his inconsistencies are striking—even glaring —but they are not as significant as superficially they may be esteemed. They are in the first place often superficial in themselves, and anyone who takes the trouble—as, in his lofty way, Emerson would have scorned, did in fact scorn, to do—can reconcile them by the exercise of attentive discrimination and, above all, of cordial good faith. I say "cordial," because goodwill is needful to illuminate even essential perspicacity when on the surface of things the case might so easily be adversely adjudicated. In reading over the Essays recently I must confess I have been extraordinarily impressed by the frequency of these apparent inconsistencies. One grows tired of noting them. Cumulatively they convey the impression of irresponsibility. Consistency, one says vainly to oneself, is the vice of feeble minds;[22] indulged to this extent, it almost suggests the sportiveness of literary bohemia. *But,* after a time—an apprenticeship one may say—you perceive that inconsistency is inseparable from Emerson's method. If a record had been kept of the oracles of Delphi, would they have been found to hang together? Besides, the Pythia, however abstractly, dealt with the concrete. She was not consigned, like Emerson, to the oracular in general, so to speak—the oracular apropos of every imaginable abstract consideration. On the whole it seems too much to ask that the oracular should also be consistent. Too much ingenuity would be requisite to make it so, and the association of ingenuity with oracle involves a contradiction in terms. The mouthpiece of the god is not concerned about matching its inspirations. If ever there existed a seer whose mental activity was in a perpetual state of ferment, Emerson was such a one. Yet he conceived of himself as a passive medium of transmission for divine messages to humanity. He conceived thus of everyone worth attention at all in the intellectual world, and even commended the attitude to the humblest of his audiences. Why not, indeed, if the farmer to whom he lent a volume of Plato returned it with the reassuring remark, "He seems to have a good many of my idees"?

We speak of a mercurial temperament, but really temperament is a constant quantity compared with the intellect, pure and simple, unbalanced by, unweighted with, its steady pull and pressure. Logic itself hardly takes its place as a check on the irresponsible and the experimental. And, as I say, Emerson eschewed logic. Obviously either logic or feeling is requisite for the control of intellectual caprice—a phenomenon mainly noticeable in the unsentimental and the active-minded: precisely Emerson's category. And the thinker who frames a system or even compasses a coherent body of doctrine is probably indebted even more than to his logic to those general appetences that make up a temperamental personality. Left to itself, without concern for consequences either to logic or predilection, the intellect is tremendously adventurous, and as hospitable to the strange and the subversive as the nomad or the outlaw. Emerson had a splendid scorn for the consequences of any of his thinking. His thinking was in truth a series of perceptions, so directly visible to his mind—undirected by any bent, unsteadied by any controlling prejudice, so unselected temperamentally that is to say—as to need no matching or comparison, no holding in abeyance, no tentative consideration preliminary to complete adoption. With him modication means a new view, more light, still another perception. Philosophically thus, and constitutionally, this preacher of individuality is himself the most impersonal of individuals. Everyone in his *entourage,* everyone who came in contact with him, noted, in the measure of his powers of analysis, the absence in him of the element of personality—the element *par excellence* that centralizes, unifies, and renders communicable any set of ideas, or even any particular point of view. Mlle. Dugard says of him very truly: "Il réalise avec sérénité le type de l'objectif dont l'âme est une forme vide que traverse l'influx divin." [23] He is himself as elusive as his philosophy is fluid. His own introspection, busy enough with his mind and seeing the universe in as well as through it, pauses at the threshold of his nature and, instinctively shrinking from looking for fixity in anything so subtly undetermined, even professes ignorance of its constitution. The matter, however, was probably simpler than with his mystic turn he was ready to admit. His nature was flooded with light, but it lacked heat. It had animation without ardor, exaltation without ecstasy.

His deification of intellect, indeed, inevitably involves a corresponding deficiency in susceptibility, and defective sympathies are accordingly—and were as a matter of fact with him—as characteristic of Emerson's order of moral elevation as is this one enthusiasm to which his susceptibility limited him. Distinctly he lacked temperament. His was a genial but hardly a cordial nature—in personal relations, indeed, more amiable even than genial. As he says, "the intellect searches out the absolute order of things as they stand in the mind of God, and without the colors of affection." [24] "Something is wanting to science until it has been humanized," he asserts, but by humanization he means "union with intellect and will" [25]—quite formally neglecting the susceptibility, the necessary transition between the two. Will comes next to intellect in his esteem—he praises action on occasion—but it is a distant second. Virtue itself, he says, "is vitiated by too much will." [26] He was poise personified, and both will and feeling impair equilibrium. The ether that he breathed habitually was too rarefied a medium for the affections to thrive in. He was in love only with the ideal—and the ideal as he conceived it, that is, "the absolute order of things." In all human relations, even the closest, a certain aloofness marks his feeling. As to this the testimony is unanimous. It was far from being shyness in the sense of diffidence. He did not know what diffidence was. On the contrary, it proceeded from an acute sense of self-respect. Mr. Cabot's Memoir contains a delicious letter to Margaret Fuller, who sighed for more reciprocity in him.[27] Plainly he was to be neither wheedled nor bullied into intimacy. He was himself quite conscious of his innate unresponsiveness—as indeed what was there that escaped his all-embracing, all-mirroring consciousness? He was twice married, and received his life long the deferential devotion of family and friends. But he undoubtedly felt that "my Father's business"[28]—or his equivalent for it—had claims upon his preoccupation superior to theirs. The essence of love is self-abandonment, and such an attitude is quite foreign to him. It was in fact inconsistent with his idea of the dignity and importance of his own individuality, which he cherished with a singleness quite exactly comparable with the saint's subordination of all earthly to divine affection. He did not care enough for his friends to discriminate between them—which I imagine is the real reason for the extraordinary estimate of Alcott that has puzzled so many of his devotees. Aloofness is no respecter of persons. Seen from a sufficient height ordinary differences tend to equalization. He shrank even from having followers and all his friends felt his detachment. He was silent for the most part in company—not constrained, not abstracted, just resting, one fancies, in a temporary surcease of meditative activity. And at home, he says, "Most of the persons I see in my own house I see across a gulf."[29]

Such temperamental composure it is perhaps that saves him from the fanaticism regnant around him through much of his life, and more or less directly derived from the disintegration of conservatism whose elements he had himself set free. We owe him our intellectual emancipation in all of its results, no doubt. But he himself never lost his equilibrium. His enthusiasms did not enthrall him, nor did he ever become the slave even of his own ideas. Of theories he had practically none. And his lack of fixity was not only too integral for fanatical determination but too frigid for volcanic disturbance. Common sense—of the recognizably Yankee variety—was less his balance-wheel than a component part of his nature, and gives to his intellect its marked turn for wisdom rather than speculation. It is this element in his writings that prevents his oracular manner from arousing distrust and makes his paradoxical color seem merely the poetizing of the literal. On all sorts of practical things he says the last word—the last as well as the *fin mot*. With the eloquence and enthusiasm of youth—no writer is so perennially young—he had the coolness of age; and this coolness is as marked in his earliest as in his latest writings, which indeed show increased mellowness and a winning kind of circumspect geniality. But, to adopt the terms he himself would have sanctioned, if not employed, his susceptibility was really stirred by the reason alone —the self-knower, the organ of immediate-beholding—and was in no wise responsive, even in dealing with the most practical matters, to the conclusions of the understanding, or the report of the senses. "There is no doctrine of the Reason," he exclaims with tender fervor, "which will bear to be taught by the Understanding." [30] Being thus stimulated in the main by only a portion (to speak anciently again) of his beloved intellect, his feelings really glowed, one may say, within extraordinarily narrow limits. When he could exercise his *Vernunft* in complete neglect of his *Verstand* he reached the acme of his exaltation. The direct perception of truth—meaning, of course, moral truth—suffused him with something as near the ecstasy he so often seems to aspire to without ever quite reaching, as his extremely self-possessed temperament would suffer. "God, or pure mind," [31] is one of his phrases, incidental but abundantly defining his conception of Deity, and it is this central conception that colors his philosophy and on its religious side makes it so strictly ethical.

Professor Woodberry—whose "Life of Emerson" [32] is in my judgment not only a masterly study of a difficult subject but one of our few rounded and distinct literary masterpieces—maintains that Emerson is essentially religious. I cannot myself see it. Perhaps it is a question of definition, but surely it is an accepted idea that religion is a matter of the heart, and one is confident that no religious or other emotion ever seriously disturbed the placid alternation of systole and diastole in Emerson's. It is fortunate probably that it is so little a matter of the intellect; otherwise the mass of mankind whom it guides and consoles in one way or another, *tant bien que mal,* would distinctly be losers. The wise and prudent themselves, as a matter of fact, to which class Emerson eminently belonged, have mainly manifested a susceptibility to it in virtue of that side of their nature which they share with the babes to whom it has been revealed. What the unaided intellect has ever done for it, except by way of occasionally divesting it of the theology it had previously encumbered it with, is difficult to see. Certainly no secular writer, even, ever cared less about it, however defined—unless it be religious to aggrandize the moral sentiment and insist on it as the *summum bonum* and the *suprema lex* of life—than Emerson. Matthew Arnold called it "the most lovable of things," though in describing it as "morality touched by emotion" [33] he seemed to many to eliminate its divine and therefore most characteristic sanction. With Emerson neither morality nor anything else is "touched by emotion" in any other sense than that of exaltation. He counsels the "scholar" to be "cold and true." [34] And though on the other hand he is in constant communication with the divine element in nature, what he understands by this is not the power that makes for righteousness, but mind—universal mind, whose sole manifestation is not goodness, or beauty, but truth, of which goodness is altogether a concomitant, and beauty a mere manifestation. "No law can be sacred to me but that of my own nature. Good and bad are but names very readily transferable to this or that; the only right is what is after my constitution, the only wrong what is against it." [35]

IV

It would, indeed, be hardly too fanciful to find Emerson's philosophy very considerably derived from the natural man in him—using the terms in the "orthodox" theological sense and not in his nor in Rousseau's. Bland angel as he was, he very much wanted his own way. One is tempted to say that he invented or elected his philosophy in order to get it. At all events it exactly suited him. He had no sentimental needs. It satisfies none. He had, to an inordinate degree—as how should he not have?— the pride of intellect. It magnifies mind. He was assailed by no temptations, knew no "law of the members." [36] It contemplates none. He was impatient of constraint. It exalts freedom. He suffered from the pressure of traditional superstition. It lauds the leading of individual light. He felt acutely, with an extraordinary and concentrated intensity, the value, the importance, the dignity of his own soul. It invents the "over soul"—surely an exercise in terminology!—to authenticate it. The natural man, however understood, is the undisciplined man. And discipline is precisely the lacking element in his philosophy. The philosophers are very impatient with it. One of them, certainly one of the most instinctive, erudite and expert of American members of the guild—practitioners of the art, I was about to say—informs me that "no one who has worshipped in the shrine of Kant can put up with that loose sort of practical 'philosophy.'" "Practical" in his view is manifestly not a laudatory epithet for philosophy —Carlyle's "moonshine" indeed, more so. But so far as Emerson himself was concerned I suspect that it is an exact one; for him it was extremely practical, even essential. In the silver shimmer of his "moonshine" the whole moral world lay argently if not effulgently illuminated, and if objective truths were not revealed in their completeness, they were essentially defined with a shadow both sharper in outline and fuller of suggestiveness than sunlight secures or permits. Logic has been said—not very scientifically, it is true—to be a justification of one's instincts. But vigorously and indeed airily eschewing logic as it does, Emerson's philosophy may nevertheless be called the justification of his intuitions to himself in more or less obscure logical fashion; concatenated intuitions involve a kind of deductive logic. Essentially novel his ideas cannot be called—though it should be said that he never claims novelty for them, merely advancing them, in serene independence, and disregard of their to him doubtless "secondary sources," as drawn from the fountain of truth. "Fragments of old thought that have been long in the world, like boulders left by the primeval streams of man's intellect," Professor Woodberry picturesquely if rather hardly calls them. Even the theory of Nature, perhaps his most personal philosophic contribution is, he continues, "not without copious illustrations in mystical writers." [37] But however strictly he had inherited them, Emerson had undoubtedly, in Goethe's famous phrase, "reconquered" them for himself.[38] And out of them he had composed what for him was an eminently practical working hypothesis which it pleased him to regard as the constitution of the universe. Is there as a matter of fact any "over soul"? one may ask. As a matter of fact there was for Emerson. But I imagine that he did not reach it by the revelation of intuition but by the convenient road of inferential if not rigorous logic, proceeding from postulates particularly agreeable to his own very peremptory predilections. Indeed it is when he abandons his intuitions—or attempts to give the order of sequence to their succession—that his genius, which is ineradically fragmentary abandons him. An unoriginal philosophy of shreds and patches may be welded into effective coherence by systematic logic alone. And Emerson's so far from being rigorous was thoroughly fanciful. All his metaphysic is fanciful. When he differentiates his philosophy and diversifies its structure into a semblance of metaphysical system, it becomes, I think, as nearly insipid as the functioning of a really great mind can be. His love of mystery, the poetic element in his thinking, is manifested in mystification, and his "circles" and "polarity" and "compensation" and differentiated "oneness" and "over soul" and so on wear less the aspect of august Laws than of the elementary varied by the trivial—having their genesis, too, in a demand as superfluous as the supply is essentially supposititious. Certainly they add less than nothing to the literary value of his writings, which—since the philosophers will have none of him—is after all the important matter. They make even less ponderable what is already on the verge of volatility.

Nevertheless if much of its *fioritura,* as his more personal contributions to it may be called, was, thus, more or less obscurely deduced—since man is after all a reasoning animal, as well as inspired by "Reason" in the Hegelian sense—his philosophy was in substance and practically altogether intuitional; and, as such, as sound as traditional authority could make it. That is to say, it was good for the general use as well for his own. Any kind of "ontology" will serve so long as its associated philosophy is sound, and however an intuitional philosophy may be depreciated, it has this in its favor that the mind itself recognizes its central postulate as its own habitual process. It has consciousness —"the light of all our seeing" [39]—on its side. Whatever the ultimate origin of ideas, in other words, introspection *empirically* attests them as at any rate not immediately proceeding from experience. Otherwise the world, given over to introspection for so many ages, would have anticipated Locke even before Bacon. Ideas "swin into our ken" [40] and it is quite impossible for consciousness to derive them from what has evoked them. The nexus escapes it. We conceive as unexpectedly as we perceive. That is to say, even if Newton really *inferred* gravitation from the fall of the apple—as so many had failed to do!—what filled his consciousness at the instant was not inference but cognition. It is this that makes Emerson's philosophy so generally attractive—its harmonious accord with the report of the general consciousness of even the unreflective and the inexpert. It preaches what common experience approves. On the other hand of course the way in which ideas reach the mind or are revealed within it having nothing whatever to do with their validity, Emerson's implicit trust in them—unexampled, in the immense and varied use he made of it, since Aristotle's discovery of their need of testing—has in him its naive, and in his disciples its incontestably fatuous, side. But if he mistook guesses at, for glimpses of, truth on occasion, it cannot be denied that, given his intense love of it—in itself the most powerful clarifier of mental vision—and his altogether remarkable good sense—inherited perhaps from generations of intellectual ancestors who knew not whim—his own extraordinarily gifted intelligence worked with a minimum of insecurity, as it undoubtedly worked in its freest, its happiest and its most congenial possible way, within the elastic framework of an intuitional philosophy, and would have been strangled by an empirical one. His philosophy at any rate, as I say, suited *him*. It fostered the expansion of his native genius and fructified as any thing other would have sterilized, the luxuriant efflorescence of his meditation. Without it, without the certainty his direct vision enabled him to feel, his wisdom would have far less authority and would have suffered from the inevitable enfeeblement of speculation. Induction is impertinent to the seer. "Without the vision" he loses his office quite as inevitably as "the people perish." [41]

His philosophy also suited the time and environment of which he was in turn a product as well as a prophet. Elusive as he is, Emerson was of the essence of New England, and the New England of the early nineteenth century. Generations of militant

Protestantism necessarily intensified the essence of non-conformity without, of course, necessarily transmitting its traditional expression. It is of course the type that persists, and the type is not a set of opinions, however rigid, but the attitude of mind in which they are held. Emerson's catholicity extends to indifference rather than to tolerance, and in itself is distinctly intellectual rather than sympathetic or voluntary. He is constitutionally less a descendant of Erasmus than of Luther. His protest against titular Protestantism, against dogma in general, is identical in nature with the Reformers' protest against specific dogmas. Its expression is in scope chiefly an evolution, though in temper a miraculous variation from type. It allows him, to be sure, an occasional return to the Puritan luxury of oppugnation and excess, as in his remark that John Brown had made the gallows as glorious as the Cross,[42] or in an ironical reference to history or culture or "Europe," or tart censure of the "Oriental" way in which "the good Jesus" has been deified [43]—instead perhaps of being "ground into paint" for more specific use, as he says was the fate to which Plato subjected his relations.[44] But in general it is needless to say he has retained the mental attitude of Puritanism purged of its polemic and contentious temper. And this attitude is illustrated in the two chief objects of his consecration—individualism and the ideal. Nowhere else could the preacher of this conjoint gospel—into which all Emerson may be run up—have been developed in Emersonian perfection outside the New England of his day. Individualism is confined to Anglo-Saxon Protestantism, and in English nonconformity the ideal is of necessity obscured by the practical difficulty of sustaining life and flowering amid obstacles instead of fostering favor.

On the other hand exactly what the soil that had produced this gospel needed was the enrichment of renewal. In a new embodiment Emerson furnished this. Modified and adapted to new conditions and new occasions—subsequent phases inevitably, with time, become as static as those they themselves supplanted—above all, tinged with poetry, vital with eloquence and softened into suavity, the old Protestant gospel of the individual and the ideal responded accurately to the actual need of his country in his time. The period of colonial growth had been succeeded by that of national condensation and aggrandizement, and in the pressing interest of its quite indispensable aims its society had come to tyrannize the individual, and material progress to obscure the ideal life. Undoubtedly too much has been said of the alleged pusillanimity of this period of our history, and cruel injustice has been done to the patriots who but for the fanatics might have held the nation together by the cement of compromise instead of that of blood. Professor Burgess has made it difficult longer to refuse them their meed of just praise.[45] At the same time the general peril naturally produced the situation which Emerson quite truly as well as solemnly characterized in one of his earliest utterances, declaring, "This country has not fulfilled what seemed the reasonable expectation of mankind." If it has in greater degree done so since it is largely due to the self-reliance and the ideality with which his dauntless clairvoyance inspired it, and made to appear rational as well as attractive. It has at least presented his career to mankind and mankind in profiting by it can hardly fail to acknowledge that in one respect at least his country has more than fulfilled its reasonable expectation.

Specifically one of his greatest services both to us and to mankind—chary as he was of specific service:

> "He that feeds men serveth few;
> He serves all who dares be true," [46]

and subtly as this one is rendered, being in fact rather an implication of his writings than anywhere explicit in them—is what may be called the rationalization of democracy through the ideal development of the individual. His defective sympathies qualify his own democracy which thus rests wholly on an intellectual basis, and for this reason his service to it will perhaps some day be perceived as one of the greatest that have been rendered to this greatest of modern causes. Too modest to conceive his mission as otherwise benevolent than is involved in the conversion of life into truth, too fastidious to respond to the elementary appeal of philanthropy, he was yet bold enough and detached enough to recognize the injustice of privilege, and the claims of every human potentiality for development into power. Besides, his philosophy of the identity of mind and his gospel of individualism imposed democracy upon him. The very fact that he was no respecter of persons protected him from illusions as to classes, and the finality of feudalism was alone enough to lead his revolutionary and independent spirit to see it as an arrest of development and not an ideal. Association with God and his own higher self naturally induced contempt of artificial human distinctions, and a theologian who did not divide mankind even into sheep and goats had no disposition to fix them in categories of complicated interdependence, where to preach to them his favorite doctrine of self-reliance would be derision. If his emotional nature lacked warmth, what eminently it possessed was an exquisite refinement, and a constituent of his refinement was an instinctive antipathy to ideas of dominance, dictation, patronage, caste and material superiority whose essential grossness repelled him and whose ultimate origin in contemptuousness— probably the one moral state except cravenness that chiefly he deemed contemptible—was plain enough to his penetration.

He hated the mob, and shrank from the vulgar. No doubt Tiberius Gracchus did. "Enormous populations," he exclaims, "if they be beggars, are disgusting, like moving cheese, like hills of ants, or of fleas—the more, the worse." [47] He certainly could not echo St. Francis's: "My brother, the ass." [48] But if his democracy was not founded on sentiment, it was perhaps all the more firmly established in principle by penetrating vision, and, as I have intimated, perhaps it is only in this way that democracy will be able to complete its conquest of the human spirit, that is to say by convincing the mind; the heart of mankind has often been persuaded even to ecstasy, but pure sentiment is subject to striking, not to say, tragic, reaction. From the democratic point of view, I know of no finer spectacle than that furnished by the procession of Emerson's lecturing years. All over the North and West of the country, as well as in his own New England, "the people"—there were no others—gathered in cities and villages and in substantial numbers to listen to the suave delivery of his serene message, to enjoy each one after his capacity, the honeyed extract of his assimilated culture, the fruit of his claustral meditation, on various phases of all sorts of topics, but always the Ideal. However much or little they comprehended, they at least savored it, and their eagerness to breathe its rarefied air and experience its elusive stimulus, witnesses a corresponding idealism in his public. His public was no doubt as eminently naive as he was subtle, but they met on the common ground of the dignity of the individual and his indefinitely great capacity for development through divine illumination. Truly a different social phenomenon altogether from that of the University Extension movement, say, whether or no as valuable measured by its fruits.

Measured by its fruits, Emersonian doctrine must certainly be, and it cannot be contested that some of these have not been fair. There can be no doubt of the preponderance of beneficence in his influence, and rightly apprehended it can have no other quality. His every understanding reader must receive from him a spiritual quickening that combines moral earnestness with intellectual exhilaration, a purified sense of the pricelessness at once and the attainability of the very best, and a corresponding disregard for the second-rate. He shrivels mediocrity for us as no other writer does. His exaction is almost exorbitant, but the courage and the consciousness of capacity he stimulates echo "the youth" who in his own famous line—unparalleled in literature, I think, for its tonic effect—"replies, 'I can.'" [49] But he has not always been rightly apprehended, and where he has not— where, against his repeated protest, he has been accepted literally and formally as a guide rather than as a stimulus—his extreme non-conformity has been disintegrating. The disposition to execute ideas instead of keeping them in reserve for general purposes of illumination and edification—a disposition which, it need not be said, Emerson himself, who held them in solution as it were, did not share—has resulted in many quarters in a flagrant individualism that is but a caricature of that which Emerson preached. All the same it is to be charged to his account, I think. Doubtless he never realized that a philosophy born of protest could become so positive, and indeed in its way ultramontane, as to have its own rigidities and restrictions. We may almost say that what now passes strictly for Emersonianism is the antithesis of the flux in which he joyed to see the universe whirl. Emptied of imagination, Emerson's philosophy is infallibly transformed. Almost all the "perky" people one knows are Emersonians, and in cruel truth, a numerous progeny of pedants may claim descent—at least by the sinister hand—from a parent to whom above all things pedantry was an offence. Just at present multitudes of those who are caught up in the contemporary current that is drifting away from materialism—and in whom the discovery of spiritual forces produces the same enthusiasm it doubtless did in the primitive man—feed or at least browse upon a literature that curiously caricatures Emerson. Everyone would agree that the crying, the notorious defect of these zealots is lack of culture. Culture and nothing but culture is precisely the cure for the mental condition illustrated in these and other eccentricities of the spirit of nonconformity. And when one sees the excess to which Emerson's central doctrine of self-reliance is capable of being carried, even more important than that one should "be content with one's own light" [50] seems the result desired by Mrs. Shelley—who had had an experience quite otherwise illuminating than was attainable at Concord!—for her son: "Teach him to think for himself? Oh, my God, teach him rather to think like other people!" [51] When Emerson affirms "Whoso would be a man must be a nonconformist," [52] it is permitted to wish, thinking of some of his disciples, that he had spent at least one day in explanation.

V

Culture, however, did not enter into Emerson's philosophy. His philosophy, indeed, following his instinct does not so much neglect as positively impeach it. There is no denying the fact, which is vaunted rather than dissembled. He has a hard word for it always. Culture means on the one hand discipline, which irked him, and on the other acquisition, which to him could only have a disciplinary function. In either aspect it involves effort and effort lay quite outside his ideal of surrender to intuition and impulse. "I would not degrade myself," he says, "by casting about for a thought nor by waiting for one." [53] And it is far less a transient than a prevailing mood in which he affirms, "I would write on the lintels of the door-post, *Whim*." [54] And this spirit informs not only his intellectual but his moral philosophy, so far as these are separable. What he holds in reserve in the one case is the "explanation" in which he "cannot spend the day," and in the other the postulate that impulse should of course be pure and good. His own being angelic, he assumes integrity in that of the world in general. "Our moral nature," he insists, "is vitiated by any interference of our will." [55] The curbing, directing, developing of instinct and impulse by the effort involved in disciplinary culture is to him as superfluous as it is held by the Perfectionist and the Antinomian. He would either have controverted Froude's comparison [56] of the moral life of man to the flight of a bird in the air which sustains itself only by effort, or have contended that the exertion on whose cessation man falls should be as instinctive and unconscious as the skylark's upward winging.

But even for culture that involves a minimum of effort, he feels no particular friendliness. Although it is at the least the other side of the shield of self-reliance, it is one of the few that he rarely turns around. "Obey thyself," "Trust thyself," are adjurations he never qualifies. Bishop Wilson's caution, after saying "Act in accordance with the best light that you have," namely, "be sure that your light is not darkness," [57] is one he never adds. He establishes egoism on a basis of practicable infallibility. Everything external, in fact, is valued so strictly for what it educes and evokes as to minimize its importance as augmentation and even illumination. Education is of course essentially as well as etymologically thus to be conceived. But even thus conceived culture is its complement, and the education of others may advantageously correct, modify and enrich, as well as stimulate the mind—increase its store as well as strengthen its powers. Knowledge *is* power as well as a source of it. It is only emphasis doubtless that saves the distinction from barrenness, but in such a matter emphasis is everything.

Emerson's whole stress and accent belittle culture in both its aspects, but especially in its aspect as acquisition. The essay on "History" is certainly not designed merely to state the trite truth that education is educative, but to deny that it is anything else. Yet in maintaining so rigidly that the educative is the sole function of history, he is really belittling this function itself. It is eminently not the kind of education he can consistently prize, since, even considered in the least material, and therefore to him most congenial, way as "philosophy teaching by examples," his philosophy eschews "examples" as the fleeting phenomena they no doubt are compared with Nature's "eterne," though surely less coherent and articulate, undertakings. How he really feels is shown in such a passage as the following in which if it be pedantic to note flippancy one may surely remark the absence of the historic sense:

The professor interrogates Sylvina in the history class about Odoacer and Alaric. Sylvina can't remember, but suggests that Odoacer was defeated; and the professor tartly replies: "No, he defeated the Romans." But 'tis plain to the visitor, that 'tis of no importance at all about Odoacer, and it is a great deal of importance about Sylvina; and if she says he was defeated, why he had better a great deal have been defeated than give her a moment's annoy. Odoacer, if there was a particle of the gentleman in him, would have said, "Let me be defeated a thousand times." [58]

It is perhaps fortunate for the visitor that it is of no importance to him about Odoacer. The history seems a little mixed. And though in general so far as any equipment he may need is concerned Emerson illustrates culture nearly as much as—*bien à son aise!*—he depreciates it, it is no doubt in his lack of the historic sense that he illustrates it least. "Representative Men" is critically penetrating, but the treatment is characteristically summary because it stops with what is to the critic himself generally provocative and suggestive; especially characteristic is the title of the introduction: "*Uses* of Great Men." [59] One follows easily the trend of his predilection: Art in his view, for instance, is chiefly valuable as recording history; history is of value so strictly as fuel for his own intellectual combustion that it is of small importance in even this regard; his mind in its creative and not its acquisitive aspect is his central concern; and in this aspect is tinder to which any spark suffices. No doubt occasionally—and impulsively—he forgot that many of his "own spirits in prison" were less happily constituted.

His neglect of the furniture of the mind, the material it has to work with—hardly less important than the condition of its muscles, so to speak—, his peremptory rejection of all that is not plainly addressed grist for the individual's own mill, appears elsewhere as plainly as in his view of history. It appears in his literary prejudices, certainly the most whimsical that could be predicated of a really great mind, whatever its temperamental defects. "He could see nothing," Mr. Cabot records, "in Shelley, Aristophanes, Don Quixote, Dickens." [60] Dante whom he conventionally celebrates in verse, he called obscurely "another Zerah Colburn"—described in the dictionaries as a youthful mathematical prodigy of the day. He finds that Landor, Coleridge, Carlyle, Wordsworth all lack the intuition of religious truth, adding: "They have no idea of that species of moral truth [identifying 'religious' with 'moral,' one perceives incidentally] that I call the first philosophy." [61] His race prejudices are also plain, as appears especially in "English Traits"—a work distrusted by the English themselves almost as much as "Our Old Home" [62] is disesteemed, and though surprisingly full of instructive data as well as distinctly entertaining, distinctly less penetrating and sound than it might have been had he had even a touch of cosmopolitanism wherewith to modify its rather loose panegyric. He knew German and Germany of course. His philosophy issued thence on its way from Plato, though he caught a good deal of it in rebound from Coleridge; his positive preference for translations is well known. But one may almost say that he appears never to have heard of France, except as an appanage of Napoleon, of whom he had a curious and curiously enlightened appreciation.[63] Social questions also left him cold. "I have no social talent," he says of himself and might with equal truth have added, no social interests.[64] Culture prescribes an interest in the present and future of mankind as well as in its past. But mankind, as such, interested him very superficially. Unlike his ally Nature he is careless of the type [65] and though it is his individuality that chiefly he cares for in the individual he certainly emphasizes this in a way that minimizes all the relations of fellowship. His social sense, in a word, has always been found by his critics even more defective than his historic, and attests even more plainly to the present time his deficiency in culture, which alone could have modified his instinctive individualism and to which in an essential respect therefore his philosophy appears provincial and, however vital, barbaric. Individualism is currently, it need not be said, a waning force in all "practical" philosophy, in whose domain on the contrary the social sense has strongly entrenched itself.

It has done so in no small degree in virtue of its substantial

accord with what culture recognizes as the survival in society of
the spirit of fraternity, which Christianity inherited perhaps
from Stoicism and, enriched with its own emotional opulence
and elevation, transmitted to the modern world—one of its
latest embodiments being in fact expressly labelled "Christian
socialism." And Emerson, to go one step further, whether or no
his devotion to the "moral sentiment" be exactly characterized
as religious or as merely ethical, is as distinctly un-Christian as
he is unsocial. The orthodox of his day followed a sure instinct
in distrusting him, however pusillanimous the form the feeling
took on occasion. The orthodox distrust of him has largely passed
away, partly through its own transformation, partly through the
extreme winningness of his eloquence and his personal saintli-
ness, partly through its failure to perceive that his variety of
idealism is as hostile to the essence as to the ecclesiasticism of
Christianity. From the point of view of culture Christianity,
denuded of its ecclesiastical sanctions, is still more to be explained as a force, a factor in evolution, an element of progress.
It is impossible not to reckon with its principles, its discoveries,
its modifications and deflections of the Pagan current of tendency
and constitution of moral attitude. Goethe, for example, passes
with the orthodox for a Pagan in virtue of his culture. But culture
includes the orthodox and Goethe's web of life lost no single
thread furnished by Christianity. The profound contribution to
the philosophy of existence made in the utterance "He that
loveth his life shall lose it" [66] finds its echo across the dissonances
of twenty ages in

"Entbehren sollst du! sollst entbehren!" [67]

—the keynote of the greatest modern poem.

Goethe, however, was in the full current of the stream of
culture—not as Emerson, a complacent spectator on its banks,
intelligently interested in the chips that floated by on its surface,
but really preoccupied with truth. He had never been extruded
from conformity by a doubt as to whether he had a right to
administer the Lord's Supper to a Unitarian congregation. Self-
assertion even of the serenest sort never occurred to him. He
was engaged in doing things—that is, writing things—that had
relations to their before and after congeners, not in contemplating

the importance of his individuality. Hence he felt the force and pressure of the things that had been done—and written—before him, and applied himself to building another chamber in the nautilus-shell of culture [68]—that culture to which Emerson penetratingly accuses him of sacrficing truth. What has Emerson added to that? The answer is capital in any consideration of him, though it in no wise obscures his undoubted invigoration of the sinews of the soul. The two achievements are, however, far from identical and it cannot be too clearly perceived that Emerson and culture are at war. That is to say, he is at war with the greatest force in the modern world—he who passes in general for the most modern of men. He is modern, however, in virtue of his wonderful catholicity of appreciation, not because of his temperamental sympathy with the way the world is going. It is going in quite the contrary direction from that which he indicated to it; the individual *is* withering and the world *is* becoming more and more,[69] in virtue at least of a growing sense that whatever is individual is necessarily partial and lacks the authority of synthetic co-operation.

The gospel of self-assertion, therefore, which is but another name for Emerson's stirring "self-reliance," has less virtue to-day than in a period of traditional tyranny especially blind to the ideal. Its virtue is incontestable, but it is already practically relegated to the category of "subsumed" and presupposed *principia* of all thought and conduct. His optimism, accordingly, remains tonic, but it is no longer daily food. It is marked rather by elevation than depth; and his philosophy, taken as a whole, which it pervades and indeed unifies, is thus marked. In its concentration on the ideal and its corresponding neglect of the actual, it is not philosophically central and complete. It stimulates aspiration, but does not sustain realization. It would be shallow to describe it as superficial. Nothing in Emerson is superficial. And to the sense that marks his lack of depth, his elevation is quite as clear if not wholly compensatory. Moreover, his lack of depth is always felt as a temperamental coldness, never, it need hardly be said, as intellectual aridity. There is nothing of which he fails to take account, but his accent and stress—an immense matter—are not dictated by feeling, and consequently have the less weight. The ascription of optimism to him in the Pangloss sense would be absurd. A view of the actual as the best possible world can hardly be ascribed to a revolutionary and reformatory spirit, always and systematically a critic of the established order—a writer whose work is full of allusions to the ineptitudes of human imbecility (not an infrequent word with him) and who asserts that "a person seldom falls sick but the bystanders are animated with a faint hope that he will die." [70] "We live," he maintains, "in a very low state of the world," and, in his excessive way, asseverates, "The highest virtue is always against the law." In fact his whole work originated and continued in a protest against institutional circumstance, as he experienced it in his own environment and perceived it in the world at large, historic and actual. His optimism consists in his confidence in the *natural* constitution of things, in the exhilaration its contemplation gives him, in his persuasion that *Nature* is the best possible Nature, and that man though "fallen," has infinite potentialities, his perfectibility being dependent only on the transformation of "masses" into individuals, on ignoring the cultivation of his garden and, not to put too fine a point upon it, brushing up his wits. With intellectual illumination thus obtained his salvation is secure. Moreover, he understands man as "fallen" in the sense of fallen from his *native* estate more in the Rousseau and not at all in the theological sense, except of course that Rousseau's view is, so to speak, historical and Emerson's naturally purely ideal. Had Pangloss heard of this variety of optimism, far more subtle but also far less vulnerable than his own, it is not unlikely that he would have consented to adopt it as a wholly acceptable compromise; in which event literature would have lost "Candide." There is no way of impeaching the view that there exists an order of Nature—"an absolute order of things as they stand in the mind of God"—which "the intellect searches out without the colors of affection," [71] and which is a harmony coestablished with the perverse order known to experience, quite as absolutely real though wholly ideal, and needing only to be perceived by the mind whose vision penetrates the veils of material phenomena. Just as to Kant the moral law was as real as the starry heavens. Only, to hold this view with enthusiasm is to be an optimist, and an optimist far otherwise convinced and inveterate than either the genial or the cynical type of indifferentist. Besides, *ex vi termini* the revolutionist is an

optimist. It is the conservative—temperamental or purely philosophic—who is the pessimist, as being less content than timorous.

Fear, however, is as fundamental as courage in the constitution of the universe. It is at least the salutary complement of
courage of the adventurous order, which is rather the instrument
of crises. It is the fear of the Lord that is the beginning of wisdom.[72] It is fear that conserves and guides and shields from peril
and destruction, and fosters growth and protects from error, and
whose service is over only when perfect love hath cast it out and
the child is reassured in the arms of its mother and the weary soul
at rest in the bosom of God. The fact that fear is rational is what
makes fortitude divine. Emerson's optimism as to the constitution of the universe—essentially unmodified, as I have said, by
his asperity toward both human kind and human institutions—
is too blithe, too bland, too confident. His ideal of independence
and non-conformity is easily made to sanction guerilla skirmish-
ing in the conflict of life, which is serious enough for a concerted
campaign. It undervalues the enemy's strength. Doubtless one
can so station the camera of his mind as to catch the universe at
Emerson's angle and identify his "perception" of positive good
everywhere with negative evil as an insubstantial and illusory
shadow—"captive ill attending captain good." [73] The youthful
Goethe, aged six, at the time of the Lisbon earthquake did so,
and reported his vision of the truth that a mortal accident cannot
affect an immortal spirit.[74] But it is difficult to "hold the position"
—which requires a dervish tension and its accompanying insensi-
bility. The slightest shifting of even the purely intellectual point
of view discloses the old panorama. Pain hurts, poverty pinches,
bereavement is bitter, injustice cruel, remorse torture. If evil is
but the shadow of good, its blackness leaves any but an invincibly
optimistic temperament sadder still by minimizing the moral order in rendering it less substantial and therefore less apt a field
for calculable conflict. Moreover, how explain sin—the *choice*
of evil? To call sin "good in the making," to ascribe it to some
"circle" or other in following which the "ways of the wicked" are
made to serve the harmony of the spheres, is to minimize its
gravity and "wither" the individual with a vengeance. But Emerson is always minimizing when he is not magnifying the individual—an inevitable alternation, perhaps, in an intellectual phi-

losophy that ignores *conscience*, and considers potentialities to
the exclusion of responsibilities. As a part of the universe, you
are a veritable *mouche de coche*, and whatever you do is muted
in the celestial symphony. As an individual, consciousness itself
gives a glowing, an almost incredible account of your capacities.
Conscience, however, is another matter.

Emerson was "all his days," says Henry James, Sr., "an arch-
traitor to our existing civilized regimen, inasmuch as he unconsciously managed to set aside its fundamental principle, in doing
without conscience. . . . He had no conscience, in fact, and
lived by perception, which is an altogether lower or less spiritual
faculty." [75] His neglect of conscience is undoubtedly due in large
measure to his personal immunity from its mordant functioning.
Unlike the youth—tenderly nurtured in the lap of Calvinism—
who expressed surprise at hearing of an *approving* one, his own
must have been radiantly commending. It was easy for him to
affirm that "no man can afford to waste his moments in compunction." [76] Personal blamelessness conjoined with modesty, which
in Emerson was correspondingly marked, naturally induce optimism. There is nothing like sin to give one a gloomy view of the
universe. It is the ally and often the parent of cynicism, doubtless,
and its natural tendency is to impair philosophic integrity—
since its concomitant is suffering and suffering of any sort deflects and distorts. But culture as well as experience feels the lack
of depth in any philosophy that ignores conscience. This is a far
more essential difference between Emerson and Carlyle than the
greater suavity of the former by which, aptly coupling them as
exponents of "personal idealism," Professor Eucken [77]—the latest
German authority on philosophy—distinguishes the two. Carlyle
surely has more depth. Nor with all his arrogance did he have
less humility. It is impossible to have less. In the sense in which
the word that epitomizes Epictetus is fortitude, Marcus Aurelius
resignation, early Christianity renouncement, the "ages of faith"
humilitas, the Renaissance emancipation, the eighteenth century
enlightenment—Emerson is summed up in *confidence*. He is as
much outside the current of ethical evolution as of Newman's
trend of doctrinal development. He has the pride which Meredith aptly called Pagan. He is not arrogant in spirit but autocratic
in attitude. The attitude of "The Problem" [78] is even exultant. He

has not the defiant note of Henley's "Invictus" or the *insouciance* of Stevenson's *gaudium certaminis*.[79] But his confidence indubitably recalls writers of this slightly aggressive order, rather than the deeper notes of the masters who interpret life with more deference, if not with a greater sense of dependence on, than of unison with, the divine. No wonder Nietzsche habitually carried one of his volumes in his pocket. If Socrates is "terribly at ease in Zion," [80] Emerson is elate there. And only those for whom elevated elation is an equivalent of depth, will find in a philosophy of intellectual pride and moral confidence the soundness and substance for which culture as well as conscience calls. In this regard those on whose hearts at the present day the sentences of, for example, the "General Confession" of the Anglican ritual no longer

"Fall like sweet strains—" [81]

will echo more spontaneously than the elation of Emerson's confidence, the deeper solemnity of such a passage as this of Fitzjames Stephen's:

We stand on a mountain pass in the midst of whirling snow and blinding mist through which we get glimpses now and then of paths which may be deceptive. If we stand still, we shall be frozen to death. If we take the wrong road we shall be dashed to pieces. We do not certainly know whether there is any right one. What must we do? "Be strong and of a good courage." Act for the best, hope for the best, and take what comes. If death ends all, we cannot meet it better. If not, let us enter whatever may be the next scene like honest men, with no sophistry in our mouths and no masks on our faces.[82]

VI

Its genesis naturally furnishes the key to Emerson's style. It is that of the pulpit modified by the lyceum, and the forensic element struggles in it with the literary. Its ideal is eloquence, not exposition, and it is more than likely that this ideal affected his thought as well—manner so marked inevitably reacting on matter. Now-a-days it is an effort to recall this ideal of but a generation ago, in the light of which however it sometimes seems as if our current literature were quite content, so far as style is concerned, to be thoroughly second rate so long as it is simple and

clear. Style indeed, properly so called, may be said not to have
survived Spencer's philosophy of it.[83] But a few decades ago, in
New England at least, it was very generally esteemed an essential
element of writing, and—no doubt to its detriment in a certain
degree—inextricably associated with eloquence. How it sounded
was hardly less important than how it read, in the consideration
of a composition even of an exclusively literary character. Oratory was still studied and practised, and imposed its criteria outside its own confines. In early days I do not myself recall that
Plato or Thucydides was ever signalized as a master of style,
though the simplicity of the one and the compression of the other
were of course noted and commended. The models set before
youth, at least as late as Emerson's prime, were Demosthenes,
Isocrates, Cicero, Burke, Webster. In point of style no purely
literary influence exerted over the youth of that day was more
marked than that of Phillips.[84] And certainly I have never encountered since, in whatever field of activity, any artistic expression that produced the effect of perfection at once more singly
and more fully than one of his lectures did. We went to his lectures in preference to the theatre. His reserve and dignity; his
concentrated power exhibited in grace, and intensity manifested
in suavity; his serenity which simulated elevation and the court-
liness with which it clothed absolute venom—every trait of his
technic was the acme of that taste which Emerson identifies with
the love of beauty and which realized for his hearers their purest
ideals of eloquence as an art. It was small wonder that for so
many of them the distinction between oral and written expression
even as an ideal was only disclosed later, by wider and different
experiences, and that exclusively literary prescriptions should
have seemed to lack vitality in the presence of a living model of
such commanding quality.

A similar influence, during his formative period, was undoubtedly exercised over Emerson by Everett.[85] In early days he admired Everett—to a degree which, since the episode of Everett's
overshadowing at Gettysburg, perhaps, has been popularly incomprehensible. He testifies that "the word that he spoke, in the
manner in which he spoke it, became current and classical in
New England." "Not a sentence," he continues, "was written in
academic exercises, not a declamation attempted in the college

chapel, but showed the omnipresence of his genius to youthful heads." [86] Everett and Emerson—it is hard to think of a more incongruous association! The connecting link is the ideal of eloquence. Like many more important writers, Everett is no longer read. But Emerson's eulogy of his style is specific and convincing. There are many echoes in this panegyric of his own procedure: "He had great talent for collecting facts, and for bringing those he had to bear with ingenious felicity on the moment. . . . All his learning was available for the purposes of the hour. . . . It was so coldly and weightily communicated from so commanding a platform as if in the consciousness and consideration of all history and all learning—adorned with so many simple and austere beauties of expression, and enriched with so many excellent digressions and significant quotations . . . All his auditors felt the extreme beauty and dignity of the manner, and even the coarsest were contented to go punctually to listen, for the manner, when they had found out that the matter was not for them . . . He abounded in sentences." [87] I have quoted so much because it is all so strikingly applicable to Emerson himself. In the matter of style a writer never fully recovers from his early admirations; they are such, doubtless, because his nature responds to them. And perhaps the seven preachers of his ancestry had transmitted to Emerson the taste and the talent for treating the written as if it were the spoken word and predisposed him to admire, and later to emulate, the oratorical manner of which Everett was—with whatever reservations in respect of artificiality, unappreciated by his youthful adorer—the most admirable exponent in his day.

To the present generation it is almost needful to protest that eloquence and oratory are not, normally, varieties of tasteless inflation and tropical excess, that they are not of necessity alloyed with the meretricious. At all events in Emerson's case, his early ideals and his subsequent practice in the lyceum pulpit, are undoubtedly largely responsible for what is the salient merit of his style—for the fact that what he wrote has the vitality of the spoken word. Every sentence is addressed to the mind directly. It has a complete value in itself, and is not merely contributory to any general cumulative effect. So far, accordingly, as the prevailing blandness of his nature permits, it is decidedly a sententious style. But blandness is also an obvious element of it and bridges the absence of transitions, or at least softens it, so that while your attention receives really a constant succession of stimuli, they almost blend in the equivalence of tendency. As there is no reasoning there is no appeal to the reasoning faculties and you turn the pages even more submissively than you follow an orator, conscious only of a series of apprehensions. And each paragraph, each sentence—sometimes nearly every word—is instinct with individual effectiveness, often conceived with a wonderful intuitive sense of beauty and fitness, always chosen with a wonderful felicity of selection, incisive, apt, illuminating and on occasion fairly vibrant with charm. His vocabulary is a marvel of eclecticism—drawn from all fields, from poetry to science, from the country of the imagination to that of every day existence, ranging from the most exotic to the most familiar, the most ornate to the most ordinary, and excluding nothing but the pedantic and the mediocre. No writer ever possessed a more distinguished verbal instinct, or indulged it with more delight. He fairly caresses his words and phrases and shows in his treatment of them a pleasure nearer sensuousness, perhaps, than any other he manifests. Everywhere his diction is penetrated with these essential traits of eloquence—traits enduing mere expression with values of force, of weight, of heightened and intensified vigor, that in Emerson combine to weave the garment of vitality itself.

On the other hand, the lack of continuity is obvious. His inconsequences of expression image his inconsecutiveness of thought with even more than the natural closeness. They increased in the transformation of his lectures into essays, which with him, owing precisely to his sense for form in the restricted degree in which he possessed it, was a process rather of pruning than development. The lectures that became essays were fastidiously and relentlessly compressed instead of expanded and the method is another demonstration of his individuality—the usual method being the extension of notes into fuller and rounder completeness. At times the effect of his page is that of a series of ejaculations, so exaggeratedly episodic, indeed, as to be more comparable with the aphoristic style of La Rochefoucauld or Vauvenargues than with that of even La Bruyère, and when he sinks below his level, not without suggestions of what he himself, I think, somewhere speaks of as the style of the almanac. Sometimes, indeed, this manner acts with him as a kind of auto-infection, owing to his very sensitiveness to *nuances* of the kind, and you feel pelted with particles rather than presented with any whole whatever— not to speak of organic completeness. But it is to be borne in mind that the lack of continuity in Emerson's style in general does not exclude *passages* of such substantial extent as really to count as periods. And such passages so count in virtue not only of extent, but of character; they are in construction and rythmic sentiment truly periodic. His eloquence is not merely pointed, but on occasion—when in fact he indulges the weakness of lingering over a thought instead of uttering another—sustained. It is needless to say this is a disposition he does not abuse. Nevertheless his habitual and prevailing elevation of mind and mood is such that in the kind of passage to which I refer, hardly any prose is richer than his. No writer ever had in more opulent measure the unusual power of maintaining throughout varied thematic modulation a single tone, a central thought, until the expression of its strict implications was complete, and one after another of its phrasings apt for echo in eloquent unison. Eloquence, in fact, either of word, phrase or passage, pervades his style as a flavor; it is present as a distinct, and, indeed, dominant element and governs the entire technic, already germinant in its inspiration.

What his style lacks is art in the larger sense. It is distinctly the style of a writer who is artistic, but not an artist—to apply to himself the useful distinction he applied to Goethe.[88] He had no sense of composition; his compositions are not composed. They do not constitute objective creations. They have no construction, no organic quality—no evolution. He is above the "degradation" of resort to the elementary, but in some guise or other fundamental, machinery of rhetorical presentation—the succession of exordium, theme, conclusion. His essays often begin happily with an arousing, stimulant utterance, but there is no graded approach to any distinguishable middle, followed in turn by some end; they do not terminate, but cease. His sense of form— exquisite where purity and simplicity are concerned—disappears in the presence of complexity and elaboration. The impressiveness of a work of art resides largely in the relations between its larger values, but Emerson has no larger values. The details themselves—often, as I say, beautiful, and caressingly burnished —are not grouped in active interdependence, and consequently do not constitute parts. A *fortiori* there is no whole, and as a rule, the essays do not leave a very definite single impression, so far as the reinforcement of the theme by the treatment is concerned. You get the idea that "self-reliance" is a fine thing, but not how, or why, or with what qualifications. The detail of such essays as "Power," "Success," "Greatness," is almost interchangeable. His way of working, combined with his depreciation of effort, made this inevitable. He read, walked and meditated eight or nine hours a day, thus accumulating golden nuggets of thought, but without the direction of the will his meditation was of necessity desultory, and when subsequently he subtracted from his accumulation of nuggets enough for a lecture or an essay their classification was perforce rather arbitrary. It is only nature that can be trusted to work thus at hap-hazard, and even Pactolus was a stream, not a moraine. For man's creation art is rigorously requisite. And art in the constructive sense found no echo in Emerson's nature.

In general terms, to be sure, he says the most searching things about it. About what subject of human concern, indeed, does he fail to? There is no witness of his wisdom, of the wide embracing character of his intellect, more striking than some of his deliverances about its character and scope largely considered, for, being temperamentally without sensuous strain, he looked through things rather than at them. It is true that any writer coming after Goethe, has small excuse for error as to essential and constitutional æsthetic principles. And in part no doubt, he owes his felicity in dealing with these to the culture he depreciates, to his having read Goethe. But he read him with sympathetic comprehension and the preparedness due to his own extraordinarily unerring intuition. Sentences such as these occur in his earliest book: "The love of beauty is taste," "The creation of beauty is art," [89] "Thus is art, a nature passed through the alembic of man," "The integrity of impression made by manifold natural objects," "There is no object so foul that intense light will not make it beautiful," "The sensual man conforms thoughts to things; the poet conforms things to his thoughts," "The charming landscape I saw this morning is indubitably made up of some

twenty or thirty farms. Miller owns this field, Locke that, and
Manning the woodland beyond. But none of them owns the
landscape. There is a property in the horizon which no man has,
but he whose eye can integrate all the parts, the poet." [90] If he
had here taken one step further and added that the artist is he
who can express this integration, unfold this involution, he would
have established the exact category of art. This step, however,
undoubtedly implies—even with Claude [91]—the effort he disesteemed. He never took it himself, nor did he value the results
of others in taking it.

His remark of Goethe, just referred to, that "this law-giver of
art is not an artist" is far more applicable to himself, though his
perception of the lack of art in Goethe's works is creditably
paradoxical in him. One argues that its absence in Goethe is
perceived and not felt by him—*more suo;* if to acuteness of
perception were added the sincerity of feeling, he would have
been less sweeping. Is not the first part of "Faust" artistic? And
are not Goethe's classical productions correct to the point of
coldness? In his own case, at any rate, what he betrays in his
attitude toward art is sapience, not sensitiveness. The fact—
considering the New England of his day—is still another, and
not the least significant, evidence of his powers of intellectual
divination. As to these one is constantly tempted to ask oneself
in reading him, if after all intellect *enough* is not all-sufficient.
But when we come to his own appreciation of art in the concrete, we realize how little it meant to him. He could, as in the
case of Goethe, recognize, and even regret, its absence, but
actively and positively it was quite indifferent to him. The real
and fundamental reason for this I suspect to be that he was, so
to speak, his own artist, and had as little need of or use for
others, in other realms of practice, as in his own. Perhaps, by his
favorite law of compensation, his aloofness and independence
were balanced by a corresponding self-sufficingness, which established his equipoise by developing the extraordinary—though
of course far from vain-glorious—egoism that is so marked in
one nevertheless so serenely unassuming. What he delights in
is nature, and in nature for what it says, not what it shows, to
him. He can perhaps make his own synthesis—his own picture.
He was inexhaustibly synthetic and hardly functioned otherwise.

He knows precisely, as I have said, what constitutes the picture. But whether he can or not, he is not enough interested in it to communicate it, and when some one else paints it, it is not his, and therefore it fails to interest him at all. Nor does he take art quite seriously enough to comprehend what may be called its physiology, academically alive as he is to its essential principles. When he first saw the old masters, he was surprised at their simplicity, which approves his penetration—the philistine note simply never appears in Emerson—but it is plain that he deemed this end easily attained by them, and ascriptible to the direct vision of genius. His maxim is that one does best what is easiest for him to do—surely a transcendental view of art, aside from the notorious truth that what one does easily is not worth doing, unless indeed one has done it before with difficulty. He did not linger among the aforesaid old masters, moreover. Mr. Henry James records that on walking with him through the galleries of the Louvre and the Vatican, "his perception of the objects contained in those collections was of the most general order" [92] —doubtless not an overstatement. Europe, indeed, said little to him in any way. Its chief interest for Americans is probably its monuments and museums. And for him these treasures were negligible as having served their purpose—a purpose in the nature of things, according to his philosophy, needing ceaseless renewal, continuous change. Anything static tends to impede the flux that was his ideal. Doubtless he took his world—the kingdom of his mind—with him on each of his two visits abroad, but one fancies him glad to be at home again, where the concrete forced itself less on the attention. At Concord, certainly, so far as art is concerned, he could escape it altogether—cultivate his cherished propensity for whim, and listen to Alcott, and call Dante "another Zerah Colburn" [93] at his ease.

VII

It is the absence of art, too, that is the most obvious weakness of his poetry, where it is of much more moment. Imaginative art is precisely what his poetry lacks to give it classic color and substance. The Poems, taken as a whole, constitute an expression altogether inferior to that of the Essays, of which they are,

indeed, a kind of intimate reverberation. They are largely
Emerson's communion with himself, as the Essays are his communication with the world. And since, so far as form goes
certainly, even communication was not a matter on which he
"wasted the day," he is naturally more esoteric and elusive in
what one is inclined to call, for the most part, merely articulate
meditation. Poetry was distinctly an avocation with him. "The
rhyming fit seldom comes to me," he acknowledged. He wrote
it to please himself—overflowed tricklingly in verse often more
careless even than awkward, cadenced to measures that could
have gratified only a tuneless ear, and constituting an exercise
rather than an expression. I do not mean that he did not take
it seriously. On the contrary he labored it now and then, revised,
rewrote, suppressed on occasion. I fancy, however, that he did
this with very little expenditure of the effort that he so depreciated, and precisely in the spirit of revising an exercise
rather than by the more arduous process of "taking thought"
which, indeed, had he taken the Muse seriously *enough* he might
easily have found quite as "degrading" in verse as in his truly
native expression. It can't be said that he materially bettered
what he changed. Taken in the mass, the Poems have precisely
the experimental, tentative, adventurous air with which this
afterthought order of treatment in the case of a few wholly
accords. It is a surprise to find that this was certainly not his
own view, and the fact argues the insufficiency of his poetic
ideal as well as performance. His verse has assuredly high
qualities, and in elevation and eloquence ranks with his prose—
qualities that carry their own justification with them, and need
to be buttressed by no illusions as to the native felicity of their
vehicle of expression. He insisted that he was a born poet, "of
inferior rank, no doubt, but all the same a poet," by "nature and
vocation," and maintained that everything in him proceeded
from that. But he was mistaken. In the exact sense in which he
called Goethe artistic, but not an artist,[94] we may say of him
(what indeed also he precisely says of Shelley) that he was
poetic—oh! distinctly—but not a poet. It is not a little significant
that in the appreciative and really monumental work Mlle.
Dugard has recently published—"Emerson: Sa Vie et Son
Œuvre" [95]—there is scarcely a reference to the Poems. And if,

considering their highly idiosyncratic quality, one could hardly count on their passing the border of another tongue, the strictures of Swinburne and the cool estimate of Arnold have at least the weight that competence and comprehension carry. In this country the elect consensus would perhaps rank Emerson with the greatest of English poets. But this is one of the literary estimates that the present generation has inherited from Emerson's own, in which the more exclusively intellectual ideas imposed themselves rather imperiously. Such an estimate will infallibly be revised when it is realized that, quintessential an element as intellect is in poetry of a high order, it is not the characterizing element of poetry at all—when in fact we either produce more poetry that is distinctively poetry or come to have a deeper and more exacting sense of it.

It is idle to maintain that a true poet, a poet, that is, to whom verse is his native medium, would have written so much indifferent and so little real poetry as Emerson. The conclusion from the obvious data is irresistible that his extremely exceptional achievements proceed from an equally exceptional inspiration. This is to say that a writer of unimpeachable genius, whose native medium is prose, may occasionally receive from the high gods the impulse and the capacity to transmute into the gold of perfect and beautiful musical expression the silver of his habitual elevated and eloquent substance. It is not at all to say that he is a great poet. Nor, of course, on the other hand, is it to say that he is incapable of great poetry. But the aim of criticism is correct characterization, and to characterize as essentially a poet a writer whose greatness is almost invariably apparent in his prose, and only occasionally in his verse, is misleading. Professor Woodberry, a poet himself, maintains that Emerson was "fundamentally a poet with an imperfect faculty of expression." [96] One differs with so good a judge with diffidence. But as a matter of fact wherever Emerson shows himself a poet at all, his faculty of expression is perfection. "When Emerson's line is good," says Mr. Gilder—another expert and practitioner—"it is unsurpassably good—having a beauty not merely of cadence, but of inner, intense, birdlike sound: the vowels, the consonants, the syllables, are exquisitely musical." [97] The adverbs are enthusiastic, but the description is just; just and extremely accurate. The difficulty is that his line so rarely is good, or at any rate, that his goodness, from the point of view of poetry, is so generally confined to his "line." And as I say it is the "mass" that counts, here as elsewhere.

So slight is the proportion of admirable to negligible verse in the Poems that one feels like saying that he can repeat all of Emerson's poetry that repays reading. It is true that of the poetry one knows by heart, the proportion of Emerson's to that of other poets is more considerable. At least this is true in America, partly no doubt because, as with Lowell, patriotism and nature —particularly our variety of each, one may say—are the twin inspirations of his muse. The "embattled farmers" lines or "Muscatequit" [98] would naturally be less popular in England. But the popularity of some of his lines with us contradicts Arnold's contention that Emerson fails to answer this elementary but essential test. Almost any lover of poetry among us can repeat "Brahma" and "The Problem" and "Terminus"; and a substantial number of more isolated "lines" than those aggregated under these titles, is as familiar to most of us as the instances of household words given by Arnold:

> "Things are in the saddle,
> And ride mankind," [99]

for example, as familiar as

> "Patience on a monument, smiling at grief." [100]

Emerson's aptness in aphorism, so marked in his prose, naturally serves him to the same good purpose in verse. He can pack his thought so close that when it is exceptionally elevated in idea, it almost falls of itself into lyric expression. When it is not, the compactness itself remains attractive, as in the lines just quoted, while the poetry evaporates. As poetry of course one can only contrast these with Shakespeare's charming image. And though other collocations more favorable to Emerson might readily be made, this answers as well as any to indicate the distinction between Emerson's verse in general and such imaginative art as that of the poet to whom poetry is a native expression, who sees truth in images rather than in propositions and whose imaginative faculty is at home in construction rather than exclusively in statement—artistic or other. Mr. Gilder says Emerson is "preëminent in his power to put a moral idea into artistic form," and—perhaps reading "eminent" for "preëminent" —very truly, I think.[101] But not often in imaginative form. The noble figure he cites of the Departing Day silent and scornful "under her solemn fillet" [102] has almost too few congeners to be called characteristic. In any case a great poem is composed not of a moral idea but of many moral ideas, however single the central motive. The poem is a construction of their interrelations imaginatively treated. For imaginative construction, however, Emerson naturally had as little faculty as for the more mechanical analogous requirement of mere rhetoric. The seer is not constructive. He is the instrument of inspiration, the exponent of intuition, the channel of celestial wisdom, not the artificer that, equally with the artist on any plane, the poet— the maker—must be.

The poet thus parallels the ideal and abstract world by an imaginative counterpart of his own creation. He does not interpret it in verbal terms, rhythmic or other, of merely energetic and illuminating, or even beautiful, rational exposition. He must create rather than merely convey, and to create he must know not merely to "sing" but "to build the lofty rhyme." [103] So imperative is construction in poetry indeed that what we feel in the Essays as mere lack of continuity we note in the Poems as positive fragmentariness. Emerson's genius has not the opulence that is profitably compressed by poetic form. His thought needs no condensation nor confinement and in metrical order acquires no energy—as substance that is rich and full so often does. The constructive imagination is replaced in him by no small degree of fancy, but whereas the material of the former is the concrete, fancy, in Emerson at least, revels in the abstract and frolics—to use one of his favorite words—in the realm of the inner not the outer sense. Even in nature it is not the concrete that attracts him. Consider these lovely lines—the oasis of "Woodnotes:"

> "Thou canst not wave thy staff in air,
> Or dip thy paddle in the lake,
> But it carves the bow of beauty there,
> And the ripples in rhymes the oar forsake." [104]

Even here the poet is not so much noting the beauty of the
phenomena he records, as inviting our attention to the law
underlying them, apparent to the fancy of the inner sense, and
declared not without a truly poetic but distinct tinge of the
didactic. It is the poetry of the poetic seer. And the lines are
exceptional in Emerson's verse in which, in general, significance
excludes all sensuous alloy; whereas the poetic ideal insists on
the fusion of sensuousness with significance. The latter element
in fact can, by definition at least, be better spared than the
former. No one doubts for example the titular claims of Swinburne's verse. The claims of the sensuous element in poetry are
unimpeachable since the concrete is its corollary and blindness
to the concrete is as fatal to poetry as to plastic art. It is the
concrete, in fact, that makes poetry an art. Of course it is the
abstract in art as well as elsewhere that supplies significance,
and all art that surpasses the *merely* sensuous is a statement, as
well as an image, of truth. For that matter, philosophically speaking, everything constructed ought, of course, equally with everything existent to mirror the macrocosm—as Emerson would, and
probably does somewhere, insist. But art is a magic mirror that
contributes as well as reflects, and if it does not count in, as well
as for, expression, if in other words it lacks or even dilutes the
concrete, it loses its characteristic sanction.

But Emerson not only has no sensuous strain. He is deficient
in sentiment. Of love, as understood by the poets—and the mass
of mankind—he had his habitual intellectual and not emotionally
enlightened conception. He quite comprehended its physiology.
To the question once addressed to him: "Do you believe in
Platonic friendships between the sexes?" he replied with quaint
sapience: "Yes, but 'Hands off'." Surely wisdom is justified of
her children! He had, however, no *sense* of the feeling, and of
the two great instincts from which all the rest that actuate
humanity are derived it is extraordinary how exclusively he was
possessed by that of self-preservation. Emotional expansion—or
even concentration—was plainly not a need of his ethereal nature, but of all directions in which soul or sense expands that
of romantic love was the most foreign to his constitution. Rather
striking confirmation of this, were any needed, is furnished by
his own blindness to the fact—almost the only instance in which

he betrays blindness of any kind. "I have been told," he says, "that in some public discourses of mine my reverence for the intellect has made me unjustly cold to the personal relations." [105] And he protests with gentle but not convincing fervor. We owe him the charming phrase: "All mankind love a lover." [106] But the kind of lover he means is he who feels warmly "when he hears applause of his engaged maiden." [107] "Engaged" is charming, too; it connotes Concord and its regularity in essentials whatever its theological heresies. Yet Emerson's Muse herself never shows any such *sense* of the universal passion as, to take almost the first instance that comes to mind, is evinced in the lines:

"Then there were sighs, the deeper for suppression,
    And stolen glances, sweeter for the theft,
And burning blushes though for no transgression,
    Tremblings when met, and restlessness when left." [108]

His nearest approach to this is where, in describing with penetrating frigidity the disillusionment of finding "that several things which were not the charm have more reality than the charm itself which embalmed them" he speaks finely of the lover's youth "when he became all eye when one was present, and all memory when one was gone." [109] But given any theme he could be eloquent upon it. He is less himself in his figure than in the remark that precedes it. The latter savors more of the "new and true" to which in this sphere as elsewhere, in the main, he consecrated his expression. The passions are too primitive for him. He moves more freely amid higher differentiations. "There, that is done" one can fancy him exclaim, in finishing his essay on "Love," [110] which, however, agreeably avoids the commonplace—a genuine distinction for a "cosmic" writer. But Emerson achieves this distinction too easily, too readily. Beautifully wise things he occasionally utters about love. "Do you love me, means do you see the same truth," [111] for example, records exquisitely the lover's longing for spiritual fusion. But even here a part stands for the whole and we gather that a negative reply would merely lead the inquirer, not too disconsolately, to seek elsewhere his other self. Had it been he, one is persuaded that he never would have pleaded for "a last ride together," [112] and at most would have proposed a walk. Such an admonition as "we must not contend against love or" [113]— what he seems to imply is the same thing—"deny the substantial existence of other people," certainly witnesses no temperamental ardor.

And for the pathos as well as for the passion of love his emotional equability is too perfect to suffer any real concern. Neither passion nor pathos, nor indeed any depth of feeling properly to be called human fell in with Emerson's scheme of things. His idealism was essentially intellectual and his optimistic philosophy excluded emotional elements so distracting to serenity and so menacing to what he probably conceived as true spiritual success. One may almost say that he shrinks from feeling, and when it seems imminent swiftly substitutes an idea. It is true that the world is passably familiar with the contrary practice and that here as elsewhere he eludes the conventional. As another American poet observes:

> "If love alone would save from hell,
> Then few would fail of heaven." [114]

Without distinction, thus—commensurable with his genius— in art, in imaginative construction, in concrete imagery, in sensuousness or in sentiment, Emerson's poetry is, like his philosophy, very largely an affair of the intellect. And even as such it is fragmentary, inconclusive, and only now and then lighted by felicities, mainly of "line" and rarely long enough to satisfy the sense they stimulate, though within their narrow limits they are felicities of a penetrating, thrilling pungency, inspired by a peculiar spiritual elevation, which have been never perhaps surpassed, and certainly never quite matched. But, save fragmentarily, the intellect unaided will not produce great poetry. Browning's poetry is great poetry and no one will deny that it is intellectual poetry. Its secret, however, is disclosed in Browning's expressed conviction, "Little else is worth study save the development of a soul" [115]—a statement of which all three terms are distinctly un-Emersonian: study, development, and—in Browning's sense—the soul. The heights Emerson sometimes attains—never, I think, the depths he sounds—cause his missing true greatness in poetry to arouse a sense of frustration. He seems

to have rented a lodge on the slopes of Parnassus and never to
have taken the fee of it, and his home is elsewhere. Well, then,
on Olympus, perhaps? Certainly of the two, yes. Even so, he
should have left some masterpiece, whereas in no one of the
formal categories of poetry can he be enrolled as a master. His
place is with Epictetus, Marcus Aurelius, Montaigne, Rabelais,
Pascal, Sir Thomas Browne—with the wisdom writers of the
world, not with the poets. And just as, had he been a great
writer, his essays would have been constructed by toil however "degrading," some at least of his poetry, had he been a
great poet, would have had a monumental character—whereas
his whole work, his *œuvre,* is rather a cairn than a structure, with
of course dire loss from a monumental point of view. Of all the
shortcomings of his poetry, indeed, the greatest, I think, is this
lack of any architectonic quality commensurate with his vision
and vitality. A great poet who never wrote a great poem is an
anomaly. One who never tried to is not fundamentally a poet,
however poetic the angle from which he viewed the universe
and whatever the radiance that plays about it in the interpretation he essayed. Emerson's real greatness appears in the Essays
in which, of course, as I have said, imaginative art is less essential and which his poetic fancy lifts as much above "Proverbs"
as his formal poetry falls below "Job."

VIII

The Essays are the scriptures of thought, the Virgilian Lots [116]
of modern literature. To open anywhere any of the volumes (including "Representative Men," which very strictly belongs with
the Essays) is to be at once in the world of thought in a very
particular sense. The abruptness of the transition is a part of
the sensation—like that of landing from a steamer, or leaving
a city train at a country station with the landscape stretching out
green and smiling in the morning sunshine. The completeness
of the contrast deepens as you go forward with Emerson into
the day, and surrender yourself to his influence in the spirit of
his surrender to his inspiration. This is the mood in which to
read him—the one, that is, in which he wrote. Soon you are
thinking almost in his diction. Any approach to the contentious

spirit you feel would affront opportunity and denounce your denseness to the benignity around you. Even the critical spirit with its scrupulousnesses is far behind, its most delicately balanced scales a rude apparatus, and the thought of *weighing*, an impertinent blindness to the imponderable iridescence that shimmers in the atmosphere, electric with uplift and aspiration. For it is the world of moral thought that you are in. The phenomena around you lose their usual aspect and individual meaning, and what you are beholding is their relations in principle and law, now clear, now confused, now co-ordinate, now conflicting, but always significant and superior to "mere understanding and the senses."

It is this that most saliently characterizes the Essays—the way in which in spite of *lacunæ* of rhetorical connection the relations of things are elicited, their relations to each other, to the cosmos, to the individual. Every statement stimulates thought because it is suggestive as well as expressive. Everything means something additional. To take it in you must go beyond it. The very appreciation of an essay automatically constructs a web of thought in the weaving of which the reader shares. All its facts are illustrative, all its data examples. The world of phenomena is lifted to the plane of principle, where if it loses the material substance with which, through the imagination, art and poetry deal, it is the object of a classifying vision that distributes and arranges it in accordance with mutual affinities and general laws, and in this way draws out its utilities for the mind. Every thought is pollent rather than purely reflective. And if Emerson does not preach action and ignores emotion, the state of mind he induces is of an energetic and exhilarated character, out of which such emotion as aspiration may be called and such action as resolve may implicate issue of themselves. He stimulates a mood at all events, in which effort seems needless, compunction useless, conscience superfluous, logic a fetter, consistency negligible, fear contemptible, courage instinctive, culture exotic and what normally we recognize as unattainable within easy reach of one's hand—a mood, that is to say, that dissipates all possible criticism of him. To those who can convert such a mood into a permanent state of mind and habit of thought, or even make it occasionally the springs of conduct and performance, the

Essays are a priceless possession. Those who cannot can hardly
fail to find it exhilarating that instead of walking crowned with
inward glory and finding merely his own content in meditation,
he should have walked and meditated his daily stint out of reach
of the working world and out of touch with its concerns—beholding them in the wise candor of perspective—and should
nevertheless have had the naiveté or the sapience—which is it?
—to take this exceptional, this unique experience and procedure
as normal enough to be preached practically and commended
confidently to weary and struggling mankind.

And scarcely less notable than the method that gives it such
vitality is the material of the Essays. Emerson's mind is as
spacious as it is active, and as stored as it is spacious. Not a
scholar in any strict sense, he read as much as he reflected and,
owing to his extremely catholic appreciativeness, as widely. His
extraordinary power of assimilation and conversion somewhat
obscures the opulence of his spoils. Whatever his depreciation
of culture and its results to his philosophy, the tapestry of the
Essays is wonderfully figured with it. Dr. Holmes gives the
number of citations they contain as 3,393, taken from 868
writers.[117] And the abundance of this harvest of his reading is
less impressive than the aptness and fecundity of everything—
everything—quoted. One almost sees it in its process of transformation into the proverbial manifold enrichment of good seed,
and views as seed the grain but freshly reaped from the ripest
fields of the world's thought. He dips into the bins of every store-
house and draws on all treasuries, though with an eclecticism
so personal and a usage so prompt that one fairly loses sight of
the origin of the material with which he sows and builds. It is
there nevertheless—an encyclopædia of others' thought, however
combined, developed, refined, and utilized by, as well as em-
bedded in, his own. And the lessons of experience he drew from
every source, from the most familiar as well as the most recondite.
As he said of Plato he kept "the two vases, one of ether and
one of pigment, at his side" and illustrated his own assertion:
"Things used as language are inexhaustibly attractive." [118] Consider merely the titles of the ten volumes of Essays. They form
a *catalogue raisonné* of wisdom, of wisdom divined and wisdom
garnered, and the whole beautifully and winningly as well as

pungently alembicated by an indisputably great mind. And if the Essays are, as they seemed to the wisest English critic of the nineteenth century, the most important work in English prose of that century,[119] it is because they are the work of the master genius of wisdom among the writers of his time.

POE

POE

I

THERE is no more effective way of realizing the distinction of Poe's genius than by imagining American literature without him. One is tempted to add there is no other way. It is in the historic rather than in the critical estimate that his eminence appears. It owes more to its isolation than to its quality. He was extremely individual, the entire character of his mind and nature is acutely, almost painfully, certainly perversely, personal; but his originality appears chiefly in relief against the background of his environment. If he did not feel intensely, he thought energetically, but to a purport more familiar in older societies than in our own. His figure acquires outline and edge from its contrast with the prevailing Philistine screen which he sedulously kept behind it and on which he made it the business of his life to cast the sharpest possible shadow. He was from the first in complete disaccord with his environment and lived in a perpetual state of warfare with it. His parentage was bohemian, his childhood and youth dependent, his associations—in the half savage, half aristocratic society of his boyhood—expressly favorable to the development of the imperious beneficiary whose sense of his own powers and of his lack of claims brought him through a rather irregular and not very grateful adolescence to the threshold of a manhood of revolt. There is a whole literature of revolt in older countries. Our only Ishmael [1] is Poe. But if not unprecedented in the history of letters he was sufficiently salient among us, and the fact that so generally his hand was against every man accentuated his individuality in the natural course of apology and polemic.

The established was with us still the moral and the didactic. Poe's antagonism instinctively inclined him to art. He is in fact the solitary artist of our elder literature. This is his distinction and will remain such. Hawthorne is in a degree a rival, but in form rather than in *fond* as his addiction to allegory attests and in any case his puritan preoccupation with the moral forces invalidates his purely æsthetic appeal. Poe's art was unalloyed. It was scrupulously devoid, at any rate, of any aim except that of producing an effect and often overspread if only occasionally clothed with the integument of beauty. As such it was in America at the time an exotic. His great service to his country is in a word the domestication of the exotic. Color, rhythm, space, strangeness, were his "reals;" they fascinated his mind and took possession of his else unoccupied soul. In the large sense thus his art is in strictness to be called exotic rather than original. French, German, English romanticism had preceded him. He pillaged and plagiarized freely. In the matter of literary phase, his most convinced admirer and most thorough-going apologist observes that he came at the close of an epoch, he did not introduce one. But in his hands the method and even the material that he adopted resulted in a very striking body of work, which still has the compactness and definition of a monument. And if he contributed little he passed on the torch. Incarnated in the vivid forms his pronounced individuality imagined, illustrated by the energy of his genius, the spirit of romantic art entered the portals of our literature and illuminated its staid precincts to the end of variety at the very least. Whatever her responsibility for the subsequent riot there, her vivifying influence is clear, and for it we are indebted to Poe.

II

The artist, by definition, exercises his activity in exclusive concentration upon his effect. In so far as his attention swerves from that he modifies his distinctive attitude. He may, of course, soar as well as sink in so doing. He may, for instance, forget his effect in the rapture of expression and rise to poetry. But unless, in so doing, his sub-consciousness at least keeps its hold on his effect— as, for example, Tennyson's always did—he pretermits his purely artistic function. This is why, in a world of imperfections, the most nearly perfect act is so often the least satisfactory—assuming the poetic to be the ultimate standard; why the perfection of Vermeer fades before the irregularities of Rembrandt; why we turn from Veronese to Tintoretto; why in only an occasional miracle of genius like Raphael at his best do we find a stable fusion of spirit and statement; why—to descend from august illustration—readers more sensitive to art than to poetry are deceived by the poetic disguise of that arrant artist, Walt Whitman, who achieved a fairly radiant degree of perfection in never yawping his commonplaces off the key, in spite of the variety of their modulations. Like Whitman's, Poe's attention never wandered a moment from his effect—even in his poetry. Now the effect in poetry, as in any fine art, is largely a matter of technic, and a great deal of poetry is naturally over-valued, because it answers the technical test, because in short it sounds well.

In the first place its technic is so difficult that, when it is achieved with any distinction, it is rewarded with at least the temporary appreciation that inevitably rewards the *tour de force*. The technical test has in truth a good deal to say for itself practically. Winckelmann objected to artists' criticism of art that it naturally made difficulty overcome the test of achievement.[2] But as a matter of fact, one may ask, is not this at least one test, since it is clearly one source of the superiority of the superior artist, whose laurels, without it, would be worn equally by the mute and the inglorious, not to say the manifestly incompetent? What one can say is that it is in no sense the test of the artist's inspiration, and that this is, after all, the main thing. The prodigious difficulties of the art of poetry, at any rate, are sufficiently attested by the abounding surplusage of unsuccessful attempts to surmount them. Everyone accordingly—except apparently the deluded practitioner—is struck by the exceptional victory when he encounters it, and apt unconsciously to ascribe to inspiration the effect really due to energy and skill, forgetting that even inspired skill is not poetic inspiration. Much of the admiration of Poe's poetry is of this kind. Much of his poetry itself can be admired in no other way.

Moreover, the technic of poetry is so multifarious, so full of possibilities, so capable of producing pleasure by mere rhyme and rhythm that with many readers at all times and with all readers at some times its content is lost sight of. English literature has a wonderful example of this in the poetry of Swinburne. Swinburne is incomparable, but Poe has something—a tithe—of the same richness of rhythmic resource, though his numbers are artificial at times and at times tenuous to a degree that removes them from even superficial classification with the opulent spontaneity and splendor of the English poet's diction. They are, too, though less richly, more exclusively, technical, leaning thus all the more heavily on technic. And his technic, being thus the main factor of his verse, lacks a little the native felicity only to be secured by keeping it in its true relative position. Forced out of its proper subordination it loses its grace as a contributing element of a larger entity. It, instead of the subject, being the poet's main concern, its theoretic quality becomes obvious. It acquires a positively notional air with Poe at times—the air of illustrating the notions of his negligible "Philosophy of Composition" and "The Poetic Principle." Its resources seem devices. Every effect seems due to an expedient. The repetend and the refrain are reliances with him—not instrumental, but thematic. At least they constitute rather than create the effect—which has therefore something otiose and perfunctory about it.

Technic of all sorts interested Poe tremendously. He had what might be called the technical temperament—a variety perhaps more familiar than widely recognized. It is the temperament that delights in terminology, labels, little boxes and drawers, definitions, catalogues, categories, all ingeniously, that is to say mechanically, apposite and perfectly rigid. It illustrates the passion for order run to seed—activity of mind avoiding the drudgery of thought by definiteness of classification. Manner being more susceptible of classification than matter, how the thing is done interests it more than the thing itself. Such a temperament on larger lines than common, with a certain sweep as well as system, Poe possessed. It rose to the pitch of positive genius with him. He pondered, himself, and lectured his contemporaries on how literature should be written, how a tale should be presented, how a poem should be built up. His criticism is largely, almost exclusively, technical. He pursued it quite in the detective spirit. His review of "Barnaby Rudge," [3] of which to Dickens's amazement he divined the dénouement, is worthy of M. Dupin and is historic.[4] His long criticisms of Cooper and Hawthorne are craftsman's criticism. And as such they are extraordinarily good. They contrast refreshingly with the general run of literary praise and blame in his day—and in ours—in being specific, pointed and competent and avoiding the vague, the sentimental and the commonplaces of moralizing, though of course they have none of the overtones, so to say, of either culture or philosophic depth that enrich criticism as well as give it a creative value. His own craftsmanship considered strictly as such is excellent. He proceeds with perfect self-possession and deliberation; and there is this to be said for his philosophizings about it, that at least they disclosed his own method and show conclusively that his art was an art of calculation and not the spontaneous expression of a weird and gruesome genius that it seems to so many upon whom it produces its carefully prepared effect.

His theory of poetry is stated within his account of the composition of "The Raven," [5] which is as a whole probably in no better faith than the anonymously published editorial reference to the poem that accompanied it on its appearance. Both are mystifications which if "The Raven" were finer would tend to vulgarize it, and are only saved by being possibly derisory from being actually as risible as Mrs. Browning found the poem itself.[6] But the theory advocated and illustrated by Poe is undoubtedly as sincere as his perverse pursuit of originality at any cost, and his temperamental revolt against what is staple and standard, not to speak of what is classic, would permit. It is briefly that poetry has absolutely nothing to do with truth, (to which he had an intellectual repugnance) that it is concerned solely with beauty (which he does not define, but assumes, in opposition to more conventional opinion from Plato to Keats, to be absolutely divorced from truth), and that its highest expression is the note of sadness—the sadder the better. Of these notions only the last need arrest attention. It is true that the most perfect beauty has often the note of sadness. The reason probably resides rather in its effect than in its constitution, being largely the recipient's subjective appreciation reacting even in, or especially in, the presence of perfection which contrasts so bitterly with

> "—the heavy and the weary weight
> Of all this unintelligible world." [7]

But it is not true that this is always the case. Who is to decide, for example, between the "Ode to a Nightingale" and the "Ode

on Immortality"? [8] Poe's theory, however, and its elaborate working out, involve the inference that "The Raven" is a finer poem
than either, since Wordsworth's ode is actually joyous, and the
idea of "The Raven" on the other hand sadder than anything in
Keats's. He proves it by *a* plus *b*: Of all melancholy topics, he
says, death is the most melancholy; it is most poetical when it
allies itself with beauty; "the death then of a beautiful woman is
unquestionably the most poetical topic in the world."

Any force his theory might abstractly be supposed to have, assuredly evaporates in his illustrative exposition of it and "The
Raven" is certainly superior to either. But two things are made
perfectly clear by such theorizing one, that the theorist is primarily not a poet but an artist—concerned less with expression
than with effect, that is to say; and, the other, that he is not a
natural but an eccentric artist, since sadness voluntary and predetermined is artificial and morbid. The poem itself—undoubtedly Poe's star performance—confirms these inductions. It is not
a moving poem. It has, as Mrs. Browning herself admitted,[9] a
certain power, but it is such power as may be possessed by the
incurable dilettante coldly caressing a morbid mood. To be moving melancholy must be temperamental. Even a mood will not
suffice. Whatever injustice is done its real genesis by Poe's farrago
about it, "The Raven" is in conception and execution exceptionally cold-blooded poetry. But, distinctly on the plane of artifice,
it is admirable art. Less remarkable as a pure *tour de force* in
linguistic luxuriance than the extraordinary "Bells," which in its
way is quite unparalleled, it is nevertheless a noteworthy technical achievement. Its rhythms and rhymes are more than clever
and together with the recurrent accent of the refrain—already
used by Lowell—combine in the production of a sustained tone
and effect of totality, which may almost be said to epitomize Poe's
genius.

Both "The Raven" and "The Bells" have enjoyed an enormous
popularity among readers impressionable by effects and insensitive to distinctions, and their poetic strain has not saved them
from being the natural prey of the professional elocutionist—also
an elaborate technician in his more or less humble fashion. Poe's
more personal verse has less interest. Some of it deserves Stoddard's verdict of "doggerel," [10] for where his own work, verse or

prose, was concerned he had no standard. The lines "For Helen" written when he was a boy are not only astonishingly precocious but charming, far better than those "For Annie" written when he had matured and for the most part overlaid his inspiration with artistry and encrusted it with technic. The idea and inspiration of "The Haunted Palace," however, amply sustain the happy technical art that expresses them with not only admirable musical aptness, but with a beautiful fusion of restraint born of taste and ease springing from fulness that makes it an indisputable masterpiece. Its reserve, indeed, secures an objectivity that is exceptional in Poe and, since his art was fundamentally more genuine than his inspiration, exceptionally moving. For once he got himself out of the way and let his genius guide him to complete success. "The Conqueror Worm" is less successful, I think, in being more a *tour de force*. It shares a little the "staginess" of the *donnée* and his taste shows its fickleness by deserting him, though it is certainly a spirited piece of *voulu* pessimism and—no slight praise—the last two lines are among the classics of the "catching." On the other hand in "Ulalume" one feels the sincerity latent in the most artificial and abnormal natures—though a sincerity that throws into sharper relief than usual the element of artifice in Poe's art and seems itself in the shadow that perhaps befits remorse, behind the apparatus of repetend and empty assonance that tries the reader's nerves. Even here one feels the aptness of Emerson's bland reference to him (in conversation with Mr. Howells) as the "jingle man," [11] and notes the artist rather than the poet and the technician rather than the artist. In any case the volume of his verse is so slight as to confine his claim to its quality, and its quality is, in general, hardly such as to place him very high up on the fairly populous slopes of Parnassus where there is more competition than he met with in his lifetime. Competition is fatal to Poe. His cue was distinctly to function outside of it, and he was wise to cultivate originality at any price.

III

As a technician his most noteworthy success is the completeness of his effect. He understood to perfection the value of tone in a composition, and tone is an element that is almost invaluable.

In this respect he has no American and few foreign rivals. All of his writings attest his supreme comprehension of it—prose as well as poetry, the ablest and the most abject. Such rubbish as "The Duc de l'Omelette" with its galvanic rictus of false but sustained gaiety; such elaborate and hollow solemnity as the parable "Shadow," which ends, however, on a note of real pith and dignity; such a crazy-quilt of tinsel as "The Assignation," all have this unifying quality which makes art of them. His very deficiency in the qualities usually present in the romance-writer and absolutely vital in romance of a high order, enabled him to cultivate his own special excellences the more exclusively. Many of the tales are tone and nothing else—not even tone of any particular character but a reticulation of relations merely in admirable unison. The false note is the one falsity he eschewed. Tinkling feet on a tufted carpet is nonsense, but it is not a false note in the verbal harmony of the artificial "Raven." In "The Cask of Amontillado" the tone is like the click of malignant castanets. And in "The Fall of the House of Usher" it reaches Poe's climax of power —a diapason of gloom, wholly voluntary, and ending none too soon perhaps, but maintained to the end with the success of a veritable *tour de force*. What on the other hand he did not understand was modulation. He has no variety. Probably he realized this limitation and confined himself almost wholly in prose to the short story, grotesquely prescribing, too, one hundred lines as the limit of a poem. A novel by Poe is inconceivable, and would be even if he had had the feeling for character and the human interest that the novel demands. This is partly because he lacked sustained power, and the larger art of organization and dynamic development, but it is also due to the monotony that results probably from the predominance and prolongation of the mood, which makes it so easy for him to secure tone.

Thus he achieves atmosphere but an atmosphere which is less the envelope than the content of his work, and which so enwraps the detail as to blend its accents and minimize the force of such variety as it has. Nothing takes place in "The Fall of the House of Usher" that is not trivial and inconclusive compared with its successful monotone, its atmosphere of lurid murk and disintegrating gloom. And as a consequence of this inversion of the normal artistic relations of content and envelope I must say I think that

even here, where we have Poe at his best, he refuses us all satisfaction that lies beyond the scope of purely scenic art. In this one
respect "The Cask of Amontillado" is better. It, too, is most remarkable artistically for its tone, the cascade of brilliant chatter
that sustains its suspense. But it contains some psychology, devil-
ish rather than human, to be sure, and therefore as usual ringing
false, yet imaginatively thrilling in its malignity, though its mon-
strousness is rendered somewhat insipid by the perversity and
characteristic inadequacy of its motive. And it has a situation
both moral and material and a rapidly conducted, however
meagre, action. But even these two tales as they stand do not take
their author out of the rank of the purely scenic artist, comparatively high as they may place him within it. The truth is that no
writer of anything approaching Poe's ability has been content to
remain in this rank.

There is unquestionable power in his best tales, but it is a re-
pellent power. Its manifestations are either unsympathetic or
repulsive—unsympathetic where successful because they make
their effect by attacking instead of charming the sensibilities, repulsive where they fail because nothing but success can excuse
such sinister assault. The complaisant mental attitude of the
reader who co-operates with a writer so systematically bent on
his conquest instead of on his captivation is singularly innocent.
And I do not think the experienced share it. Mainly, I imagine,
Poe's stores are read in youth and rarely returned to—except by
patriotic critics of a tendency to dithyramb, and too solicitous to
magnify the salient figures of our literature to reconsider their
own early evaluations. A mature judgment must discern, and a
mature susceptibility resent, the writer's manifest motive. In fact
his most characteristic limitation as an artist is the limited character of the pleasure he gives. He has a perverse instinct for re-
stricting it to that produced by pain. Pain and pleasure have no
doubt an equivalent æsthetic sanction. Metaphysically they are
sometimes, indeed, difficult to distinguish; desire, for example,
which superficially classes itself as pleasure being probably pain
in reality. The discussion of such a question would have delighted
Poe; but it is unnecessary to quarrel with the legitimacy of painful effects in art—in which as in life no doubt, as Mrs. Browning
declared, "pain is not the fruit of pain"—in order to appreciate

the perversity of Poe's practice in this regard. The production of pain is with him an end, not a means to the production of pleasure. His design is, crassly, to wring the withers of our sensoriums. Such a design is the delight of the degenerate. Decadents, such as Baudelaire, discern it readily and naturally—or unnaturally, as one chooses—savor it and enjoy to the full "the generous pleasure of praising" it.[12] The naive and hearty and good natured and uncritical with a weakness for the romantic at any price, such as Gautier, fail to note it and admire its results as revolutionary simply. Doubtless Poe did not himself realize this perversity in its fulness. Doubtless nothing would have surprised him more, and more evoked his scorn, than the assertion that such a foe to philistinism as himself lacked ideality. He had ideality but it was exclusively artistic. It was entirely consistent with unscrupulousness. No doubt the most loathsome subjects are susceptible of artistic treatment and may serve the ends of beauty. But a preference for them in the artist raises a presumption against his competence in the circumstances—a presumption amply justified in Poe's case. Not whatsoever things are lovely and of good report,[13] but whatsoever things are effective were his preoccupation. Intensity of effect was accordingly his end, and artifice his means. And fine things are not thus produced. The law of the universe in virtue of which the beautiful, the true, and the good are inextricably interrelated forbids it. Matthew Arnold maintained that it was "lost labor" to inquire into a writer's motive. Undoubtedly errors have been made by allowing the real or supposed springs of a writer's production to color one's appreciation of them. Thackeray's view of Sterne,[14] for example, is rather summary. But with Poe the case is different. The only reason for its being lost labor to inquire into his motive is the fact that his motive is in plain sight. And to neglect it would be to neglect what not only colors, but is the constituent element of a large portion —a large proportion indeed—of his writings.

In the most characteristic this motive is exactly that of the fat boy in "Pickwick" who announced to his easily thrilled auditors that he was going to make their flesh creep.[15] To accomplish this result, however, is more difficult than to announce it, unless one deals with an altogether higher order of material than Poe's, and is possessed of an altogether different order of powers. The ele-

ment of awe is not, of course, in question, and there is no need
to cite more august examples than that of Victor Hugo, for instance, to remind ourselves by contrast of the difference between
the flesh-creeping effects produced by a master and those obtained by a charlatan who addresses not in the least the mind,
but exclusively the nerves. In fact the comparison of any great
writer to Poe, it may be incidentally remarked, results in the
sense of contrast, and would undoubtedly instinctively be called
unfair by his admirers, many of whom "do not," as the phrase is,
"know very well what they want." His success in accomplishing
his desired effect at all events is fatally compromised, usually, in
two ways: his motive is too plain and his means are too primitive.
He makes his motive so plain, not only by its constant undisguised
and obvious recurrence, but by actual profession (see "The Philosophy of Composition" and "The Poetic Principle," for example) as to defeat its own end. It is impossible to meet halfway an
artist whose efforts to surprise, shock, startle you are all the while
in full sight. He must perforce forego the unconscious reciprocity
of concern that is the essence of appreciation. A writer who declares at every turn, as the inveteracy of Poe's practice, his constant harping on the string of "horror," declares, that he is "going
to make your flesh creep" can hardly succeed in doing so. In the
face of such an announcement any flesh at all jaded by the extravagances of romanticism remains stationary. In the case of
some of Poe's stories, in fact, positive paralysis ensues in the face
of almost hysterical efforts on his part at galvanism; "The Pest"
for instance. For this carnomaniac purpose, too, his means are as
primitive as his motive is plain. He can certainly produce his effect
when the material he treats is of a nature to produce it in anyone's
hands. The subject itself of "The Premature Burial" is full of horror, and can be trusted to come home to the imagination of the
reader under any treatment of it. So with the idea of being walled
up alive as presented in "The Cask of Amontillado." So also with
the situation in "The Pit and The Pendulum." But in most instances it may certainly be said that one does not get enough pain
out of Poe to receive any great amount of pleasure from him.

He carries his "unscrupulousness" very far indeed—much farther than even in Arnold's estimation Kinglake could be said
to! [16] In fact, if throughout his work you feel the artist, you also

feel the artistic liar. He is the avatar of the type—a type tolerably well known in a multitude of examples from Mandeville to Münchausen [17] and establishing perhaps through its mere existence, if anything could, the absence of any necessary connection between art and truth. Truth stood between him and originality. It irked him equally in pursuing the egregious, in which he delighted, and in eluding the commonplace, which he abhorred. The esoteric attracted, and the ecumenical repelled him. He was fascinated by the false as Hawthorne was by the fanciful. He was, as Henri Martin said of the Celt, "always in revolt against the despotism of fact." [18] He was an artist in whom the great purpose of art, making the unreal appear real, became the end of making the false appear true. At this flagitious game he evinced the superior cleverness of the children of this world. Nowhere is his skill more noteworthy than in securing verisimilitude for the improbable, the incredible, one of the most obvious of his expedients being the auto-biographical form, for which he shows the notorious partiality of the so-called habitual liar. I have not made the calculation, but I should think there were not a half-dozen of his sixty-eight tales in which this form is not employed, and these are not among his comparatively few successes; when the material is extraordinary this personal presentation of it gives it great plausibility in the esteem of the credulous, though it is to be said that it arouses a corresponding distrust in the sceptical. The same fondness for the false appears in his occasional inversion of the process, whereby the truth is made to seem incredible —marvellous beyond belief, "too good to be true," in a word, but true all the same. Here of course the falsity of effect, merely takes the place of falsity of material. It was all one to Poe, provided he satisfied his passion for mystification. The shortest road to producing the sensational effect that alone he sought is to controvert the established order and for that road apart from its being the line of least resistance he had a native affinity. The key-note indeed of his nature is revolt.

In instinctive recalcitrancy to the general constitution of things he passed his life in kicking against its pricks [19] and produced his literature in the process. Inevitably the false, the ugly and the wrong attracted him, since the established standard is of the good, the beautiful and the true. But as the established is the only conceivable standard he was naturally forced to treat the former trinity in conjunction with, if not in terms of, the latter. The effect he aimed at being exclusively a sensational effect, he could best secure it by falsifying his material, and thus circumventing the reader's tranquillity of expectation. The fact that such sensation is valueless was of no concern to a philosopher who attached value to sensation as such and to sensation only. Hence he devoted the powers of an extraordinary intellect to producing what is to the intellect of next to no interest. The abnormal, in its various manifestations, the sinister, the diseased, the deflected, even the disgusting were his natural theme. He could not conceive the normal save as the commonplace for which he had apparently the "horror" he would have liked to inspire in others by the presentation of the eccentric. Dread of the commonplace, as was pointed out centuries ago by a far otherwise penetrating critic than Poe, is fatal to the sublime. And there is assuredly no sublimity in Poe.

Yet the tales of horror and those of the weird and the fantastic probably stand in the widest popular estimate as especially characteristic. And it is true that it is of these one thinks when one speaks of a Poe story. They have, many of them, the evil eminence that wilful morbidity lends to the production of its votaries of genius, and except for the effect on the nerves which a few of them are able to produce on "suggestible" sensoriums, they hold their place among other writings of a similar sort—there are none precisely like them, because of their meagreness—chiefly on account of their scenic quality. More has been claimed for the "tales of ratiocination" [20] as they are called. Writers before Poe have "grovelled in the ghastly and wallowed in the weird" with considerable effect if with an art inferior to his. But he has been called the inventor of the detective story, and thus decorated with a badge of unique distinction in the hierarchy of literature. It is always difficult to assign with certainty to any individual the invention of a literary or plastic genre. "Doubtless Homer had his Homer," remarks Thoreau.[21] M. Dupin was certainly preceded by Zadig, and Voltaire is said to have invented "Zadig" after reading an Oriental prototype. And even ascribing to Poe the invention of the detective story, the lover of literature may justly exclaim, "*la belle affaire!*" and feel disposed rather to

charge than to credit him with it. However, to start or even ac-
celerate a literary current of magnitude, whatever its merit, is an
accomplishment so rare as to be noteworthy on that account
alone. And though it is, no doubt, the detective story that is most
indebted to him in this respect, it is by no means the only fruit of
his remarkable inventiveness. "No man," says a writer in the London *Spectator*, "struck out so many new lines in the region of romance," and he proceeds to derive Jules Verne's stories from
"Hans Pfall," "She" from "A. Gordon Pym," "Treasure Island"
from "The Gold Bug," "Dr. Jekyll and Mr. Hyde" from "William
Wilson," Zola's, Flaubert's and even Mr. H. G. Wells's realism
from Poe's minute detail, etc. This does not of course modify his
own conclusion that "it is an inhuman and perverse judgment
that finds in Poe the springs of truly great writing;" [22] and it
should also be pointed out that there is a considerable element
of fancifulness—the fancifulness of the literal—in such romantic
etymology. It is quite conceivable that neither Jules Verne nor
Stevenson, nor Mr. Rider Haggard nor any of the other writers
in question was conscious of any specific or general indebtedness
to Poe, whom also in the different *genres* in question, save perhaps that of "The Gold Bug," they one and all altogether surpassed. Mr. Wells, for example, might excusably prefer to derive
his mystification from the minute detail of Swift. Nevertheless,
such analogies are eloquent witness of Poe's inventive genius—
characterize, in fact, his genius *as* inventive rather than imaginative.

For that reason he seems to me, as I began by saying, more
personal than truly original in the higher literary sense, since,
though he was extremely idiosyncratic, nevertheless what he
originated lay definitely in the sphere of invention. His imaginative writing is far less original. Having the imaginative in mind
we may say that originality consists in taking a fresh view, origi-
nating a new conspectus, a new synthesis, of life and the world
—turning objective material around a little and exhibiting it with
a different silhouette. It is in this way that real contributions to
literature are made, and it is thus that the really great writer
serves literature as the savant advances science. There is nothing
of this kind to be looked for in Poe. The true material of literature
he left precisely where he found it, for all his fantastic stirring of

it and uneasy striving with it. On the lower plane of invention, his mechanical and mathematical turn, his fecundity in ideas, conceptions, experimental notions certainly devised new modes, new fashions as it were, in fiction—which, indeed, was precisely what he himself understood by the originality he pursued and declared universally attainable. And in this field "ratiocination" is distinctly his forte. Here he excelled if he did not, narrowly speaking, invent; or rather, broadly speaking, excelled as well as invented. In this respect "The Gold Bug" is probably an unsurpassed masterpiece; a masterpiece, at any rate—which is no doubt eulogy enough, though M. Lemaitre's characterization of Maupassant as "à peu près irréprochable dans un genre qui ne l'est pas," [23] is certainly applicable to it. So in a less degree is "The Murders in the Rue Morgue." "The Purloined Letter" is decidedly inferior and "The Mystery of Marie Rogêt" quite unworthy the inventor of the detective story. In "The Purloined Letter" the effect of M. Dupin's contemptuousness dominates that of his skill, and in "The Mystery of Marie Rogêt" the arrogance of the author is destructive of all interest in a tale that is also otherwise tedious. When Poe's personality comes to the surface the effect is always unpleasant, and it is the absence of temperamental color that gives an agreeable relief to such exhibitions of his purely intellectual activity as "The Gold Bug" and "The Murders in the Rue Morgue;" just as among his weird and fantastic tales the best are those in which there are the most evidences of his art and the fewest of his disposition.

However, the extraordinary disproportion of inferior work in his prose does not obscure the fact that he was essentially an artist. The fact that there are hardly a dozen good ones among his sixty-eight tales is not due to any deflection of his artistic attitude. He had no other attitude—save that of necessity involved in his contentious exposition of artistic principles and his temperamental reprobation of practitioners of a different turn. Polemically he certainly shows little of the detachment so often prescribed to the artist. But even in polemic whenever he is in the least impersonal and disinterested it is the artistic for which he is contending. He is not averse to "abusing the plaintiff's attorney," [24] but the plaintiff's case he attacks on artistic grounds. Even in his poorer work, even in his poorest, the workmanship is always the best element. It is poor enough in some of it, but in such tales as "Four Beasts in One," "Loss of Breath," "The Man that was Used Up," "Never Bet the Devil Your Head," in fact almost all the "tales of extravaganza and caprice," there is assuredly nothing else. In such inexplicable "extravaganzas" as "The Duc de l'Omelette" and "Lionizing" its stark salience gets on one's nerves. The excessive predominance of this kind of thing in his tales is due obviously to failure in inspiration. But more obscurely it is undoubtedly due to alcohol. "Bon-Bon," for example, seems definitely characteristic of inebriety. The effect of alcohol is well known to be the relief of that tension which the maintenance of equilibrium imposes so painfully on such organizations as Poe's, and a consequence of excessive indulgence in it is therefore the loss of that balance of the faculties which secures correct judgments. It is impossible to account for much of Poe's writing except on the theory that both in conception and in execution it was in this way transfigured to his mind and sense. He saw it through the mist of mental congestion and saw in its incoherence the significance that escapes sobriety. Even his egotism would be insufficient otherwise to explain it. The effects of opium in stimulating and coloring the poetic imagination—as in Coleridge's case [25]—are familiar. But those of alcohol are pathologically quite different and quite inferior, and it does not seem to have been sufficiently remarked that in Poe's case they were undoubtedly responsible for the deterioration of his literary productions as well as for the pathetic disintegration of his life. It is a generous instinct that shrinks from dwelling on the latter, but the naiveté that ignores the obvious origin of much of his "extravaganza and caprice" is less generous than blind—and above all slightly ridiculous. The explanation at all events seems to reduce *ad absurdum* the sanction of being "thrilled" for the "thrill's" sake.

IV

The truth is it is idle to endeavor to make a great writer of Poe because whatever his merits as a literary artist his writings lack the elements not only of great, but of real, literature. They lack substance. Literature is more than an art. It is art in an extended sense of the term. Since it is the art that deals with life rather than with appearances it is the art *par excellence* that is art plus something else—plus substance. Its interest is immensely narrowed when it can only be considered plastically—narrowed to the point of inanity, of insignificance. Poe was certainly an artist, but the fact that he was exclusively an artist and an artist in an extremely restricted sense, of itself minimizes the literature he produced. Shakespeare, for example, is neither exclusively nor supremely an artist. M. Jules Lemaitre informs us how much better in some respects—in artistic respects—Racine would have written "Hamlet." [26] Every art of course, has its conventions. It rearranges them from time to time, it is subject to the law of evolution, but it depends on them always. And in so far as literature is an art it, too, leans upon them. It has its schools, its phases, its successive points of view, its academic perfections, its solecisms. But the fact that it deals with life itself rather than exclusively with appearances— which may be arranged, organized, systematized, controlled far more easily through their greater preliminary simplification— gives it so much more range, so much greater freedom, such an infinitely greater miscellaneity of material of so much more significance and vitality, that it is comparatively independent of conventions, and finds its supreme justification in giving anyhow, in any way, well or ill one may almost say, the effect of life, the phenomena and significance of life which constitute its substance. Thus it is that in literature substance counts so much more than it counts in any other art, however much any other may also be in its degree "a criticism of life." [27] Mr. Henry James has curiously illustrated the principle in later years. Beginning as pre-eminently or at least conspicuously an artist he has become so overwhelmed by the prodigious wealth and miscellaneity of his material—that is to say, the phases of life which his prodigious penetration has revealed to him—that his art has been submerged by it. The trees have obliterated the forest. All the more important is it, one may argue, to cling to conventions of treatment, that your picture of life may be definite, coherent and effective. Yes, but one of these conventions is a certain correspondence with reality. Life being the subject of literature more fully and directly than it is of any purely plastic art that deals with appearances—which are necessarily more ordered and adaptable and in a sense art themselves, or a stage of it—being indeed the substance as well as the subject of literature, this correspondence with reality is exacted by it of any treatment of it that is, even as art, to have any interest or value. The doctrine of art for art's sake applied to literature is apt to have particularly insipid results.

In short, however extravagant and capricious, any work of art is necessarily subject to its material and the hand of every artist must like the dyer's be subdued to what it works in.[28] But a literary composition, especially, cannot be conceived and executed *in vacuo*. The warp must be "given," however wholly the woof may be invented, or the web will be insubstantial and the pattern incoherent. Poe could transact his imaginings in environments of the purest fancy, in no-man's land, in the country of nowhere, and fill these with "tarns" and morasses and "ragged mountains" and shrieking water-lilies, flood them with ghastly moonlight and aerate them with "rank miasmas." [29] Nevertheless, he could only avoid the flatness of pure phantasmagoria by peopling them with humanity. His landscape might embody extravagance and his atmosphere enshroud caprice, his figures demanded to be made human. The overwhelming interest of fiction is its human interest. Since it is peopled with human figures neglect of its population is a contradiction in terms. Even in the fiction of adventure, in which the personages are minimized and the incidents the main concern, even in fiction in which plot figures as the protagonist of the drama, plot and incident would be sterile but for the characters that figure in them. However subordinate and undifferentiated these may be, they must make some intrinsic appeal, or we should not care what happened to them. The game even as a game is not one that can be played with counters. Yet, that is precisely the way in which Poe played it. And his stories have no human interest because humanity did not in the least interest him. Neither man nor woman delighted him enough to occupy his genius even incidentally. His tales contain, of course, no "character"—that prime essential, and most exacting *raison-d'être* of normal fiction. But what is surprising is the absolute inhumanity of the personages he is compelled to incarnate and the absolutely inhuman way in which he sets them forth. In almost every case of importance, as I have said, the chief personage is the narrator and—perhaps a little from this substantially unvaried practice, though mainly, I think, because of the real resemblance —the narrator suggests Poe himself. Each is very baldly the centre of his universe. The two take pretty much the same view—an astonishingly external one so far as human nature is concerned. The illusion of the story is subserved, but of the story quite apart from the personages. What it gains in illusion, it loses in significance. Indeed, so great is the importance of human character to a story that deals with it at all that I think those of Poe's tales in which the personages are the least shadowy, the least like algebraic symbols, the least characteristic, that is to say, are greatly helped by the fact. The stories in which he figures gain greatly from M. Dupin, who has a pedantic and censorious temperament, though his differentiation is as inferior to that of his successor, M. Lecocq,[30] as the meagre and mathematical medium in which he exists is to the varied and entertaining field of activity, full of character and crowded with incident, that Gaboriau furnished for the latter—without, however, reaching eminence as a "world-author" in the process. "The Fall of the House of Usher" gains greatly from the characters therein, though these are merely sketches for the reader's imagination to fill out. One thinks of "Wuthering Heights" and of the place in literature that would have been assigned to Emily Bronte by Poe admirers, had she had the good fortune to be born an American. "The Pit and The Pendulum," one of the best of the tales, it seems to me, owes much to its exceptional "psychology" as an imaginative study of real torture to which ingenuity gives real point instead of merely displaying itself as ingenuity. It is helped, too, I think, by being localized in real time and space; by the fact that there was such an institution as the Inquisition, a fabric also quite otherwise "thrilling" than any of Poe's imagination, and that the victim's rescuers had an actual and the correct nationality, though I fear these considerations would seem philistine indeed to the true Poe worshipper. Furthermore, "The Murders in the Rue Morgue" forfeits a large part of its interest, the moment it appears that the murderer is an ape and not a human malefactor. *Ce n'est que ça*, one feels like exclaiming—and repeating even when William Wilson's double dissolves into his conscience, though of course allegorically that is the point of the story, as well as being very

cleverly, very ingeniously, managed. Finally one of the tales—
"The System of Dr. Tarr and Dr. Fether"—has an exceptional
interest because it is an intelligent, though it does not pretend
to be a profound, study of a phase of mind and character under
certain conditions and in a certain environment, executed with a
wholly unaccustomed lightness of touch and an aspect of gayety.
The scene, however, it will be remembered, is a *maison de santé*
and the personages are its inmates. And nothing is more characteristic of Poe's perversity than that his most normal fiction
should be the representation of the abnormal. The abnormal was
essential to him, and he only varied his practice of achieving it in
his treatment by securing it in his material. Taken with the whim
of depicting human nature he could at least select its deflected
types. Even here, however, his interest is clearly in treating his
material in a rather ghastly vein of contrasting and contra-
indicated *bouffe*. He cares nothing for his "types," and his real
success, such as it is, is incidental.

Similarly with his preoccupation with crime—almost an obsession with him. He is never concerned with sin, which is too
integrally human an element of life to interest him. Crime on the
contrary is in comparison of an artificial nature, and of however
frequent still of exceptional occurrence. Undoubtedly it furnishes
apposite material to the novelist of character as well as to the
portraitist of manners, and is a personal as well as a social factor
in human life. But this aspect of it Poe, whose criminals are only
criminals, completely ignores. He uses it not naturalistically but
conventionally. It is his conventional machinery for his story.
Like Mme. Tussaud and Mrs. Jarley [31] he finds in it the readiest
instrument of his most cherished effects. And so far as he "psy-
chologizes" it he increases its inherent artificiality by treating it
with morbid imaginativeness, endeavoring after his favorite
method to give the illusion of reality to its abnormal repellency,
and not at all concerned about demonstrating its real character.
Here he is measurably successful in such a tale as "The Imp of
the Perverse" where he utilizes the well known tendency of the
criminal to confess, and totally fails in such absurdity as "The
Black Cat," a story that could hardly have "thrilled" Ichabod
Crane; but one illustrates his lack of human feeling as well as the
other. And of almost all the stories into which the element of hu-

manity enters perforce, it may be said, finally, that the residuum is not so much worth while as to earn neglect of his shortcomings in a respect normally vital to the kind of thing he is doing. In a word the "Poe" in his stories could only be moving and effective, if this element were present also.

For the only thing that can give any significance, any vital interest, any value, in a word, to the weird and the fantastic themselves is to establish them somehow in some human relationship —as Hoffmann does.[32] Otherwise they are simply phenomena that appeal strictly to the nerves. Poe's treatment of them negatives their sole sanction. "He can thrill you as no one else can," says one of his admirers. As to that there are several things to be said. In the first place it depends a good deal on who you are whether you are "thrilled" or not. In the next place how are you "thrilled?" As you are by the knocking at the door in Macbeth, or as you are by a bad dream or a gruesome sight in actual life? Thirdly, are you thus affected because the story *is* thrilling, or because, as I have already noted, your own imagination is set at work as to how you would be affected by experiencing what you are reading of—"The Premature Burial" for example—forgetful of the fact that personal application, than which nothing is more common, notoriously vitiates any objective judgment. Finally of what value after all is "gooseflesh" as a guide to correct estimates in art? Is this hyperæsthetic reaction a trustworthy measure of real æsthetic merit? To ask these questions is of course to answer them. But even accepting this effect on the nerves as evidence of Poe's power, even of his unique power—for I think no other writer ever essayed it so baldly—its essential insignificance must be admitted because it is wholly divorced from any element of interest outside of itself. Instead of itself being an element in a composition, as with Hoffmann, Poe's weirdness is the whole thing. An occasional discord has its uses in a work of harmony, but the scrannel shriek of a locomotive performs no function but that of irritation, though it may "thrill" or even deafen a listener. It is certainly more important to be moved than to be moved pleasantly, but to be moved to no purpose, to be agitated aimlessly in no direction, is an unsatisfactory experience.

It is needless to specify instances among Poe's tales that illustrate this exclusive appeal to the nerves. It would be difficult to

find any among those of the weird class that do not. Besides, in
them it was his theory, his "scheme," to create this precise effect
and no other. The particularly crass one of "Berenice," however,
shows his method in particular relief. It is that product of his
genius in which a madman recounts his fascination by the beautiful teeth of his mistress and his exhumation of her remains for
the purpose of extracting them as a last exercise of his faculties
before losing these completely. Poe sometimes went too far and
did so in this instance, naively admits one of his earlier editors!
As if it mattered where along that line one stopped. The partly
ridiculous, partly repulsive, wholly inept quality of the performance is stamped as such at the start. The serious workmanship
only emphasizes the fact that the personages are lay figures, the
motif insane, the story incredible. As a ship-shape and coherent
account of incoherent horror it may contain a "thrill" for the predisposed, but it is fully as fitted to wake a smile as a shudder and
there is obviously no standard by which to admeasure this sort
of thing except that of technical execution. Any reader of "Berenice" not a neurasthenic must inevitably ask, "What of it?" Having no import it has no importance.

V

"Berenice" epitomizes very well Poe's lack of substance, and
the insignificance of the fantastic element in his work which this
lack of substance involves. It also illustrates the aridity of his
imagination. Imagination is, in the view of most of his admirers,
probably his most striking, his most salient possession. But it is
darkening counsel to stop with this mere ascription as if imagination were an invariable rather than a protean faculty. Poe's imagination was of a peculiarly personal kind. It intensified his divining powers, but never extended his range of thought. It was thoroughly, integrally, analytic. His "Tales of Conscience," [33] as they
have been called, deal mechanically so far as they do not deal
conventionally with conscience. There is no largely imaginative
treatment of it. They summarize phenomena deduced from remorse and fear as forces and, confined to crime as they are, involve little imaginative psychology. His imaginings are largely
inventive, and important as the imagination is to the inventor, the

tendency to invention is apt to imply an inferior order of it. The
poets are sadly lacking in the inventive faculty. It is essentially
logical, concatenated, mechanical. It has no spiritual and no
sensuous side. Poe's inventiveness is his chief mental trait and
his imagination was its servant. He is perhaps at his best in "The
Gold Bug"—to Poe's partisans a miracle of imaginative invention
but only to his partisans anything else. His spiritual side is illustrated by his "Ligeias," "Eleonoras" and "Morellas"—which measured by a serious standard are scarcely more than morbid moon-
ings. The ingenuity of his one spiritual tale, "William Wilson"
is far more in evidence than its imaginativeness. It is an extremely
artistic piece of workmanship and shows what Poe's art could do
in the service of truth instead of mystification. But only up to the
point when you perceive it *is* mystification after all. Curiously,
then the effect deliquesces—when its meaning appears—with the
entrance of avowed allegory. The whole thing becomes insubstantial because his imagination is unequal to conducting his fine
conception to its conclusion without destroying his illusion. His
sensuousness is distinctly rudimentary, all glitter and tinsel, ebony
and silver. His consecration to beauty seems a little ironical in the
light of his too frequent conception of it. Witness "The Assignation," with its "mingled and conflicting perfumes, reeking up
from strange convolute censers, together with multitudinous flar-
ing and flickering tongues of emerald and violet fire" its "thousand reflections from curtains which rolled from their cornices
like cataracts of molten silver," its "beams of natural glory" which
"mingled at length fitfully with the artificial light and lay welter-
ing in subdued masses upon a carpet of rich, liquid-looking cloth
of Chili gold"—all of which "richesse de café," as Balzac would
call it, suggests Thackeray caricaturing Disraeli and Bulwer combined [34]—those twin sources of Poe's style according to his latest
editors, who, however, must have been thinking only of its extravagances, as his style in general is admirable.

In any case such writing is not sensuous but scenic. And Poe
had no more the sensuous than the sensual strain. The sensual as
commonly understood does not exist for him, apparently, as it is
apt not to in persons of his variety of nervous organization, and
his writings it is to be pointed out have this signal negative merit.
But he perhaps pays for it in some degree by an extraordinary

aridity in the whole sensuous sphere. When he enters this he is either perfectly insignificant or else his taste deserts him. He is too insincere to succeed in it. His nature requires the element of the artificial which distinguishes the scenic. His genius was certainly a striking one and if he was a charlatan he certainly had a genius for charlatanry. He revelled in the specious. The vivid aspect of reality he gave to his creations is due to his skill in its use, for he never *felt* reality and was impervious to its appeal as the true constitution of the universe, moral and material. What he desired was to be striking. He says so in so many words in one of his disingenuous (or merely perverse, who knows?) argumentations, contending that any one can be original if he will. And his usual means of accomplishing it was by giving through speciousness the semblance of reality to the unreal and incredible. He relied on this far more than even on his scenic imagination, though his scenic imagination gave him great power of vivid material realization; his landscapes are stereoscopic. The scenic, however, demands scale. With Poe the scale is too small. His stage is lilliputian. He is so fond of the lime-light in itself that he floods his picture with it. But for the proper play of this illuminant more time and space are needed than his cabinet canvas contains. His imagination is not rich enough to engender extension, endue it with continuity and crowd it with action. His action is always meagre and, one may say, deduced from, rather than largely illustrative of, his idea. Or else it is conventional, as in the "Adventures of A. Gordon Pym" which is the acme of stereotyped "adventure," imitating even the religious out-givings of "Robinson Crusoe" with grotesquely mechanical effect.

On the other hand he was full of ideas. If he lacked the visualizing moral power of the image-making faculty, if his action and incidents are meagre and gain their aspect of reality through a specious art of presentation rather than by the actual incarnation of artistic vision, what eminently he did not lack was fertility in intellectual conception. Sixty-eight stories, whatever their average quality, are a good many. His picture might be vague, but it never lacked subject. He cannot be said to have lived in the world of ideas, in the accepted sense of the phrase, for he had but a smattering acquaintance with its established consensus. Predeterminedly original, however, he created his own. Artist as he was, he was nevertheless far more predisposed to the abstract than to the concrete, except in the purely material sphere; he began with principle and proceeded to phenomena, in irreproachably deductive fashion. Analytical as he was, he conducted his analysis deductively; he had a passion for ratiocination, but he argues synthetically. His conclusion is always his own point of departure—artistically withheld till the climax is reached in the verification of hypothesis. This is the difference between M. Dupin and the inductive Zadig, for example. He was tremendously concerned with theory, a circumstance that gives point to his criticism and coherence to his tales, however it may devitalize his poetry. His mind was highly speculative, inquiring, even inquisitional. He had a prodigious interest in problems, puzzles, rebuses —an interest that to those who do not share it is apt to seem inept. He was in a way a conjurer in literature. He delighted in mystification—which is as much as to say he had no other interest in mystery. He was less of a mystic than any writer who has ever dealt with the mysterious. He had vastly more affinity with Cagliostro [35] than with Hoffmann from whom—inexplicably—he is so often said to derive. Without the vanity he had the conceit and enjoyed the complacence of the prestidigitator.

In his early studies, mathematics, and in his later reading, science in general, attracted him most genuinely. With all his gift for language it interested him mainly as syntax, and his knowledge of languages was as superficial as his care for letters. His French for example—which is not infrequent—is what he would censure in another as culpably ignorant. He may be said, indeed, to have indulged his mathematical turn in his philosophy of life —or whatever may serve to pass for it with him; of course as such he had no philosophy of life. His interest in ideas did not extend to moral ones, of which he had none. The whole world of morals was a terra incognita to him—not at all the same thing as saying, which is also true, that he had no morals. Coleridge, for example, has been said to have had none, but he was immensely concerned with their philosophy. Poe's personal egotism accentuated by his indulgence freed him from a sense of personal responsibility no doubt, but the singular thing about him as a writer is that man's moral nature made no appeal to his imagination. Morbid psychology, to be sure, was a part of his material, but he used it almost altogether as a means mainly mechanical to the production of a dramatic effect. And even here his general ideas have not the scope and freedom they have in the purely intellectual sphere, but evince the succinct specific quality that marks the "notation" of phenomena. So that even his determination to the abnormal does not in the unfamiliar moral sphere remark any law of general import—except such commonplaces as the tendency of the criminal to confession already noted. And of course, as regards morals in the extended sense, he had, about man's habits and customs, around which the imagination of the normal literary artist plays perpetually, no ideas at all, either general or otherwise.

In brief, his lack of moral imagination accounts for the vacuity of his writings. A writer's product is characterized in great part by what he lacks as well as by what he possesses, by his defects as well as by his qualities. It is no reproach to a theological writer to be ignorant of the fine-arts unless he refers to them. On the other hand it would be an insufficient characterization of a landscape painter to say that he could paint clouds if he could not paint trees, though certainly if he painted clouds extraordinarily well, that would be the most important thing to say about him, as it would signalize his contribution to landscape art, besides which his failure in any respect would be more negligible. The theory of criticism, however, which holds that the excellences of a performance are alone worth attention, that it is, unlike a rope, to be judged only by its strongest part, and that the function of criticism is really the judicial dispensing of rewards of merit, is unsatisfactory and provincial. The whole work is there calling for critical account and, due attention paid to the matter of emphasis and accent, its sins both of commission and omission are germane to critical consideration. In practice the other theory leads to notorious confusion and—as Americans at least must be constantly reminded—the distinction between good and bad is obscured by mechanically ascribing to a failure the characteristics of a performer's successes. At all events it is pertinently illuminating to find a writer of tales, criticism and poetry deficient in the philosophy of life, letters and feeling, not only because this at once ranks his product and measures its value, but on account of the light it throws on his productive faculty itself—his imagination. It is a just reproach to Hawthorne that he suffered the genius that produced "The Scarlet Letter" to produce little or nothing else comparable with it. But the case is quite different with Poe, because tales, criticism and poetry of real value cannot be written or can only occasionally be written with Poe's equipment. The wonder is not that he did not succeed oftener, but that he succeeded at all, as assuredly he did in his own way—one can hardly say his own *genre,* since he had no congeners.

It is a mistake to try to classify him. He is very strictly *sui generis.* So appalling an egoist could hardly fail to be. No more superficial association was ever made than in relating him to Hoffmann, in whom the weird and the fantastic are always in close and generally in affectionate companionship with sentiment and humor. "Where form dominates" says Balzac, "sentiment disappears," and in the temperament of the technician humor has as little place as sentiment. Notoriously Poe had none of either. He was an artist with a controlling bent toward artifice, exaggeratedly theoretic, convinced that the beautiful is the strange and the sad the poetic, and exercising his imagination through every expedient of ingenious invention, to the end of producing effects of strangeness to the point of abnormality and of sadness to the point of horror. Compact of neurotic sensationalism and saturated with the specious, Poe's "thrilling" tales taken in the mass illustrate the most detestable misuse of imaginative powers within the limits of serious literature, and only fall within these limits by the intellectual vigor which oftenest they argue rather than evince. "It's a weary feast," says Thackeray, "the banquet of wit where no love is." [36] And Poe's banquet is as bereft of wit as it is destitute of love. He lacked humor and he lacked heart.

VI

If even his imagination was thus limited it was perhaps partly because the field of its exercise was naturally limited by his lack of culture. He had no culture properly so called. He applied the schoolmaster's rod to others with the gusto of pretentiousness, but discipline is precisely and *par excellence* what he lacked

himself. He is the notablest example to be found among men of
letters of a writer living exclusively in the realm of the intellect
without developing or enriching his own. His first work is as
good as his last. He read much but without purpose. In this
single respect his editors have perhaps done him somewhat less
than justice in saying "His sources were, at first, books of which
Disraeli's 'Curiosities of Literature' [37] is a type, and in science
some elementary works; generally he seems to have read books
only for review, as they came under his notice at random, but
he paid much attention to the magazines, home and foreign,
throughout his life." Desultory as his reading was it was not
indolent and hap-hazard. Devoid of sentiment, he eschewed
"trash." And without any spirit of *suite,* or any persistent amass-
ing of knowledge, still less with any ordered and philosophic
acquisition, his purely intellectual organization led him into the
realm of learning, where he was distinctly at home without,
however, possessing the moral purpose to benefit by his stay.
He satisfied his curiosity, following an indubitable natural bent,
without engaging his responsibility or really increasing his
knowledge. There is no such absurd *fatras* in literature as the
absurd "Eureka." He found his practical account in these excursions. All was grist that came to his mill. Just as he read the
current product for journalistic ends, he pursued in literature
out-of-the-way paths in search of the odd and the unfamiliar
with a similar motive—at least with a similar result. What he
found there served to decorate his own writing with the un-
conventional and the recondite. His writing is bedizened with
the frippery of learning often, but one suspects that most of the
goods, in familiar phrase, are in the shop-window. And his
étalage of learning is that of the literary charlatan—an arsenal
of the occult and the obscure, the abstruse and the exotic, above
all the esoteric and the technical, the whole chosen and cal-
culated to impose on the credulous and mesmerize the impressionable.

But it is doubtful if any one of his circle had as much reading.
In this respect he belonged rather in the New England that he
constantly jeered at as provincial and hated with a genuine and
sometimes clairvoyant hatred. The weaknesses of Isaac are apparent enough to Ishmael and though his railing at them may

seem Bedouin to the Brahmin, it is not to be called Bœotian.[38]
There was probably no one within the purview of Transcendentalism capable of writing the following: "Sculpture, although in its nature rigorously poetical, was too limited in its
extent and consequence to have occupied, at any time, much
of his attention." Possibly Poe was not and got it from Goethe,
as almost certainly he did the remark on the next page of "The
Domain of Arnheim:" "No such paradises are to be found in
reality as have glowed on the canvas of Claude"—a landscape
by whom he had probably never seen. It is difficult to determine
the true inventory of the predatory, but appreciation of Goethe's
æstheticism is in itself a distinction for Poe's time. Nor is he to
be called bohemian. His habits were irregular enough, but the
bohemian has no intellectual curiosity, and Poe was made of it.
The bohemian is content "merely to bask and ripen." Poe was
a worker. His irregularities have obscured for us his exceptional
industry. They interfered sadly with his accomplishment, but
with its amount far less than with its character. In spite of them
he kept at work—or at least returned to work when he could.
His indigence and the heavy pressure of it on the two beings he
cared for were a constant stimulus to a nature that, whatever
its faults, knew not supineness. With even less urgent need he
would have worked as hard—perhaps even, considering the in-
stability of his nervous organization, to better purpose, since he
would have been less harried by the cormorant care. He had the
disposition of the fighter, and his failings did not mine his
fortitude nor his failures discourage, however they might tran-
siently deject him. He was not an idler or a dreamer. His mental
activity was constantly informed with purpose, and directed with
assiduity. He was always full of energy when he was not ham-
strung by exhaustion. No bohemian produces ten volumes. When
his ambitious and sometimes arrogant plans met shipwreck,
owing in general no doubt to his own evil genius, he made new
ones. Never handicapped by modesty or even the prudences
of self-distrust, he was undeterred by obstacles and undismayed
by misfortune. If he did not have a proud soul, at least his
egotism conserved his identity unimpaired, even in the disintegration of his faculties, and to the last made the most of what
his errors had left him. Next to his art it is his energy that by

demonstrating his capacity distinguishes him and makes him a marked figure in our literature.

He had an English experience in impressionable school-boy days—which served him to real purpose in "William Wilson," probably the solidest of his tales. But he never travelled, and in this respect he inevitably seems limited, even boyish, in comparison with many of his contemporaries. It is hardly necessary to say that this was a limitation he did not himself feel. But if his egotism amounted even to bumptiousness, as it did, it was naturally associated with great independence. He did his own thinking. He was constantly "sizing up" everything, especially others, and could on this account alone hardly have been popular, even among the lowly spirited to whom arrogance and imperiousness, or even the caricature of those vices, seem not defects but qualities. They were especially evident, along with more amiable ones, in his criticism, which forms several volumes of his complete works, which he wrote more incisively, not to say more successfully, on the whole than any of his few contemporary competitors, and for which he certainly showed the aptitudes of real penetration and a philosophic stand-point. He lacks, to be sure one of the chief qualifications of the critic, the critical temper. It is in his criticism that his "journalism" appears most obviously. And his journalism was that of his day, the farthest possible removed from the critical temper. It has instead the polemic temper. And his polemic was extremely personal. Its tone is often extremely contemptuous. The lining, as the French say, of his praise is sometimes abuse of those who differ with him. His praise of Hawthorne is highly spiced with contempt for the neglect of Hawthorne that he charged upon New England. He felt the sectionalism of New England as of course no writer, not himself a New Englander, could fail to do. But he treats it with a self-answering excess in his references to "the Emersons and Alcotts and Fullers." [39] His treatment of Longfellow is another instance. Longfellow is something of a quack himself, he says, but his reputation is what mainly strikes him, and this he thinks almost altogether due to the quackery of Longfellow's friendly environment. He makes elaborate accusations of plagiarism against him, and then at the conclusion of his philippic takes it all back or at all events whittles it down to a negligible point, with the obvious result, of course, of making his own article negligible. Perhaps he had not enough purpose to be called malevolent. He was rather irritable than imperious, perhaps, in his lack of any feeling of responsibility, in which case he must be acquitted of more malign motive than that of the strutting and consciously clever Ishmael bent on self assertion. To call Carlyle an "ass" and Emerson his imitator [40] was but a way like another of calling attention to himself. So, possibly, were his equally extravagant eulogies. Such primitive "methods" were certainly more in vogue in his day than in ours. The journalism to which his work formally belonged or with which it had notable affiliations bristled with "personalities," so-called. But Poe has claims inconsistent with the cloaking of his faults by the mantle of his time, and certainly no writer of his time, even, of anything like his powers wrote criticism of this particular order of simplicity. If it had been as prevalent as it was primitive we may be sure he would have avoided it in his consecration to "originality" and aversion to custom and the common.

Cavilling came naturally to him. He began it early. It was perhaps the edge of his adolescent cleverness. "I never heard him speak in terms of praise of any English writer living or dead" says a fellow cadet at West Point—testimony to a natural bent, at least.[41] As he matured and began to write he necessarily modified it, but never beyond clear recognition. He was in fact, rather better in its practice than when he varied it with eulogy. There is more truth, for example, in his remark about Carlyle, whom he did not in the least appreciate, that his manner "is conventional—with himself," [42] than in his characterization of Tennyson, whom he adored, as "the greatest of all poets living or dead." [43] His laudation of the galaxy of female poets whose praises he sang so enthusiastically is ascribed by Stedman to his chivalry—an admission that he did not take either the sex or his function very seriously. And in truth his various judgments, favorable or other, are less trustworthy than those of any other critic of his general eminence. He could not have learned much from his contemporaries here if, as he says, "Our most analytic if not altogether our best critic (Mr. Whipple, perhaps, excepted) is Mr. William A. Jones." [44] And in fact, in his day criticism among us—and measurably in England—had even

closer relations than it has to-day with the function discharged
by professors of rhetoric and was rather elementary and of a
hole and corner character. On the whole, it may be said that
in spite of his penetration, which was keen within narrow
enough limits, he indulged his propensity to personal irresponsibility rather more than less in his criticism than in his tales
and—naturally—much more than in his poems; yet that on the
other hand his criticism shows incidentally the same alert mental
activity and intellectual curiosity.

His mental activity was indeed extraordinary—so much so as
apparently to be deemed by him almost an end in itself. To what
purpose or upon what substance his mind was engaged was of
small moment so long as it functioned. But to the fact that it
did function so actively is probably due the specific excellence,
as his penetration is the specific quality, of his criticism, namely,
that like much of his fiction it is ratiocinative and neither ca-
nonical as so much past, nor impressionist as so much current,
criticism is. He was dogmatic enough, and absurdly autocratic,
but his dogmas were not conventions. On the other hand he had
ideas about the matter in hand and did not "recount the adventures of his soul among masterpieces" [45]—though it is to be
said that acknowledged masterpieces did not greatly interest his
soul to which they doubtless afforded too little polemic material.
His ideas were often mere notions. With his theoretic bent they
could hardly be otherwise. But in form, at least, they were conspicuously rationalized. Reasons with him were as plenty as
blackberries. He delighted, in French phrase, to *remuer* them—
fussily, perhaps, rather than profoundly and largely, no doubt, by
way of what he himself calls "kicking up a bobbery," [46] but
energetically and unceasingly. And though whistling as one goes
even from excess instead of want of thought is still only whistling,
nevertheless the phenomena of so much mental activity occupied
with something quite other than Transcendentalism, exalting
beauty to the point of declaring its incompatibility with truth,
must have been interesting in his day. In fact it still has a certain
piquancy. But his reasons were not the fruit of inquiry. They
were "immediately beheld" justifications of his preferences, and
his mental furniture was not rich enough for the production of
any *a priori* reflections of range and moment. He never speculated

as Balzac, in similar case, observing: "There must be a cause for this singularity." He was only too pleased to rest in the singularity, to establish and flaunt it. He was much impressed by the saying he cites more than once from "Lord Verulam:" "There is no exquisite beauty which has not some strangeness in its proportion," [47] but he does not press the matter further, and is too content to get authority for "strangeness"—which was precisely his affair—to appreciate that its service as an accent does not involve its value as an element even, to say nothing of his own practice of enforcing its predominance as a factor. The portion of his reasoning that—naturally—has most interest is that concerned with linguistic technic. He would have made a stimulating professor of prosody, in spite of his "crotchets," as Stedman calls them,[48] and his extravagance is in this field altogether more suggestive than in any other.

VII

He had, in short, a fine mind which he neither disciplined, nor stored, nor developed; the unusual activity of which was stimulated and guided by intellectual curiosity; of which invention and logic were more marked traits than imagination and poetic feeling; and of which he made effective but unscrupulous usage to no particular purpose. There is nothing very sinister in Poe, except the desire to produce sinister effects. And since these, as I have said, are apt to fail through the obviousness of their motive and the crudity of their means, they leave a merely disagreeable and not a sinister, a morbid and perverse not at all a satanic, impression of the genius they express, though it is undeniable that a good many of the tales recall Emerson's description of Mephistopheles: "pure intellect applied—as always there is a tendency—to the service of the senses." [49] His literary and artistic far exceeded his personal temperament, and he had appetites rather than passions. His lack of sensuousness was agreeably accompanied by an apparently complete emancipation from the sensual. There is simply no sex in his writings, and was not in his life till he went completely to pieces. His unscrupulousness and indelicacies with regard to ways and means, to be sure, began early, but his attitude toward them, if it betrayed a

ferocious egotism, showed also the distinctly unmoral nature—
the shallower side of the instinct for self-preservation, not its
perversion. If he was a charlatan he never saw any harm in being
one. The candor of his duplicity emulates sincerity. And he
looked on literature as the adventurer views his field of operation, not as the enthusiast his cause or the regularly enlisted his
profession—a fact wholly germane to any consideration of his
success in it, quite apart from its bearing on the character of the
man behind his writings.

His legend has grown curiously since his death. The reasons
for it are of course largely romantic, personal rather than literary.
He is distinctly so much the most, as to be almost the only,
romantic figure of our literature; and his romantic interest has
greatly influenced the critical estimate of his work. In the first
place it has led to the production of an unusual amount of
criticism of this. And this criticism has been increasingly favorable. His contemporaries took a much less extravagant view of
it. For them there was less mystery about Poe himself and they
entertained none of the illusions that time, instead of destroying,
as usual, in Poe's case seems to have multiplied. Then, too, the
appreciation of literary art has greatly increased with us—to an
excess, at present, I think, that fairly matches our earlier
provincialism. Moreover, the spirit of literary generosity, particularly abounding in America toward our own authors—our
own *sommités* in all fields—touched by the hard fate and possible injustice which Poe endured and from which his personal
reputation suffered in the eyes of his contemporaries and the
succeeding generation, has tended to exalt his literary reputation,
with no doubt the instinct that its exaltation may serve to excuse
or at least obscure his infirmities. To his contemporaries Poe was
a man and a writer like another, to be measured by his performance. To subsequent critics he gradually came to appear as
unique in a literature especially in need of the element he
represents. And now it is difficult to judge him in the interests
of truth without a melancholy consciousness of disloyalty to
tradition. To recall once more Sainte-Beuve's serviceable remark
to Arnold about Lamartine; "he was important to *us*." [50] A spot
of scarlet in a monotone of subdued hues, he naturally, as we got
further and further away from his time, came more and more

to rivet the attention which on closer scrutiny it appears he does not repay.

His reputation among us has notoriously been greatly increased by foreign recognition of his writings. If, say his admirers, we ourselves esteem him because he is an American writer, this cannot be true of his foreign estimation; quite the contrary. This is certainly plausible. But foreign recognition sets such traps for our naiveté that it is prudent to be a little on our guard in the presence of it. The theory that the foreign estimate previsages posterity's is open to some question—aside from the fact that posterity itself may make mistakes; Aldrich, for example, acutely argued from Browning's obscurity the probable injustice of posterity, preoccupied with obscurities of its own, to his incontestable merits. But foreign recognition in the nature of the case rewards to a disproportionate extent the merits that especially appeal to foreigners. If, as Arnold held, Sainte-Beuve could regard Lamartine as important to the French without implying a positive in this relative importance, it is equally true that an exotic may make an appeal out of all proportion to its intrinsic value and interest. In any event we ought to distinguish between foreign recognition of those of our writers who are classifiable with foreign ones and this recognition when it rewards with its irresponsible applause the exceptional and extravagant which appeal to its interest in the novel and the foreign *per se.* As a matter of fact foreign recognition has been most generous with regard to many of our, to us, least indispensable writers. To put the matter crudely, the appreciative foreigner has admirable writers of his own; what he most appreciates in our literature is the queer, the odd, the qualities from whose associated defects he feels an entire detachment. Foreign recognition therefore in the case of Poe's extravaganzas and caprices is not necessarily an *imprimatur* of the same authority as it is in such instances as those of Cooper and Longfellow, for example. It attests not the merit but the extraordinariness of his writings, and a little, no doubt, the extraordinariness of their being produced in America. Gautier's reference to him, besides classing him with Mrs. Radcliffe and "Monk" Lewis, is chiefly depreciation of his environment.[51] And in France, at least, his sponsors were not, as in the case of Cooper, Balzac, and Sainte-

Beuve, the foremost of Continental authorities at the time, one may say, but the genial and good natured Gautier, who was preaching the gospel of romanticism *à outrance,* and Baudelaire, as to whose authority Swinburne's praise and the current rediscovery of him by the dilettanti, mainly of Swinburne's speech, are disconcertingly at variance with his treatment by the austere Scherer,[52] our own catholic Henry James, and the trenchant but impartial Faguet, perhaps the first of living French critics, in whose admirable "Literary History of France"[53] his name does not appear. It is also worth bearing in mind—since prudence in such a matter is, as I say, commendable—that Baudelaire, whom Mr. James cruelly calls Poe's inferior both as a charlatan and as a genius, had nevertheless an even greater purely linguistic genius than Poe's and that the beauty of his translation, in itself celebrated, has been an appreciable element in Poe's Continental vogue. In France, in fact, our "world-author's" stories appear as a part of Baudelaire's complete works.

Besides the foreign appreciation, Poe's fame has been forwarded by enjoying the favor of those who take what may be called the professional—or perhaps one may say more definitely now-a-days the professorial—view of letters. This is somewhat different from that of the disinterested lover of literature, who is less concerned about classification. Tracing the tendencies and recording the phases of literary evolution, especially in a society so uniform, and with a history so short as ours, is a work in which accents of any sharpness must, one would say, be so acceptable as to be magnified out of sheer gratitude. The pleasures of classification are simpler, as well as less arduous, than those of characterization, and any intensification of their pursuit must be particularly welcome. A crisp note, a vivid patch of color, a definite *point de repère* in American literary history can but be so prized by the literary historian as to acquire in his treatment a relief somewhat independent of its intrinsic quality. Poe is the nucleus of romanticism in American letters, and in addition to his indubitable importance thus in supplying a "note" we might otherwise have lacked, he has in consequence acquired from the literary historians and the critics who take their cue from them, an adventitious aspect of real and intrinsic importance as well. And this verdict has naturally been relied on by the extremely *un*professional many who possess those "primitive tastes" to which, says Mr. Henry James—decidedly our most competent critical authority in such a matter—Poe particularly appeals.[54] After the edition of his writings by the late Mr. Stedman and Professor Woodberry, one can hardly see how they could do otherwise. This piece of editing is one of the most distinguished examples of its art and a monument in which American letters has excellent reason for taking a genuine satisfaction. There is an adequate "Memoir" condensed with additions by Professor Woodberry from his admirable "Life." There are three "introductions"[55]—to the tales, the criticism, and the poems, respectively—beautifully written by the elder editor, marked and catholic contributions to American critical literature, not quite convincing, I am of course bound to think, but of far finer flavor than is often to be found in the rather Barmecide banquet they preface; yet for this feast every scrap of Poe's writings has been collected, collated, and commented with an opulence of apparatus unsurpassed by that arranged for Shakespeare by Furness, for Bacon by Spedding, or for Milton by Masson.[56]

The cult of Poe is not in the interests of literature, since as literature his writings are essentially valueless. The interests of literature occasionally call for restraint in the indulgence of Swinburne's "generous pleasure of praising"[57] not for the purpose—quite as frequent with Swinburne—of alternating with it the delights of censure and reprehension, but in order to maintain unobscured and unimpaired the standards of literature itself. Literature has a stronger claim than any of its practitioners, and generously or ungenerously to exalt these at its expense is to belittle and betray it. Hardly any cause is nobler and treason to few so flagrant or—since the pleasure of praising *is*, like most prodigalities perhaps, a generous one—so frequent. But there is a particular irrationality in American overpraise of Poe. It is this: unlike foreign literatures and English literature as a whole, American literature—as it is, perhaps fatuously but nevertheless conveniently, not to say inevitably, called—has no background. Its figures do not form part of a pageant relieved against a rich and varied scenic setting, but stand in silhouette before the black "drop" that isolates rather than supports them and focuses attention on their individualities, from the stately lyceum lecturer

like Emerson to the genial "song and dance artist," in all strictness too numerous to mention. Lacking—within our own exclusively American ranks, I repeat—ancestors and traditions, we
are without the restrictive influences of a "stream of tendency," [58]
an orderly evolution, without that subconscious education which
saves conscious intelligence so much unintelligent performance.
Our protestant and innovating temperaments have really nothing
to protest against, nothing to break away from, no routine to
vivify. More than that, we have comparatively speaking, nothing
to maintain, nothing to keep in mind, no standards in a word.
Such a romanticist as Gautier with the whole heritage of the
noble seventeenth and the enlightened eighteenth century
French literature in his literary blood could safely practise and
preach the literary freedom which with us means license—and
consequent insignificance. No romantic artist can do more than
"pad round" the skeleton he must have derived from his predecessors—at least in our day, the human imagination on which
he leans having been so long at work. Our realists are in better
case—nature being inexhaustible. Hence our disposition to
magnify our extravagant and capricious writers—such as Poe and
Whitman—is destructive of our holds on the standards which it
is of the last importance for us consciously to keep in mind since
so only can we have them in mind at all. Only an older society
than ours can with impunity cherish and coddle "les jeunes,"
who with us are merely out of the ranks, however bravely we
may imagine them at the head of the procession.

It is true that the cult of Poe is, as I have said, largely dependent for its persistence on the Poe legend, and the legend is
concerned with his life which was romance itself and not his
writings which are considerably its caricature. But his life was
quite as abnormal as his writings. Beyond doubt it is largely to
be charged with the failures and shortcomings of these, as well
as, like them, lacking itself, however pitiful and pathetic, the
elements of permanent interest. "Through the storms and tem-
pests of his furious mind" says Thackeray of Swift in a memorable passage "the stars of religion and love break out in the
blue, shining serenely though hidden by the driving clouds and
maddened hurricane of his life." [59] We cannot write of Poe in
this vein. His powers were of a surety not comparable with

Swift's, but what prevents his tragedy from being relatively as impressive is its fatal lack of dignity. And its lack of dignity is due not to his errors and the payment they exacted but to himself. There is a tragic pathos in the ruin wrought by the empire of anodyne over the victim of an abnormal nervous organization, that couples it not unworthily with madness itself. But it is not Poe's gloomy life and its ghastly conclusion, apt extinction of a genius already honeycombed with demoralization, that robs his figure of dignity and alloys the awfulness of his fate. It is his own character—his own predetermined organization, if one chooses. In spite of his personal charm, his was a baleful spirit. For him the stars of religion and love do not break out in the blue. Spiritually, he lacked ideality. His *indignatio* is not *saeva*,[60] but fretful, jealous, egotist. He had no religion, in which respect he is marked among poets and romancers. Of course I do not refer to theology, but he had no sense of awe. The sense of awe was a plaything with him. It never mastered him. He used it as one of the tools of his trade—to create his effects, to harrow his readers' nerves. His attitude toward awe in fact is essentially blasphemous; he does not mock it, but he is impervious to its influence and handles it with the impunity of moral insulation. "My whole nature," he affirms, "utterly revolts at the idea that there is any being in the Universe superior to myself." [61] Like a soulless Undine he is on this account quite outside of our instinctive, and appeals only to our imaginative, sympathies.

It is people's imagination that has made him what popularly he seems—something quite other than the reality. The star of love did gleam fitfully for him in the frigid ether that was his sky. His love for Virginia was his one external stimulus, the only magnet of his errant course, the sole unselfish indulgence of a nature otherwise in galling bondage to egotism. His devotion to her, however, signal as it is in contrast to his habitual self-concentration, was apparently chivalrous rather than passionate. Mrs. Clemm shared it in large measure, as her own adoring affection and practical care richly entitled her to do. And essential element of every relation as chivalry is, it is not ideally adequate in the sphere of the affections—where it needs the supplement of self-surrender. In Poe's case, too, as the days became darker and darker it suffered some strain, as "Ulalume" perhaps attests. If so, though the most hauntingly mournful of any of his poems, its burden is characteristically unremorseful. Compare it with the passionate regrets of Carlyle's "Reminiscences," [62] the wild contrition of a far from loving nature. And it may aptly be remembered with regard to the various "affairs" of Poe's last years that he had already added opium to alcohol, and was the prey of vagrom impulses rather than of any profound and sincere, however transient, passion. This is at once their superficial excuse and their fundamental indictment, but in any event they serve to deepen one's sense of his lack of resource and illumination in love as well as in that general spiritual aspiration we call religion. The lack of dignity in his career from its beginning to its close, in spite of his pretensions, his arrogance and his abounding egotism, estranges sympathy as well as admiration and prevents the gloom of his wretchedness from obscuring in any effective way the comparative valuelessness of his work. His errors and misfortunes are only to be understood probably from the point of view of pathology. From this point of view they must arouse a deep compassion and one intelligent enough to ascribe the futility of much of his work to the fated frustration of his extraordinary powers. But it is the tragedy of American letters that the one absolute artist of our elder literature should, in any marked degree, require a chivalrous, rather than requite a critical, justification.

LOWELL

LOWELL

I

I REMEMBER hearing Lowell on two occasions. One was that of the address on "The Independent in Politics."[1] The substance was rather discouraged—as anyone may verify by referring to it in his works. He took it very seriously and spoke in a prophetic strain and with the prophetic manner. But he seemed rather a jaunty Jeremiah, and one could not feel that the country of which he was such a genuine product could be in hopeless estate. The other occasion was a dinner in aid of the American School at Athens, when he spoke extempore and must have been at his best. It was on occasions, great or small, in spoken or written poetry or prose production, that he was, I imagine, at his best. His speech was the happiest, easiest, most graceful conceivable, with just the right proportion of play to seriousness, the ideal combination of ingredients for a post-prandial confection. I recall an anecdote with which he began. He had been present at a large political meeting in England somewhere, Manchester perhaps, where Gladstone was to speak. The hall was packed and the air stifling. For some reason it was impossible to open the windows, which were very high, and one had to be broken. It was feared that the noise would startle the audience and the Mayor stepped forward to explain what was proposed. The audience, however, had not assembled to listen to the Mayor and overwhelmed him with cries of "Gladstone," "Gladstone!" At last the misconceived and infuriated official restored silence by shouting at the top of his lungs: "I'm not going to make a speech; I've *got something to say!*" Lowell had something to say; and it was not merely the announcement of a gift to the Athens school or some such practical matter, to which his exordium referred. He had a great deal to say always on such occasions—at least *for* such occasions. He was pithy without baldness and full without prolixity. He never said too much, or said what he had to say with too much gravity. His manner, in short, was perfection; but the real substance that his felicity of presentation clothed counted for still more. Curtis [2] was perhaps a rival, though I think Curtis was a shade forensic for the *genre,* but Lowell had no others among his countrymen and in his own day, I am quite sure. And in England his unexampled popularity was very largely due to this gift. During his official residence in London he was in prodigious demand on all occasions that afforded an opportunity for its exercise. His literary reputation, the piquancy of pardoning "The Biglow Papers," [3] even his personal charm and tact in more intimate intercourse probably counted for less.

It is a great gift—particularly rare in first-class men, perhaps, and yet to be found in its perfection in first-class men alone. Hence, Lowell's distinction in its possession and exercise. Both branches of the Anglo-Saxon race have the oratorical tradition and with them at all events the post-prandial phase is the latest in the evolution of eloquence as an art. At the present day set speeches are surely less savored. And no other art is surer of instant and enthusiastic appreciation. It is so popular that its exercise has become epidemic and there are already signs of its decadence in its decline into the perfunctory and its vulgarization by the inexpert. So soon as the practice of any art becomes universal this decline inevitably ensues. When *everyone* practises it, the mass of its production must be common; and commonness in excess is a solvent that sets free the elements of energy for new combinations. But whatever forebodings we may have as to its future, there can be no gainsaying that, taken with its extension and congener of the occasional performance of all kinds, this is an art not only of integral dignity but of unique character and satisfactions. Not the most important, but the most characteristic achievement of an artist is the best guide to the essential elements of his personality. And if Lowell was in general at his best in improvization—if in a word his occasional performance in prose and poetry, was, in general, more unrivalled than, in general, his other productions, and the foremost American man of letters was also the first after-dinner orator of his time, it was in virtue of two or three cardinal facts of his constitutional make-up.

II

Of these the chief I take to have been a certain representative rather than individual turn of mind. He illustrated on occasions of all kinds what he himself says the public asks of the poet, namely, to express for it its own feelings. It is not perhaps a comprehensive or exacting demand to make of the poet—at least of the poet of a different strain from Lowell's—but it is precisely the one made of the public speaker. Lowell answered it amply. He felt as others do, only more consciously—more categorically. He expressed what others think, but with more energy. He was not an original but an independent thinker. He had the kind of independence which even in reflecting it makes its own the general consensus. He did his own thinking, but its results were as recognizably reasonable as its processes were placid. In other words, his idiosyncrasy lay not in his mind but in his character. His reference to himself in "A Fable for Critics" [4] as addicted to "isms" and eccentricities is a complete misconception—cleverly misleading, it might be called, in view of the anonymity of the book, but for the fact of his lack of self-consciousness. Such self-consciousness as he had was at least not self-scrutiny. It was certainly never paralyzing nor even disconcerting. It was clothed in the complacence born of the most reassuring conviction in the world, that of being in essential harmony with others. He beamed and expanded in a confidence free from the fear of confutation or even contradiction. The rare controversial note in his writings is always superficially perverse and piquant, not fundamentally argumentative. He does not in fact argue, but enounces. He is never either stimulated or embarrassed by "the other side." There was for him in general no "other side," and indeed oftenest in his case there is not, for even when he is most polemic he is fired by those sure convictions attending little else so infallibly as the slaying of the slain. The function is a most important one, since nothing is more undesirable than their resurrection, to which there is always a tendency. But the inclination for it is a didactic and conservative one, quite inconsistent with the exploring instinct of the iconoclast.

Lowell's "radicalism" in politics, in social matters, on subjects theological, historical and literary, was practically and personally conservative, since it was the established attitude of his sufficing —and self-sufficing—circle. To be an abolitionist, a "rationalist," a theoretical romanticist, was for him almost a consequence of ancestry, tradition and circumstance. Following a legitimated radical programme is not uncongenial to the whig temperament. Of the extravagances due to the temperamentally radical with which every New Englander in Lowell's youth and early manhood was familiar, no one has said sharper and saner things than he. He was himself eminently sane and sound. His poise, indeed, is his chief distinction, and it is a great one. He liked whatever was sure and wholesome and eulogized it on all occasions with the zest of the discoverer. He might make a willing concession now and then to the popular demand for the idiosyncratic in the way of personal aspect or attire, just as he frolicked and sported with quips and puns in his writing, but otherwise than superficially he was even in his youth a very sedate *enfant terrible.* The fundamental quality of his mind is as practical and conservative as its lighter moods are playful. It seems to have absolutely no adventurous or interrogative side, and irresponsible as are many of its expressions, they are but the sparkle and ripple on a very staidly flowing current. Even his irresponsibilities and looseness, his superlatives and sweeping statements are due to limitation, rather than to enterprise, of thought. One can hardly "place" him in the same environment with Emerson. His passions, too, may be summed up in patriotism, books and nature, in which there is as little that deflects as there is that is differentiating. And probably the residence of a man's real passions in the realm of the abstract is rather a bond than a bar between him and his fellows, even those who reserve that region for their ideal ones alone—on the principle, perhaps, that the priest wins more confidence than the practitioner. Add to these various elements fostering intellectual commerce, to this representative turn of mind, a sterling character that gives it body and substance and a remarkable faculty of expression that gives it definition, and one can conceive no better equipment and instrument for the admirable art of telling people on any special occasion, on a high plane and in an elevated, an exquisite or an energetic way, as may be required, precisely what they wish to hear.

Other auxiliary qualities to this end were Lowell's ingrained cleverness and his extraordinary personal charm. Cleverness and personal charm are qualities that are—perhaps ominously—extremely attractive to contemporary appreciation. Nothing is more envied in the living. Nothing finds prompter interment with their bones. Cleverness cloys too quickly to be an element of abiding satisfaction in their "works." And personal charm is almost inseparable from personal presence. The writers who—like Lamb and Thackeray—establish it in their writings as a vital and preservative force, are very few. Lowell was immensely clever. "A Fable for Critics" is a youthful masterpiece—youthful enough in some of its criticism, but an extraordinary *jeu d'esprit* and so individual as to remain, with parts of "The Biglow Papers," his most characteristic, as the "Commemoration Ode" is his most consummate, production. He was always extraordinarily ready. Whether the occasion were grave or gay, serious or sportive, it never found him at fault. To unveil a monument, or respond to a toast, or consecrate a festival, or cap an epigram, and each in ideal fashion, he was equally prepared. Cleverness was the state in which habitually his faculties dwelt, not a mental exercise or phase. And it found its most congenial expression in pleasantry and playfulness. It was not quite, perhaps, what Schiller had in mind in asserting that "the last perfection of our qualities is when their activity, without ceasing to be sure and earnest, becomes sport." [5] In Lowell, one is tempted rather to say, such was the inveteracy of his cleverness, the last perfection of his qualities was when their activity without ceasing to be sport became sure and earnest. For his cleverness, though extreme and even at times excessive, is never sophisticated, rarely even subtle. It is always frank and generally gay. He began with high spirits and his youthful buoyancy stood by him to the end. His biographers record periods of gloom, even thoughts of suicide, and Mr. Greenslet finds grounds for the belief that he had a "dual nature" [6] in this as in other respects. It is not unlikely. Most people have. But it is difficult to make a mystic out of Lowell. One may as easily fancy St. Francis in Fanueil Hall. He had his seasons of melancholy, but normally and for tragically abundant cause. There is no more the mystic, than there is a morbid, note in his composition. Everything of the kind is

instinctively antipathetic to him. Apparently with all his reading
he never read, at least sympathetically, the Scriptures of any
people. He never cites the Bible. His good sense sufficed to assure
him that

> "—you've gut to git up airly
> Ef you want to take in God," [7]

and the apocalyptic was superfluous to him.

At all events, no writer of anything resembling his bookish
and scholarly turn ever possessed high spirits in any such degree,
as no writer ever so cordially conjoined the study and out-of-
doors. Among writers of distinction we should have to go, not I
think to Mark Twain and Aristophanes (the coupling is Lowell's
own), who mix things less, but to Dickens for a parallel to his
irruptive and casual gayeties in grave context. Certainly if his
high spirits are not marked by the usual exuberance, they sometimes show as unmistakably in whimsicality and extravagance,
however exhibited in playful rather than in boisterous guise.
They do not lead him astray, but they are constantly taking him
aside. He is not their slave, but they are his plaything. When
they are constrained and directed to an artistic end, as in "A
Fable for Critics" or "The Biglow Papers"—in the prefaces to
which indeed they become sedate enough, even solemn, one may
remark without fear of flippancy—they serve as excellent stimulus to sustained effort. But when, as is sometimes the case, they
are the desultory and yet deliberate accentuation of his gayety,
his general *enjoué* manner, they are less to the purpose. "Nothing," he says rather hardly apropos of Fletcher, "grows mouldy
so soon as mere fun, the product of animal spirits." [8] And we
should be tempted to call some of Lowell's sallies "mere fun" if
the high spirits from which they spring were not rather mental
than animal, and if they were not so clearly stamped with his
indisputable cleverness. They may be strained, of inappropriate
tone, of doubtful taste, distracting rather than contributory or
even decorative; there is none, it would be safe to wager, that is
not truly however studiedly clever, though sometimes, it is true,
what one feels impelled to call demonstrably so. But cleverness
is largely a matter of expression, and expression is but one element of style, which though no doubt the great preservative

of thought is in turn reciprocally dependent upon it for its own endurance and vitality. Take for example this delightful sentence: "In what may be given me to say I shall be obliged to trust chiefly to a memory which at my time of life is gradually becoming one of her own reminiscences, and is forced to compound as best she may with her inexorable creditor, Oblivion." [9] That is Lowell's cleverness at its best, cleverness with the addition of poetic and personal charm. But if one has only ten pages for an appreciation of Coleridge, it may be said to sacrifice, so far as it goes, the permanent to the occasional note. What gives the address value is the excellent characterization of Coleridge's picturesqueness, and then, too, it gains, I think, from the necessity of making it rapid "generalization," as Lowell calls it, pertinent to the unveiling of a bust in Westminster. Take on the other hand the rather elaborate essay by no means "occasionally" evoked on the now forgotten poet Percival, which leans entirely for support and even countenance on the essayist's cleverness. Among us when Percival wrote, he says, "to write a hundred blank verses was to be immortal, till somebody else wrote a hundred and fifty blanker ones. . . . Unhappily Percival took it all quite seriously. There was no praise too ample for the easy elasticity of his swallow," [10] etc. Of cleverness of this sort, in which Lowell abounds, the interest evaporates with the outwearing of the subject if not with the occasion itself.

It was, however, a constituent probably rather than merely an ally of his great personal charm, which is universally attested. Mr. Howells has borne affectionate as well as discriminating testimony to it, and Mr. James's essay on him is eloquent witness to its power to color and even gild the appreciation of a critical faculty far otherwise penetrating than Lowell's own.[11] To have inspired this remarkable portrait the sitter must have been richly endowed with qualities that the reader, familiar only with his writings, can only infer. Evidently he was the best of company and *in* the best of company. His sincerity and dignity of character, his accomplished scholarship, his frankness and optimism, his good sense and appreciation, his wit and extraordinary powers of expression, must have made intimacy with him ideal and mere acquaintance a delight. He was literally but not overpoweringly a brilliant conversationalist, and if he "did most of the talking," others—Thackeray, Longfellow, Clough, and Edmund Quincy on one recorded occasion—were more than content to listen. One certainly argues a considerable egoism from his writings, but no one seems ever to have minded or even marked it in his talk, and even in his books it never excludes the most altruistic admirations. He was geniality itself, and though undoubtedly what used to be called a Brahmin—at least by the Pariahs of the period—his sympathies were undoubtedly, in a human if not in an intellectual sense, catholic and active. His circle, however, was not large and those outside it could more easily perceive, perhaps, than those within it, that what, together with his cleverness, constituted for these latter an essential part of his personal charm was his clearly defined possession of the temperament of the dilettante. Mr. James states the fact, with extraordinary searchingness, though with, of course, the slightly august tone of the memorial "tribute." He regards his career "as in the last analysis a tribute to the dominion of style. This is the idea," he continues, "that to my sense his name most promptly evokes. He carried style—the style of literature—into regions in which we rarely look for it: into politics, of all places in the world, into diplomacy, into stammering, civic dinners, and ponderous anniversaries, into letters and notes and telegrams, into every turn of the hour—absolutely into conversation, where indeed it freely disguised itself as intensely colloquial wit." [12] One could not better describe the activities of the true dilettante temperament.

Its conjunction in Lowell with his incontestable and even salient Americanism, is decidedly piquant. There is not an exotic tinge in his nature, and if he is not representatively national in the sense in which he himself called Lincoln "new birth of our new soil, the first American," [13] it is not because in being even more sectional he is less native. Yet one would say off-hand that the American genius was incompatible with the dilettante temperament. But really Lowell was precisely the product reflection would predicate of its American modification. The dilettante is not a type especially distinguished by originality, it is true, and ordinarily originality is an essential and predominant element of what we think we are, of what—more optimistically perhaps than discriminatingly—we mean in calling anything characteristically American. But it is in the solution of new problems that our very striking originality is mainly developed. Like the "new duties" taught, in Lowell's phrase, by "new occasions," [14] it is the product of necessity and opportunity, probably, rather than due to the climate or the predilection of Providence. We have other characteristics that we share with no other people, but originality is not one of them; our invention has the same mother. It is not remarkable, therefore, except superficially, that Lowell should have been so genuine an American and so genuinely a dilettante. But we may say that the paradox has the interest of novelty and that, though no more originality than the dilettante type calls for is either usually to be expected—in the field of letters—of the American genius, or to be found in Lowell, he was a dilettante of an original type in being so thoroughly American. He had the disinterested delight in the delectable that characterizes the dilettante as distinguished from the artist, to whom the delectable is material. His singularity—as a dilettante, not as an American—consists in his being attracted by the elementary quite as much as by the differentiated. His *milieu*— which was really, in the large sense, the lack of any—imposed this upon him to a certain extent, of course. In such a society as ours, without variety of type and without background, without the many elements that Mr. James has scrupulously catalogued in his life of Hawthorne, the rôle of the dilettante can only be sincerely played—and sincerity was one of Lowell's cardinal qualities—by a nature in which confidence, eagerness, ardor, generosity, and optimism replace the sentimental, sensitive, and fastidious instincts, the divining and discriminating faculties that are less disposed to see sermons in stones and good in everything than to select and exclude. The fact that he carried "style" into some of the regions enumerated by Mr. James—in some of which certainly his "style" savored more of the amateur than of the connoisseur—both denotes and defines his temperament, shows at once its inveteracy and its limitations.

III

Of his own particular environment, to which he was profoundly attached and in which he throve, he could nevertheless

take a properly objective view. Whatever the limitations of his
temperament, his mind, which was alertness itself, instantly apprehended the suggestions of culture, though his own culture,
which was eminent, was as idiosyncratic—quite as idiosyncratic
—as his personality. "How narrow Boston was!" he exclaims.
"How scant a pasture it offered to the imagination." He speaks
of Allston, "who perished slowly of inanition over yonder in
Cambridgeport," and adds: "That unfinished Belshazzar of his
was a bitter sarcasm on our self-conceit. Among *us* it was un-
finishable." [15] The implication of the italicized "us" is candid,
courageous, and correct. Lowell himself never experienced any
such difficulty. His work could be produced and finished to its
last potential perfection in this same atmosphere, in which he
found something intimately congenial. He even took it with him
on his travels, and was, even in Europe, surrounded with the
Massachusetts aura. He had his books and he had his public.
It is probable that he was conscious of no other needs. His
acquisitiveness was among the most preponderant of his mental
traits, but books satisfied its cravings—which does not seem so
singular when we remember his enormous consumption of them.
They and the society of Cambridge and Boston, in which
"Allston perished slowly of inanition," sufficed to evoke and polish
in him those qualities that make the perfect man of the world;
so that when he went officially to Spain and England he was as
much at home in a cosmopolitan society as he was in Cambridge.
His own extreme personal charm and innate dignity counted
largely, of course, in the distinguished impression he made
abroad. But, every allowance made for these, it is particularly—
and to his countrymen it must remain satisfactorily—notable that
he should have had such a striking European success with such
an exclusively American equipment.

Books, apparently, can accomplish a great deal; books in sufficient quantity, the best books. And even books that come more
or less strictly under the head of *belles-lettres*. For if Lowell had
any other equipment as a man of letters than *belles-lettres*, taken
in the wider extension of the term, the fact does not appear in his
writings. Science, theology, art, philosophy, history, apparently
interested him in a very subsidiary degree. Never was such conspicuous culture so exclusively belletristic. Mr. James says: "He

knew his Paris as he knew all his subjects. The history of a thing was what he first saw in it." [16] If so, they never passed beyond the states of seeing and knowing into feeling; and his "subjects" were altogether literary "things." Neither his knowledge of Paris nor his expertness in Old French gave him any independent appreciation of France or things French, at any rate, with reference to which he always utters the traditional British commonplaces. Tennyson hardly phrased them in more sharply stereotyped smugness. The great facts of French history are still for him the massacre of St. Bartholomew and the atrocities of the Revolution. "He should have fought with Nelson," as Arnold remarked of some fanatic—an Englishman, however.[17] And of any special acquaintance with English history there is insufficient trace in his books to account for Mr. James's further statement: "He had studied English history for forty years in the texts, and at last [on becoming minister to England] he could study it in the pieces themselves, could handle and verify the relics." [18] The "texts" Mr. James has in mind are perhaps literary texts. In other words, Lowell had studied English literature; he was now to "check" it by a study of English life. Possibly so omnivorous and indefatigable a reader had read Freeman and Stubbs and Gardiner as well as Macaulay and Froude, Hume and Green.[19] But certainly neither English history nor Continental, ancient, mediæval, nor modern, deeply interested him except from an extension of the belletristic point of view. And even from this point of view, of course, far less than it did Macaulay, Carlyle, or Arnold, not to speak of such writers as Taine, Scherer, and Sainte-Beuve, of the value of whose "detective method" in criticism, indeed, he expresses doubts. Less even, one may surely say, than Thackeray. For, in spite of his special studies of early New England, if there is a passage in his works resembling the impressive and illuminating picture of Europe in the early eighteenth century in the lecture on George I, beginning with "The landscape is awful—" [20] I have not remarked it.

Mr. James speaks of him as "steeped in history and literature" and "redolent, intellectually speaking," of Italy and Spain. But what he means appears in his next sentence: "He had lived in long intimacy with Dante and Cervantes and Calderon." [21] That is to say, he was steeped not in history and literature, but in liter-

ary history and literature—nowadays, at all events, an unsatisfactory infusion for producing the best of even literary effects. He
relied, indeed, even for the illumination of literature not so much
on life as on linguistics, and the literary and linguistic pages of
history, which is life recorded, monopolized his attention. "As
Dante tells us," he says, "St. Francis took poverty for his bride."
He does indeed. So does Francis himself.[22] So for that matter does
Giotto. It is, in fact, a circumstance decidedly not divulged by
Dante. Such a phrase in itself implicitly glosses Mr. James's assertion that Lowell was "steeped in history." But his own words
are explicit. In one of his political essays there are several pages
of express depreciation of the value of history [23]—much in the
vein of Colonel Esmond's sentimentally sceptical old age, except
in being more systematic. In his essay on Dante he says that "one
almost gets to feel as if the chief value of contemporary Italian
history had been to furnish 'the Divine Comedy' with explanatory
foot-notes." Indeed he *quite* "gets to feel" so when the momentum of hero-worship carries him on to the statement: "For Italy,
Dante is the thirteenth century." [24] One thinks of what, besides,
the thirteenth century—the century of Frederic II, and Innocent
III, and Giotto, and St. Francis—really was for Italy, "the most
interesting," as it has been called, in the history of Christianity
after its primitive age, "more interesting than even the century
of the Reformation"; and owing not to Dante but to Francis.
Elsewhere, too, Lowell speaks of Dante as having been "produced" by the fourteenth century.[25] In strict accuracy, of course,
he would have done better to have had the thirteenth produce
him and let him be for Italy the fourteenth. And nothing could
be more definite than Lowell's association of history with the Dismal Science in his admirable and elevated address on the two-
hundred-and-fiftieth anniversary of Harvard College. "Give," he
says, "give to History, give to Political Economy that ample verge
the times demand, but with no detriment to those liberal Arts
which have formed open-minded men and good citizens in the
past, nor have lost the skill to form them." [26]

As a *philosophia ultima* of literary phenomena, that popularly
associated with Taine and Spencer is perhaps discredited in so
far as genius escapes its explanations. And it is at once a mark
of distinction and of naïveté in Lowell that, in criticism, he occu-

pied himself mainly with genius. As a subject, one may say in
racy current phrase of which he was fond, the best was good
enough for him. But however it be with the explanation, for the
illumination, the appreciation, of genius the historical method is
invaluable. Between genius thus illuminated and genius just
merely accepted as an undifferentiated prodigy, there is a prodigious difference in mere appreciation. Genius itself, in fact, has
come to be looked at a little more narrowly than heretofore.
There is commonly felt, to begin with, that there is less of it. I
remember Mr. Winslow Homer, who certainly should know, once
remarking: "Genius is so rare there is no use talking about it." [27]
Lowell was particularly fond of talking about it, and rehearsing
the accepted views about its essential difference from talent. Certainly such a difference exists and we shall never know what precisely it is. But the Germans may be relied upon never to let us
forget that its character is mystic. And a writer like Lowell, in
whose temperament there is so little mysticism, becomes conventional and superficial when he presses the matter no further
than he does. His hearty and insistent adoration of Shakespeare,
at every opportunity of mentioning whose name that he encounters or can contrive he performs a little act of genial genuflexion,
ends by fatiguing us. He has certainly said some very interesting
things, in detail, about him, without, however, fixing them very
securely in one's memory, but his admiration takes on, finally, an
aspect of adulation. One recalls Voltaire's exclamation of a
greater even than Shakespeare: "I pray you never let me hear that
man's name again!" [28] It is always genuine, but Lowell had a
"genius" for being perfunctory and genuine at the same time—
such was his zest for the sure and sound. It is true that "others
abide our question" [29] and Shakespeare does not, but other than
lecture-room purposes do not demand constant iteration of what
is best condensed in a sonnet. In all Lowell's references to or
formal consideration of Shakespeare nothing so illuminating is to
be found as Arnold's: "There is but one name for such writing
as that [citing a couple of lines] if Shakespeare had signed it a
thousand times—it is detestable. And it is too frequent in Shakespeare." Or his statement: "He is the richest, the most wonderful,
the most powerful, the most delightful of poets: he is not altogether, nor even eminently, an artist." [30] Even Carlyle's humorous

definition of "superiority of intellect" as "on the whole" Shakespeare's "distinguishing characteristic" [31] gets us nearer a satisfactory answer of "our question" than repeated obeisances to his
"genius."

It is extraordinary at first to an Anglo-Saxon reader to note how
little reference to genius there is in French criticism, how exclusively a writer's "talent" is considered in it. And extraordinary, a
little later perhaps, to observe how satisfactorily "talent" answers
the purpose in most cases. Undoubtedly this is due to the presence in the French critic's mind of the penumbra as well as the
shadow of his subject, of the life as well as the books of a people
or a period, of circumstances as well as essence, and—in the consideration of the classic, of such themes as, so greatly to his
credit, Lowell's were—of history as well as literature, of transactions as well as texts. Against a visualized background of time
and space, any one figure seems less exceptional and inexplicable
than genius is by definition required to be; more familiarity with
their history, for example, would have prevented Lowell from
asserting that "the genius of Motley has revealed to us" [32] the distinction of the Dutch. But apparently he never read any French
to much purpose, except Old French, and this but confirmed him
in his concentration upon linguistics. For the great movements,
migrations, vicissitudes of the march of mankind—its transforma-
tions, enterprises, and achievements—the grandiose drama of war
and peace, the rise and fall of tyranny and freedom, faith and
philosophy, the birth, development, and decay of institutions—
social, political, and religious—the spectacle foreshortened in
time, in a word, of general human activity caught and fixed in
the multifariously embroidered web of history he cared less, to
judge from its reflection and echo in his works, than any other
writer of his indisputably high rank that one could readily name.
The service rendered criticism by this its connotation and collat-
eral re-enforcement is, as I have said, incontestable. The work of
every important modern critic relies on it—to an extent that gives
its absence in Lowell a slightly old-fashioned air for works on so
high a plane of scholarship and intelligence. His essays, in a
word, are not historically enriched nor the product of a mind
thus enriched. They have a very particular, a very bookish, and

in consequence a rather restricted quality, for all their humanity, their elevated *bonhomie* and unaffected cordiality.

The matter is not one of erudition at all, but of culture. Lowell's erudition was great—even conspicuous, being, though always assimilated, always comfortably if not complacently displayed. Mr. Greenslet, his latest biographer, whose Life is, critically, a work of altogether unusual distinction, asserts that his scholarship was not up to current standards. One understands what is meant, but is a little impatient at having this sense of the term scholarship taken for granted. Lovers of literature would gladly have it remain esoteric a little longer, and instinctively shrink from the time when "we shall all go into the drab." [33] One would gladly postpone yet for a brief season the era of specialism, and views with misgiving the no doubt inevitable invasion of barbarian hordes from without the confines of the empire of letters. The province of history has already been overrun and the expert is established within its stronghold, haughtier than Alaric or Attila in his contempt for the superficialities and shallownesses powerless to resist him. *Belles-lettres* may, however, hold out a little longer before it is transformed into scientific feudalism or declines in Byzantine decadence. The scholar should be an authority upon, as well as accomplished in his subject. Inspiration by its spirit will not atone for ignorance of its letter. True; alas! there is no possibility of robbing an ideal of so reasonable a requirement. But there are practical difficulties. Porson on his deathbed sighed ruefully that he should have confined himself to the dative case.[34] Had he done so, however, scholarship would have lost something. Mere count of heads shows that there are not enough Porsons to go around when the number of dative case equivalents is considered. Furthermore, he never could have learned much about the dative case itself by confining himself to it. No man, says Arnold, knows even his Bible who knows only it.[35] And Professor James sets it down as "a common platitude" that "a complete acquaintance with anything, however small, would require a knowledge of the entire universe" [36]—"that tempting range of relevancies," as George Eliot calls it. But even a knowledge of the entire universe would not obviate the greater obstacle in the path to literary distinction of the expert in literature. He would still need what Bacon prescribes for the portraitist who would enhance nature—"a kind of felicity," [37] namely. Bentley's scholarship will hardly be impugned, though he might perhaps judiciously have restricted its range. But even had he done so, no amount of concentration could have prevented the perpetration of his revised text of "Paradise Lost"—a veritable pharos erected on the rocks of learning [38] to warn the voyaging expert through yet "undiscovered deeps of time."

Lowell certainly did not resemble the Casaubons of former, or their brisk analogues of present, times. No one would have been readier than he to disclaim expert pretensions; quite destitute of deference as a coloring characteristic of his nature, such an attitude as he assumes toward Professor Child, for example, about Chaucer, is witness enough of this.[39] His temper was as little authoritative as it was conspicuously complacent. But in Old French, as to a certain extent in linguistics more generally, he was an authority; and though *quicquid agunt homines* [40] (within his own field) interested him too vivaciously to permit him to pursue to its documentary fastnesses other game that he nevertheless delighted to hunt, it is misleading to lay any stress on the deficiencies of his scholarship or to impeach the genuineness of his truly scholarly tastes. He was at least a scholar in the tested and traditional sense. That his "results" were not more important from the standpoint of the specialist does not make it the less erroneous to obscure his scholarship, which was remarkable, by emphasizing his culture, which in certain respects was restricted. He was a distinguished example of what he himself calls "liberal scholarship"—a term with as definite and laudable a meaning as that of the liberal arts. His learning was great and varied. His reading was enormous. He read as Chinese candidates read their classics and commentaries—all his life long, usually for many hours at a stretch, often for more than the day-laborer toils. And he read because he liked to—not, as a rule, one guesses, as specific preparation for work of his own. When he did it did not always bring him good luck. He says that he expressly read over again, seriatim, all of Thoreau's works before writing of him, and certainly he did so to small purpose.[41] As a rule, we may be sure, he read to satisfy his curiosity—the curiosity of the scholar as well as that of the dilettante. However desultory, too, his reading may appear to pedantry, it was, owing to his curiosity, thorough-going if not systematic. He was as persistent, as patient, in it as is possible only to a man who is following his bent. There is no other explanation of ten consecutive hours devoted to "Barbour's Brus"! [42] His energy, his high spirits, his debonair possession of a reasonably thick integument to shield his nerves and allay irri-tability, all contributed to the inveteracy of his favorite pursuit. He read everything except the inept and negligible; and every-thing, ancient and modern, in its own tongue. Dulness itself had no terrors for him. He read Gower as well as Chaucer, Joel Bar-low as well as Homer. He delighted as much in his "Library of Old Authors" [43]—a formidable array!—as in the less recondite and better-remembered books that filled his ample shelves. Not a scholar! *Le moyen,* as the French say, for such a tremendous bookman not to be.

But the truth is that Lowell's eminently scholarly tastes were wholly directed by his temperamental predilections, and he fol-lowed these, I think, with an enthusiastic docility that limited his culture to a degree unfortunate for the importance and endurance of much of his work in prose. His preferences despotically dic-tated his preoccupation, which was rather exclusively with lin-guistics, taking the term of course in its widest extension. "His linguistic sense," Mr. James says truly, "is perhaps the thing his reputation may best be trusted to rest upon." And he accounts for this admirably in saying further, "He had no experimental sympathies and no part of him was traitor to the rest," and that "this temper drove the principle of subtlety in his intelligence . . . to take refuge in one particular . . . corner," linguistics, namely. One could not more delicately suggest limitations or bet-ter indicate the quality of mind of the true dilettante innocent of the artist's constructional purpose, though the dilettante in thor-oughly American disguise—robust, genial, confident, and mascu-line, without "experimental sympathies." [44]

To his lack of experimental sympathies, too, must be ascribed his apparent insensitiveness to the plastic arts. Of course I do not mean that he was blind to their beauty, feeling sure as I do that the poetic strain is the dominant one in his equipment. But he did not take them in the least seriously. There is extraordi-narily little reference to them in his works, which fact, however, is less indicative than the conjoined freedom and fatuity of such reference as there is. It did not occur to him, probably, that they have a point of view of their own. He did not set them off in his mind from other intellectual pursuits and appreciate their self-justification—as indeed how should he, expanding in an environment that stifled Allston, æsthetically modified only by an occasional reading of Ruskin, who never appreciated this very keenly himself? The great artists probably did not figure in his selected list of great men, which besides was further contracted to include mainly the poets—the poets and Abraham Lincoln, one might say. He is not even at the pains to keep their nationality in mind and—in "On a Certain Condescension in Foreigners" [45]—makes Holbein and Rubens fellow-countrymen of Rembrandt. Ravenna for him is merely the site of Dante's tomb, which, he says, "is now the chief magnet which draws foreigners and their gold" thither —Ravenna being actually, of course, for art and measurably for history, what Carlyle called Gibbon, "that splendid bridge between the Old World and the New," [46] and Dante's tomb,

"A little cupola, more neat than solemn,"

being for the generally cultivated, if not for the exclusively belletristic, gold-bearing foreigner, the least of her monuments. He has misgivings about Michael Angelo—perhaps, as he says, "bitten with the Anglo-Saxon gadfly that drives us all to disenchant artifice," perhaps because in a strange land it behooves one to be cautious about appearances. "Michael Angelo seems to me," he writes, "in his angry reaction against sentimental beauty to have mistaken bulk and brawn for the antithesis of feebleness. He is the apostle of the exaggerated, the Victor Hugo of painting and sculpture." (*Encore*, is it necessary to parenthesize his view of Victor Hugo!) "I have a feeling," he continues, abandoned altogether by what Mr. James calls "the principle of subtlety in his intelligence," "I have a feeling that rivalry was a more powerful motive with him than love of Art, that he had the conscious intention to be original, which seldom leads to anything better than being extravagant. The show of muscle proves strength not power." But he does not wish to be "niggardly toward one in whom you cannot help feeling there was so vast a possibility." The whole series of observations illustrates his independence certainly, and perhaps should modify one's impression of his lack of originality. Originality, at any rate, cannot be denied to some architectural remarks further on in "A Few Bits of Roman Mosaic." "I doubt about domes," he observes, with a tentativeness charming in Lowell. "In Rome they are so much the fashion that I felt that they were the goitre of architecture. Generally they look heavy. Those on St. Mark's in Venice are the only light ones I saw, and they look almost airy, like tents puffed out with wind. I suppose one must be satisfied with the interior effect, which is certainly noble in St. Peter's. But for impressiveness both within and without there is nothing like a Gothic cathedral for me, nothing that crowns a city so nobly, or makes such an island of twilight silence in the midst of its noonday clamors." The poet's touch recalls us to Lowell again, and him to a more congenial subject. We are as relieved as our guide at the next sentence: "Now as to what one sees in the streets, the beggars are," etc., etc.[47] We are back on firm ground once more, and our doubts about Michael Angelo and about "domes" become as insubstantial and "airy" as those of San Marco or their ancestral Turcoman kibitkas.

IV

It is not impertinent to regret the restrictedness of culture in the critic's equipment that is implied in neglect of such a splendid and such an illuminating expression of the genius and mind of man as the plastic arts constitute. It is regrettable in the case of Arnold, of English critics generally. It is regrettable in the case of Sainte-Beuve; one may resent the peevishness of the Goncourts or even sympathize with Champfleury's designation of them as *"ces cocodettes de la littérature"* [48] and all the more deplore the ground there was for their impatience with the eminent literary critic's artistic deficiencies and his ignorance of them. Without their knowledge of and devotion to the plastic arts the works of not merely such critics as Pater and Symonds, but even Taine— even Goethe himself—would have far less value. More than any other critic of his eminence Lowell would have profited by an acquaintance with them. An acquaintance with them would have broadened his view—in detail, at all events—of his special and particular field of consideration, of *belles-lettres;* and it would perhaps have given his treatment of it the element that conspicuously it lacks, the element of construction and presentation. Arnold, Sainte-Beuve, needed it far less—as well as possessing it far more. They were not exclusively concerned with *belles-lettres.* And they were, as Lowell certainly was not, saturated with history. Accordingly, when we come to consider Lowell as a critic we may almost deduce the detail of his criticism from his personality and his equipment. As I have said, he had a solid and independent character, with a turn of mind representatively sound and conservative rather than markedly individual, and a temperament disinterestedly enthusiastic without being sensitively discriminating or speculative. And his equipment, that is to say, his culture, was an extraordinarily bookish one, and, though in this sense thorough and scholarly, exclusively literary and, for an exclusively literary culture, singularly independent of the two great allies and supports of literary culture—history and æsthetics. It is evident beforehand that Chatterton will escape him, that Wordsworth will bore him, that Pope will displease and Byron disgust him, that he will delight in Gray and Dryden, and that he will never tire of singing the praises of the indisputably great, such as Shakespeare and Dante, Chaucer, Spenser, Calderon, and Cervantes.[49] It is evident, too, that his critical work will be at its best in appreciation, that it will excel more in finding new beauties in the actual than in discovering new requirements in the ideal, that it will consider personalities as fixed and final, and not in their origin, tendencies, or relations, that while being perfectly candid and genuine it will be tinctured with that order of partisanship which proceeds from dwelling on the justice of its feelings rather than on the truth of its ideas, that it will be devoid of any defined philosophic drift or suggestiveness, and that its felicities will be felicities of detail rather than of general view.

His criticism clearly grew out of his reading habit, not out of his reflective tendencies. He read pencil in hand, and as he read he annotated. His criticism is therefore largely comment, and, its original destination being often the lecture-room, its tone is largely conversational. He collected and sifted his marginalia, expanded them, wrote context (multifarious and spirited) for them, supplied them with introductions (extremely artificial in gen-

eral), and presented them to the public, having first, in many
instances, presented them to his pupils. They have thus an intimate and familiar quality and suggest the lecture-room, or at
most the lyceum, more vividly than the forum or the library. They
are on a high plane, the high plane on which habitually Lowell
lived and thought, but their glance is *de haut en bas,* and such
traits as unexplained allusions and untranslated quotations and
recondite references—a kind of *fatras* of bookish reticulation
with which they are overspread—do not disguise a certain complacence not wholly foreign to genial condescension. Then there
are the jokes, the puns, the witticisms generally of a high order
and, though sometimes "naked to laughter" rather than provocative of it in the reader, very comprehensibly the Attic salt of the
class-room. What could be wittier or more incisive than, speaking of "the average Briton" in America, "not a Bull of them all
but he is persuaded he bears Europe on his back"? [50] On the
other hand, such a title for such a grave political essay as "The
Pickens-and-Stealin's Administration" amuses the reader distant in time and place and spirit less, probably, than the under-
graduate under the personal charm of the author—presupposes,
in fact, a sympathetic relation. Similarly the reference in the
"Thoreau" to the "maggots" of which New England brains were
full in the 40's and which "must at times have found pitiably short
commons." [51] And a score, a hundred, others easily cited. Quite
so, one imagines, or rather we know, he must have lectured to
his students, of whom it is surprising—and discreditable to university youth—that he had so few. It is less surprising, however,
that his readers at the present time should not be more numerous. His essays are criticism made easy—for the critic, that is to
say, the learned and book-loving critic, and as correspondingly
hard for the reader as Sheridan declared all easy writing to be.[52]
The reader is at a disadvantage. He can only envy the experience
Mr. James records in describing how he "on dusky winter after-
noons escaped with irresponsible zeal into the glow of Mr. Lowell's learned lamp-light, the particular incidents of which in the
small, still lecture-room, and the illumination of his head and
hands, I recall," he says, "with extreme vividness." [53] The illumination of the printed page is our sole resource. And with this,
as I have intimated, I do not think quite sufficient pains have

been taken to fit it for going out into the world alone, as it were, and taking its place in the company it really belongs in.

To begin with, the critical essays are distinctly artless in both the literal and the derived sense of the word. And in the essay, as elsewhere, art is indispensable to real effectiveness and permanent interest. It is surely not the one form of literary expression that is exempt from this necessity. A critical essay is not a cairn of comment, but an organic composition. An organism is a whole of which the parts are mutually dependent and each essential to the whole. An artistic organism is one whose structure is expressive rather than expressed—its means answerable to analysis, its effect sensible in aspect. An essay of Lowell's has this quality no more than one of Emerson's has. It is not a quality that either of them sought. It is a quality, indeed, probably without special appeal to either the professor or the prophet, and Lowell was a little of a prophet just as Emerson has something of the professor. Neither is actuated by the motive of the artist, the desire to please. This desire is as much that of the artist in criticism as it is that of the designer of a cathedral. It is because rhetoric is an art that Aristotle defined its end as not conviction but persuasion. Lowell never tried to persuade any one in his life, his strong strain of didacticism showing itself rather in confirming the accepted than in commending the overlooked. The "Biglow Papers" themselves do not proselytize, but merely pronounce. And it probably comes about quite naturally, quite normally, therefore—apart from its desultory class-room origin in many instances—that whatever else a critical essay by him may be, however penetrating, instructive, valuable for admonition, reproof, or enlightenment, it is certainly not in any satisfactory sense an artistic performance. Consequently his criticism has less currency, I think, than its substance deserves. You have an active, even a vivid sense that he knows what he is talking about, but you are less—considerably less—stirred by what he says. One receives impressions from it, which he remembers or not, as it may happen, but they are not central or complete impressions. They are not informed by an idea of the subject, but are rather of points of detail, often so casual as to have almost an *obiter* effect.

It is easy to seem pedantic in insisting on organic quality as an essential of effective and agreeable composition of any kind, and so on. To do so is merely to rehearse a commonplace of elementary rhetoric. Of course, a literal exemplification of the principle would, if on a scale of any size—larger than that of a sonnet or triolet, say—incur imminent risk of becoming an extremely wooden affair. A writer who should undertake to make a composition impeccably organic must either attempt a very insignificant composition or achieve a mosaic rather than the living result that precisely, in art as in nature, an organism is and a mosaic is not. But to paraphrase the ethical ideal of the first great literary critic, there is reason in all things. As a matter of fact there is only one way, probably, of attaining this result of unity in any various work of art, and that is to keep the *ensemble* in mind. Now to do this one must first have in mind an *ensemble*. The literary or other artist is no freer from this necessity than the sculptor, to whom it is almost a physical impossibility successfully to model a detail of anything in the round without constant "reference to the profile." Some central conception is similarly necessary for the successful conduct of any composition. If it is an essay on Rousseau or Keats or Dante—a full-length portrait, a half-length, or a head—any feature or phase of his productions, his place in literature, his influence on mankind, or whatever, or all these together—a necessary preliminary will be the establishment of some general idea of the subject. The essay will be the expression in detail of this conception—in proportion to its complexity the elaborate expression of it. Reading and general undirected reflection serve merely as agencies formative of the conception itself. This is the undoubted process of all the great critics, however various their tendencies, points of view, and technical expression. Whatever may be said for the superiority of the much-vaunted historical method over the intuitive must be based on the superiority of induction in forming this central conception, and cannot apply to the evolution of the detail, which must inexorably be deduced or the practical result is heterogeneity. Arnold's reply to Scherer's contention that "out of the writer's character and the study of his age there spontaneously issues the right understanding of his work," namely, "in a mind qualified in a certain way it will—not in all minds," [54] is unimpeachable. To be qualified to express energetically and effectively any understanding at all of a writer's work, however, whether correct or not, involves the preliminary synthesis of a general conception. That at least is an artistic necessity involved, as a matter of fact, in the laws of thought, if one cared to go into that.

To say that Lowell's criticism lacks this initial central conception would be to say that it is written at random. But, indeed, it often has precisely the appearance of being written at random, and precisely because his central conception is vague. Erasmus's witty and apt complaint that "every definition is a misfortune" [55] related to the abstractions of doctrine and dogma. In art the concrete reigns supreme and nothing can be too definite—even if, or perhaps especially if, it is to express the abstract. The essay on Dante Lowell says is the result of twenty years of study. One may easily believe it—taking the statement somewhat loosely, as of course he intended it. It is packed with interesting and illuminating detail, and has been called his ablest performance in criticism. In Dante's case, more than in most others, to admire is to comprehend. Lowell's admiration is limitless and one feels that he understood his subject. But his expression of it is only less inartistic than it is uncritical. His twenty years of study have resulted in his comprehension of his theme, but not in reducing it to any definite proportions or giving it any sharpness of outline. There is nothing about it he does not know and perhaps one may say nothing in it that he does not appreciate. But he does not communicate because he does not express his general conception of Dante and he does not because he has not himself, one feels sure, thought it out into definition. He is interested in ranking his poet, not describing him. Dante is next to Shakespeare, next to Homer, above all others, and so on. Think of him in connection with Byron! "Our nineteenth century," he says, "made an idol of the noble lord who broke his heart in verse once every six months, but the fourteenth was lucky enough to produce and not make an idol of that rarest earthly phenomenon, a man of genius who could hold heartbreak at bay for twenty years, and" [56]—but no one can care for the conclusion of such a sentence as that. Lowell himself has been less fortunate than he says the fourteenth century was, but his idolatry merely consecrates the looseness that mars his admirably sympathetic essay.

For just as the artlessness, the formlessness, which his essays betray—and which Mr. Greenslet illustrates by an amusing analysis of the "Lessing" [57]—is a consequence of his lack of a central and unified conception of his subject, so this lack is itself a consequence of the absence in his brilliant equipment of the critical spirit, the critical temperament. The possession of this spirit would have perturbed him out of his Capuan dalliance with detail and spurred him to the capture of the capital, on which for life, as well as order, all the provinces of detail depend. The critical temperament is a reflective one. Criticism is not the product of reading, but of thought. To produce vital and useful criticism it is necessary to think, think, think, and then, when tired of thinking, to think more. Lowell's temperament is not unfairly to be inferred from a playful but indicative passage in "A Moosehead Journal." "It is curious," he says, "how tyrannical the habit of reading is and what shifts are made to escape thinking. There is no bore we dread being left alone with so much as our own minds." [58] Hence the predominance in his essays of desultory over consecutive thought, as well as of detail over *ensemble* in their form. Hence, too, his hospitable harboring of the partisan spirit. And as his representative turn of mind dominated his individuality, the partisan spirit blurred—or, if one chooses, gilded—his perceptions, and dulled, or at least deflected, his penetration. From the great endeavor of contemporary criticism, if it be "to see the object as in itself it really is," [59] he is constitutionally disassociated.

Accordingly, it discloses a fine trait in his character that his essays should be, in general, so compact of eulogy. Choosing, as I have said, the best of subjects, by the natural selection of an aristocratic intellect, he was here, to be sure, in the main on safe ground. It would certainly be a task almost—not quite—as idle as ungracious to attempt to pick flaws in or seriously to controvert the larger proportion of his eulogiums. They constitute a veritable literary monument, with the traditional epitaph inspiration, and might be entitled "The Praise of Great Writers," being sometimes, too, almost lyrical enough in spirit to be called poems in prose. Of his dispraise one easily feels less certain. In the nature of things—there being notoriously no standard of the false, the ugly, and the wrong—censure exacts more qualifications in the critic than eulogy. But the critical spirit may be as clearly absent from sound praise as from unjust censure, and it is only the critical spirit that can preserve criticism from that oblivion which swallows all at last but which is indecorously hungry for the partial and the partisan. Mr. Greenslet says Lowell's essays are read in colleges.[60] As if that were any augury of immortality!

There is no qualification to his praise to give it persuasiveness, to say nothing of permanence. The Dante essay (to recur to this representative example) is all patently partisan—patently therefore, in the sixth century of Dante criticism, either unsound or superfluous; the day of discrimination is never over, but wholesale consideration reaches finally its term. Lowell is, like all the temperamentally energetic but reflectively indolent, particularly fond of superlatives. Sir Thomas Browne's is the greatest imagination in English literature since Shakespeare. Hawthorne is "the rarest creative imagination of the century, the rarest in some ideal respects since Shakespeare." Milton is "the most impressive figure in our literary history." Donne "wrote more profound verses than any other English poet save one only." Dante is "the most masculine of poets"; French "the most feminine of tongues." [61] Marvell's "Horatian Ode" is "the most truly classic in our language." "Nothing in all poetry approaches the imaginative grandeur" of Dante's vision at the end of the "Paradiso." Chaucer is "the greatest of English poets save one." The secret password of all poetry "with the most haunting memory" is a distich he cites from a Spanish ballad—needing its context, too, to be "haunting" at all. English is "a better literary medium than any modern tongue." He has the tone of an official conferring decorations or degrees.[62]

Superlatives may be just, but they do not define. Obviously they state the known in terms of the unknown—a in terms of x, as Lowell might say; clearly the converse of the critical order. The general atmosphere of idolatry that they create is unfortunate because it is plainly "too good to be true," and in a world of imperfections the result is bound to lack verisimilitude. Dante in Lowell's pages ceases to be credible; or if abstractly credible is concretely very difficult to conceive as a mediæval Florentine, as well as a very different personage from the Dante of other commentators. Miss Rossetti, for example, whose interpretation Lowell praises so highly as to say that he shall only endeavor to supplement it by the "side-lights" of his own prolonged study—Miss

Rossetti acknowledges that after Beatrice's death Dante gave himself up "more or less to sensual gratification and earthly aim." [63] On this Lowell remarks: "The earthly aim we in a certain sense admit; the sensual gratificaiton we reject as utterly inconsistent, not only with Dante's principles, but with his character and indefatigable industry." What it is not inconsistent with is the known, or at all events, universally credited, facts of his life. "Let us dismiss at once and forever all the idle tales of Dante's amours," exclaims Lowell, with extraordinary finality.[64] But the reader is bound to reflect that all the "tales" are not "idle." Some of them deserve philosophic treatment—for instance, one may say, those on which, in the passage of the "Purgatorio" where she reproves him for his backslidings, Beatrice probably based her rebuke. Such treatment is this sentence by Arnold, who certainly had not devoted twenty years of study to Dante, which is unparalleled for penetration by anything in Lowell's essay— or, in fact, in Lowell anywhere: "We know," he says, "how the followers of the spiritual life tend to be antinomian in what belongs to the outward life; they do not attach much importance to such irregularity themselves; it is their fault as complete men that they do not; it is the fault of the spiritual life as a complete life that it allows this tendency; by dint of despising the outward life it loses control of this life, and of itself when in contact with it." [65] Boccaccio, who is one of the arch-offenders Lowell would "dismiss at once and forever," would have smiled assent to this. But I have cited it, as one is constantly tempted to cite Arnold in contrast to Lowell as a critic, because it shows how the definition which is lost by looseness is secured by discrimination.

Another remark of Arnold's which illustrates the same thing is: "Perhaps in Sophocles the thinking power a little overbalances the religious sense, just as in Dante the religious sense overbalances the thinking power." [66] That is a critical and illuminating statement. Having, inevitably, to compare Dante with the Greek drama, Lowell puts the matter in his conventional and figurative way, maintaining that the Greek drama satisfies "our highest conception of form," but "its circle of motives was essentially limited," it "is primarily Greek and secondarily human," whereas "the Christian idea has to do with the human soul, which Christianity may almost be said to have invented," and the "Divine

Comedy" is "no pagan temple enshrining a type of the human made divine by triumph of corporeal beauty," but a cathedral whose "leading thought is that of aspiration," or, in fact, a Christian basilica: "there is first," he concludes, "the ethnic forecourt, then the purgatorial middle space and last the holy of holies, dedicated to the eternal presence of the mediatorial God." [67] No doubt there is justice in the general contention. No doubt, in a sense, Christianity invented—or one would prefer to say discovered—the human soul. But it is just this sense that the critic would seek to determine—precisely what, in fact, Arnold's sentence hints at. Lowell's dithyramb is partisanship. He is always a partisan in allusions to the Greeks. He yields them supremacy in form with the readiness of a formless writer to whom form is "even now sour" or else unessential. But he has absolutely no sympathy with Greek substance. The best pages of his essay on Shakespeare discuss the difference between Shakespeare and the Greek drama in that Shakepeare's characters incur, and those of the Greek dramatists suffer, their fate. But he treats the subject with didactic finality, as if the insoluble question of determination were absolutely settled, and not at all as a critic, so that what he has to say is really of only exegetical value. The critic would say—as Arnold does in effect—merely that in the Greek drama the element of conscience is less developed than in the Christian. The conscience of Socrates enabled him to be "terribly at ease in Zion"; [68] that of Dante permitted him a similar tranquillity, perhaps, only in putting his enemies in hell. The subject is too large for passing treatment. My only point is that Lowell treats it in frankly partisan fashion and that the partisan rather than the critical inspiration marks his philosophic treatment in general.

This being the case, it would no doubt be fortunate that in general there is so little philosophy in his essays, if it were not for the fact that the philosophic spirit is the life, as the critical instinct is the inspiration, of criticism. The two, indeed, are hardly to be discriminated; and as the absence of the latter in Lowell is attested by the lack of centrality of conception responsible for his formlessness, so it, in turn, implies the absence of that interest in ideas as such, in and of themselves, which marks that side of the critical temperament, approximately at least, to

be called philosophic. For this there is absolutely no adequate
substitute in criticism. With it the critic may lack almost everything else. Stendhal, for example, one of the great figures in criticism, depends upon it almost wholly. He had, it is true, one or
two saving lines of thought which he held to with a passionate
fixity unknown in Cambridge and which gave all his work a consistent tendency. But nothing can be more formless than the
"Promenades dans Rome" or the "Histoire de la peinture en
Italie," [69] and they will never accordingly enjoy currency. They
are also full of extravagances—extravagance being precisely one
of Beyle's *lignes directrices*. What stamps him as a stimulating
and perennially interesting critic is his devotion to ideas. Exiled
in Città Vecchia he longed for Paris, by no means for patriotic
reasons, but because he could get the four or five cubic feet of
ideas which he said he needed for daily consumption as much as
a steamboat needs coal. Of ideas in this sense Lowell's consumption was comparatively small, altogether disproportionate to the
volumes of often picturesquely wreathed smoke into which the
alembic of his extraordinary faculty for expression converted such
as he consumed. So far as luxuriance may be predicated of them,
his ideas were in general the conceits, notions, fancies, of the true
poet, of the observant rather than the reflective order. Of philosophic ideas, general ideas, there is in his many volumes a dearth
that only ceases to be surprising when one recalls Mr. James's
remark that he "had no speculative side" [70] or his own reference,
indeed, to "speculation's windy waste." Macaulay, in comparison,
is alive with them.

They certainly can be overworked. M. Faguet has a charming
passage about them in this sense. "It is impossible," he says, "to
be quite ignorant of anything without systematizing it a great
deal or to know anything without systematizing it a little; so that
one cannot escape general ideas even by virtue and effort, and
learning itself only serves to enable us to avoid them in excess."
A certain order of truisms aside, Lowell's general intellectual superiority, his admirable culture, saved him from the mediocrity
thus satirized, of dealing with general ideas by main strength
and *à tout propos*. Also his unspeculative temperament. And as I
say, they are infrequent in his pages. An occasional distinction,
that between the poetic temperament and the poetic faculty, in

his "Percival," [71] for instance, is vouchsafed us; but, on the other hand, when he deals with ideas of a general nature he is apt to recall Mr. Howells's remark about an eminent publicist accustomed "to do his boldest thinking along the safest lines." His normal attitude is very well indicated in his signalizing as "an important and even profound truth" Webster's assertion that a coward cannot be an honest man, and calling it an example of the "metaphysical apothegms" of which he says only Chapman was fonder than Webster.[72] Ideas are certainly, if succin[c]tly expressed, "metaphysical apothegms," but to think of them as such is to take rather an unfriendly view of them.

Consequently, in his criticism one feels the lack of the element that gives it at its best what it has been said even a biography should have, namely, "a life of its own apart from the subject." Of his own general conception of life and art, we get very little. He had apparently no particular philosophic view to advocate or express and his essays have no general philosophic derivation. His critical work as a whole lacks the unity of a body of doctrine or even a personal point of view. It does not discuss principles. Its chief value is exegetical. This is why he is at his best in his "Dante" his "Chaucer," his "Dryden," his "Shakespeare," and the Elizabethans generally. For as exegesis is the strongest part of his criticism, linguistics are the strongest part of his exegesis and he is even better in discussing the language than in explaining the substance of the poets. For language he had the instinct to be expected of such a master of expression, and of archaic, recondite, or foreign language he was an admirable interpreter—being both a poet and a precisian. In this field it would be difficult to overpraise him.

V

His style lacks continuity—which is to say that it lacks style. That is the first, and I think the final, impression left by any prolonged consecutive reading of his prose. One feels the lack of continuity of presentation consequent upon the lack of sustained thought, the sense of which, also, is thus considerably accentuated. The appearance of vagrom annotation which the essays often have is enhanced by the absence of distribution and or-

ganization in the design, or rather, by the absence of design itself.
I think it is also enhanced by the brilliancy of the detail. Lowell
had an extraordinary, a wonderful gift of expression—a faculty
perhaps as often fatal as favorable to the achievement of style.
He could, as the phrase is, say anything he liked. He could follow
the turns and shadings of his lively fancy into all sorts of recesses
of refinement, and with the greatest ease. This sense of ease is the
greatest charm of his style. The reader savors it—when he can
abstract it from its associated phenomena—with the satisfaction
always aroused by the untrammelled functioning of any truly
native and effective faculty. And often it evokes the additional
enjoyment of a fine faculty at play, revelling in its own effortless
activities. Often, too, it must be said, it falls into the clutches of
excess, of which it is, of course, the natural prey, unwary as the
bird blind to the fascination of the serpent; often the sense of
effortless ease shades into that of a kind of decorous riot, which
would be distressing if it were not tinctured by a genial self-
satisfaction that renders it insipid instead. But at its best, Lowell's
gift of expression vivifies his prose immensely. It makes an occasional stretch, now and then substantially long reaches, of his
essays—especially those in familiar vein, like the "Moosehead
Journal" and the "Condescension in Foreigners" [73]—a succession
of what are known as "good things." He was himself extremely
partial to both the phrase and the fact of "good things." Reflection with him no doubt frequently took the form of preparing
them, and one can predicate in fancy the *pétillant* way in which
preliminarily his mind ticked them off—whether in a *coupé* going
to a public dinner or in his library at Elmwood, a wide-margined
"Cervantes" on his lap and nicotian spirals from his contemplative
pipe doubtless half veiling

"—a statue by Powers or a picture by Page" [74]

that must have been among its Lares. These "good things" are
also really good—and not the counterfeits that so frequently impose on a lazy and loose appreciative sense. They will all parse
according to the strictest syntax of the grammar of excellence.
They have no meretricious ring. They are not said for effect, but
from inspiration. They are free from the taint of "rhetoric"—
that compound of charlatanry and convention. At least their only

defect is the occasional error in taste, and this is due to either excess or energy. Measure and reserve are not essential traits of the "good thing," which may sin against both and still merely fail, negatively, to be an even better thing.

And Lowell's good things are curiously *sui generis*. They are not rarely the good things of the poet who is touched as well as enlightened by the truths he discovers or rather feels with personal stress and states, accordingly, in figurative fashion; for example, "Style, the handmaid of talent, the helpmeet of genius." They are as a rule, however, curiously devoid of epigrammatic quality, as that quality is displayed in the most eminent examples of epigram; a fact which proceeds, I suppose, from his constitutional neglect of the field of "general ideas." Often extremely witty, their wit is not pure wit, any more than it is pure humor, but a kind of combination of the two—wit, let us say, with the inspiration of humor. It is, like his mind, sensible and sound and unspeculative. It neither flashes nor glows, but sparkles. It does not illumine a subject with a chance light, a sudden turn, a wilful refraction, a half truth, but plays about it sportively—leaving it, besides, pretty much as it found it. No one would call his wit searching. Lowell possessed too little deference as well as too little *malice* to be distinctly penetrating. It has a very persistent judicious side, infallibly provocative in the end of grief in the judicious. For nothing will save a succession of good things considered as the web of a sustained literary production but the spice of paradox. Paradox is the only variant of the inevitable monotony. It is the life of Stendhal's essays, one may almost say, to cite again an example of formlessness paralleling Lowell's. But it never occurs in Lowell. He can, on occasion, be trivial, even flippant, wilful, even wrongheaded, but never paradoxical. One gets tired finally of the undisputed thing said in such a witty way. Nay, one must also admit fatigue with what he himself would call the perfect concinnity of all this brilliant and desultory detail and itches to cast his oyster-shell against this impeccable Aristides of expression.

But from the point of view of style its defect is that it *is* detail, and so accentuated as to nullify the *ensemble,* on which style inexorably depends. For, however one define it, style implies a sustained flight. Lowell achieves it in his poetry sometimes splen-

didly, superbly; which renders it at first thought unaccountable
that his prose should be so desert of it. Other poets have never so
conspicuously fallen down in this respect on alighting from their
Pegasus. But no doubt the reason is that whereas he was not
habituated to sustained thought, and shrank recalcitrant from its
concatenation, he delighted in sustained emotion—the simpler
the better, too. "Style," says Buffon—and one cannot too often
cite the remark in explanation of his much misunderstood *"le
style, c'est l'homme"*—"style is nothing other than the order and
movement which we put into our thoughts." [75] In Lowell's prose
either there is no order and movement or it exists only in passages. And these passages not only count as detail—like the good
things—but they are less noteworthy because they are less, far
less, individual. There are places, says Mr. James, in which "he
sounds like a younger brother of Bacon and of Milton." [76] Precisely. But one could wish for more such sentences as Mr. James
quotes in support of his remark: "Oblivion looks in the face of the
Grecian Muse only to forget her errand." They are far from un-
welcome punctuation of the prose in which, in Mr. James's words
again, "he sounds like no one but his inveterately felicitous self,"
—even such of it as this sentence, also illustratively adduced by
Mr. James, from the address on Wordsworth: "Too often . . . he
seems diligently intent on producing fire by the primitive method
of rubbing the dry sticks of his blank verse one against the other,
while we stand in shivering expectation of the flame that never
comes." [77] There are times, one feels, when Lowell's inspiration is
that of Périchole's "Oui, bonnes gens, sautez dessus," [78] and
when, I think, his style is subtly injured by his rather primitive
truculent inclinations at the expense of the obviously "par trop
bête." But his *opéra bouffe* is as Mr. James says, "inveterately
felicitous," and perhaps it is pedantry to object to Offenbachian
treatment of Wordsworth and at the same time quarrel with the
obviousness of its relevancy.

"Inveterately felicitous," in fact, is not an inexact epithet for
Lowell's figures in general. And of both the good things and the
elevated passages of his prose the figure is an unfailing characteristic. His poetic faculty follows him even into argumentation
and gilds his rhetoric with fancy. His figures are of course vari-
ably, however inveterately, felicitous, but they are always favor-

ites with him, one feels, over the substance it is their formal
function to illuminate or adorn. The logical path through one of
his essays, or such semblance of one as he follows, is fringed with
figures that count really as digressions, so much do they absorb
his zest and so thoroughly does he explore and exploit them. The
reader more easily surfeited with straying might find these loops
and excursions too frequent, but for the fact that they are not
rarely quite as entertaining as the highroad of his thought; from
which, besides, they diverge without abruptness and to which
they always return, for though they vary in felicity, his figures
are simply never inapt. A page opened at random, for example,
says of the Elizabethans: "But though fortunate in being able to
gather their language with the dew still on it, as herbs must be
gathered for use in certain incantations, we are not to suppose
that our elders used it indiscriminately, or tumbled out their
words as they would dice, trusting that luck or chance would
send them a happy turn." [79] Indeed we are not to, and probably
we should not. So that the warning to us not to think of the age
of verbal *concetti* as linguistically happy-go-lucky is less impressive than the beautiful figure about the language with the dew
still on it. The passage could be paralleled every few pages
throughout the six volumes of essays. It is characteristic, too, not
only in the superiority of figure to idea, but in the pursuit of the
figure and its transformation, like the pursuit of the genie by the
princess in the Second Calendar's tale. [80] This fecundity of fancy
and comparative continence of thought varies in felicity, however, as I have said. "The nameless eagle of the tree Ygdrasil
was about to sit at last, and wild-eyed enthusiasts rushed from
all sides, each eager to thrust under the mystic bird that chalk
egg from which the new and fairer Creation was to be hatched in
due time," [81] is more in the *bouffe* vein again, though graphic.
And Lowell's fecundity in figure by no means precludes terseness
—though I think it is oftener piquant, like his wit in general.
There is nothing loose about his lavishness with it and his meta-
phorical plethora is often a succession of pointed petards. And
though his fondness for it becomes infatuation at times, its aptness and polish command his intelligent effort. No great prose
writer ever wrote, probably, such a sentence as the following:
"Bran had its prophets and the presartorial simplicity of Adam

its martyrs, tailored impromptu from the tar-pot by incensed neighbors and sent forth to illustrate the 'feathered Mercury' as defined by Webster and Worcester," [82] but it is impossible not to discern painstaking in its composition. A good deal of Lowell's prose, indeed, has the piquancy of Pegasus in harness.

But at least it is never prose poetry. It is masculine, direct, flexible, and energetic prose. Whatever irresponsibilities of taste he might have, however addicted to a kind of racy and idiomatic order of *concetti* and overfond of figure he might be, however lacking his writing in the larger rhythm of style and the organic order of composition, his essays are admirably written from the point of view of adequate, accurate, and scholarly prose expression. His poetic faculty is an aid, not an embarrassment, to him and when he had poetry to write he wrote it in verse. His trained sense and sound instinct secured him against the mediocrity of inflated periods and ungoverned emotionality. He aimed at no meretricious "effects." He was quite without inferiority of any kind, though his partisanship in both reprehension and idolatry robs his writing now and then of that positive perfume of sensitive intellectual refinement in which self-respect and consideration seem magically fused; as in Emerson, for example. Without a tinge of austerity, despite his *concetti*, and despite, too, his wealth of literary allusion, his writing is admirably simple; so far at least as clearness is concerned it is simplicity itself. His vocabulary is extremely extensive, and often extremely personal, but I think he never exploits it. He had no pedantries. He even belittled rather than paraded his Old French. He was fond of unusual words, no doubt, but for their expressive value, and never used them inaptly or as decoration, though never restrained from taking advantage of their concise and epitomizing quality by awe of philistine resentment at the unfamiliar. When he said such a thing would have "arrided" Lamb, he was using Lamb's own word, and when he speaks of "the hermetic gift of buckling wings to the feet of their verse" [83] he is but pardonably mercurial. At all events, if he was now and then linguistically precious he was far oftener linguistically instructive, and always quite without display. His allusions are often recondite, like Carlyle's, though not, like Carlyle's, *bizarre;* he lacked the edge as well as the irritability of extravagance in its intenser forms, the relief as well as

the rudeness of the eccentric—save in the matter of taste, his
offences against which fringe the commonplace and are not so
eccentric as it is eccentric to commit them. His peculiarity of
never explaining his allusions is not affectation. He had none. He
is too bland, too broad, too complacent. It is merely bookish. It
does not in the least modify the general effect of his essays as
lectures to students or a lyceum public of docile and deferential
quality, though perhaps of a rather special sort. On the contrary,
it adds to their air of the academic close, peopled not by representatives of the reading world at large, nor even by the generally
cultivated, but by the matriculate and the novice. Nor does their
style, spite of the admirable qualities enumerated, quite take
them out of this category. They will doubtless continue to be indispensable in the college courses referred to by Mr. Greenslet,
and certainly every one should read them for the instruction
they contain, for their literary saturation. But the larger public
—so free, so fickle, so entirely irresponsible but also so responsive
to what is really addressed to it—will increasingly, I think, turn
to his poetry as Lowell's more interesting and more admirable
achievement and his more genuinely native form of self-
expression.

VI

The qualities to be found in his prose exist, of course, in his
poetry, but they make a very different thing of it. It is not to
be regretted that, unlike Tennyson, for example, he did not
confine himself to poetry. Not only did he write a great deal of
admirable and distinguished prose, not only may we say, indeed,
that there is very little of his prose that is not worth while, but
he wrote a good deal too much verse; and verse that misses the
mark has less to fall back upon than errant or superfluous prose.
If he had consecrated himself completely to the service of the
Muse, we should have lost more than we should have gained,
and have gained little properly to be called indispensable, since
the proportion of his poetry that can be so called is small. But
a great deal of it is very fine, very noble and at times very beautiful, and it discloses the distinctly poetic faculty of which
rhythmic and figurative is native expression. It is impressionable

rather than imaginative in the larger sense; it is felicitous in detail rather than in design; and of a general rather than individual, a representative rather than original, inspiration. There is a field of poetry, assuredly not the highest, but ample and admirable—in which these qualities, more or less unsatisfactory in prose, are legitimately and fruitfully exercised. All poetry is in the realm of feeling, and thus less exclusively dependent on the thought that is the sole reliance of prose. Being genuine poetry, Lowell's profits by this advantage. Feeling is fitly, genuinely, its inspiration. Its range and limitations correspond to the character of his susceptibility as those of his prose do to that of his thought. The fusion of the two in the crucible of the imagination is infrequent with him, because with him sense impressions are more vivacious than the imagination is luxuriant and highly developed. Without, of course, Emerson's fragmentariness, it nevertheless, cannot be claimed that for the architectonics of poetry he had notably the requisite reach and grasp, the comprehensive and constructing vision. Few of his compositions have any large design or effective interdependent proportions. In a technical way an exception should be noted in his skilful building of the ode—a form in which he was extremely successful and for which he evidently had a native aptitude. His sonnets are less happy—some of them, in fact, curiously routine and mechanical for so energetic a spirit. But the ode is a comparatively loose construction—witness the unrivalled success in it of the author of "the slipshod 'Endymion,'" as Keats agrees with his reviewer in calling it,[84] and the fragmentary "Hyperion." Of such a poem as the "In Memoriam" or "Evangeline," or even "Snow Bound," Lowell is incapable. The "Legend of Brittany" [85] is full of charming and touching poetry, but it has far less structure, less definition and coherence, less movement and evolution, than the "Isabella and the Pot of Basil," in which Keats has been charged with drowning all the crispness of Boccaccio. Keats, however, loses his structure in a surfeit of imaginative surplusage. In Lowell it is the imagination itself that is lacking, though in nearly every stanza his impressionability makes a brave struggle to cover its defection with genuine felicities.

The "Legend" is an extremely characteristic poem. Like the

"Vision of Sir Launfal," [86] with its charming nature detail, it not only fails in design, failing to bring out effectively the design supplied by the legend itself, but it fails in characterization; the figures are not alive; in spite of considerable elaboration they are not even distinct. A sort of *couche* of moralizing—oddly un-Breton—overlays the poem, while, singularly, there is not enough intensity in the treatment to make the tragedy stern. Intensity, in fact, is wholly foreign to Lowell's temperament, and his poetry suffers accordingly in this respect more than in almost any other. His lack of passion—almost droll in so convinced a partisan—is so pronounced as to amount well-nigh to dispassionateness. Naturally, the entire gamut of emotions excluded by a rectitude of feeling paralleling his regularity of thought is without his range and he could not be expected to "break his heart in verse every six months." But even where his feeling is lofty it is rarely exalted, and where it is profound it is not intense. The "lyric cry" is not to be heard in his poetic dominions, where the curfew of calm replaces it with its placid toll. Sentiment, in a word, replaces passion—in quite eighteenth-century fashion one would be tempted to say but for its conspicuous genuineness and often truly Wordsworthian melody. Cowper's and Cowley's at least one may call its congeners, rather than the intenser strain of nineteenth-century verse at its flood. "Auf Wiedersehen," [87] for example, is a charming poem, but compare it with the stanzas "In Switzerland" concluding with

"The unplumbed, salt, estranging sea." [88]

Its best, its most characteristic line is the admirable one,

"The turf that silences the lane,"

in which nature asserts her primacy in the poet's reflections and inspires him with a felicity his mistress cannot evoke. "The First Snowfall," too, is exquisite, but it does not strive nor cry. It expresses bereavement touchingly. But it is on the natural picture with

"The stiff rails softened to swan's-down" [89]

that the poetic stress falls.

For nature, however, Lowell *did* have a feeling justly to be
called passion. His passions, as I have said, may be summed
up in nature, books, and patriotism, and it is precisely the first
and the last of these that provide motives for song which in
their intensest expression retain still something of the abstract
and impersonal, and in their loftier and broader statement
express the universal rather than the particular. No one is a
stranger to the meaning, however he may be to the experiences,
of patriotism. And poetry at the present day can say little to
him to whom nature says nothing. These two sources of poetic
inspiration are therefore especially germane to the genius of a
poet like Lowell, who had no general point of view of his own,
no personal "message" to deliver, but whose gift of expression
was fully exercised, in all its rich luxuriance, in expressing the
thoughts and feelings of his fellow-men. To sing one's country
and its landscape; one does not need a "speculative side." And
impressionability as sensitive as Lowell's does duty here very
efficiently for the imagination. He was extremely sensitive to all
out-of-door aspects and influences. If he did not read Wordsworth's pantheism into nature's phenomena, he observed them
with a loving sentiment that eliminates all traces of vagueness
and gives a crisp and definite report of them guaranteeing its
own genuineness and forming an authentic basis for the delight
with which they filled him and which flowers in indubitably
poetic characterization. His ingrained predilection for the figurative in language, so excessive in his prose, stands him in good
stead here. In verse his figures add to their invariable aptness
a truly poetic charm. He carries his beloved Shakespeare out-of-
doors with him and speaks thus of the treachery of spring, in
lines which have more *style* than all his prose contains, and
which, like the lion on the flag of the Persian poet, "move and
march" in the sustained *souffle* that style is:

> "And winter suddenly, like crazy Lear,
>   Reels back and brings the dead May in his arms,
>   Her budding breasts and wan dislustred front
>   With frosty streaks and drifts of his white beard
>   All overblown." [90]

"What is so rare as a day in June"? Such poetry about it as this:

"The little bird sits at his door in the sun,
 Atilt like a blossom among the leaves,
And lets his illumined being o'errun,
 With the deluge of summer it receives." [91]

Nature is usually animate with him. The birds sing in the branches. Sunshine vivifies the fields and thrills the woods it filters through. The breeze blows. Life and motion are everywhere. Shelley and Wordsworth have not more worthily immortalized the skylark than Lowell has the bobolink, its New England congener. Who that has ever seen this embodiment of sportiveness at play in the zephyrs can forget the lines:

"Half-hid on tip-top apple-blooms he swings,
 Or climbs against the breeze with quiverin' wings,
 Or, givin' way to't in a mock despair,
 Runs down, a brook o' laughter, thru the air"? [92]

Joy is the sentiment that chiefly nature inspires in him. It is the birch-tree, not the weeping-willow that he celebrates, and that might almost be taken as the symbol of his nature poetry, with its crispness, its delicacy, its New England color and substance, its alert grace, its antitropical allure, its independence and breezy self-sufficiency. With the awful, the majestic, the solemn and sublime aspects of nature, her immensities of space and stillness and the drama of her storms and wilder moods, he is less in touch. Her more familiar and more benign aspects appeal to him as the New England poet which he was and—being without a trace of affectation—was necessarily. The huckleberry-bush has not quite the same suggestiveness as the laurel, the vine, and the fig-tree, but it has indefeasibly its own poetic potentialities, and these and their kindred found in Lowell an exquisite as well as an eloquent, a sensitive as well as a veridical, expositor. Lowell's constitutes, on the whole, the most admirable American contribution to the nature poetry of English literature—far beyond that of Bryant, Whittier, or Longfellow, I think, and only occasionally matched here and there by the magic touch of Emerson, who *had* a "speculative side."

And his patriotic poetry is altogether unmatched—even unrivalled. It is the loftiest expression of the American muse singing America, and in virtue of it she stands shoulder to shoulder with her English sister in her most inspired moments. Shakespeare's

> "This precious stone set in the silver sea,
> This blessed plot, this earth, this realm, this England—" [93]

is no better than some of the lines—some entire strophes even—
of the "Commemoration Ode," [94] either as patriotism or as
poetry. The ode is too long, its evolution is defective, it contains
verbiage, it preaches. But passages of it—the most famous having
characteristically been interpolated after its delivery—are equal
to anything of the kind. The temptation to quote from it is hard
to withstand. It is the cap-sheaf of Lowell's achievement. The
Agassiz Ode [95] perhaps deserves a proximate place—friendship
was a harmonious inspiration for Lowell; and the "Biglow
Papers" are doubtless more nearly unique—are unique, in fact,
as well as highly characteristic; as characteristic as the extraordinary *tour de force*, the sustained *jeu d'esprit* of his youth, "A
Fable for Critics," the *bouffe* rhymes in which are as good—
nearly—as Byron's, and which in a certain opulence of spirit
he never surpassed. But the "Biglow Papers" equal the "Commemoration Ode" neither as poetry nor as patriotism. They
contain some very beautiful poetry, as well as a sufficient amount
of rather light doggerel. They are a treasury of both wit and
humor, though now and then the humor is overdone. The idea
was a *trouvaille*, but it is overworked. The second series justifies
itself amply, but it has less spontaneity than the first; and it is
not only occasionally labored, but it is frankly and loosely partisan, the scales not being held with anything like the steadiness
that they are in "The Bridge and the Moniment," [96] for example.
With all his Americanism Lowell was scarcely less essentially,
than he was—as he was fond of insisting—ancestrally, English.
New England was not so named for nothing. And if it has been
our best section—as in the literary sense it certainly has been—
it has certainly also been, even in the literary sense, the most
sectional. The "Biglow Papers" contain some very incisive criticisms of England, but they are not bitter or unjust, and when
their author became minister to England Englishmen found it
easy to admire their sometime censor, assured that fundamentally he returned their admiration. The quarrel was a family
one. On the other hand, his own fellow-countrymen south of

Mason and Dixon's line were even more bitterly than incisively satirized in the "Biglow Papers." They were in the political articles which fill a volume of his complete works and which, save the paper on Lincoln, are only of historic interest, having only a temporary value. They contain enough "good things" perhaps to explain his wish to perpetuate them—though even these are apt to run speedily to seed; witness the extraordinary play upon the name of John Bell, the Tennessee statesman, kept up for a page and a half.[97] Otherwise they are quite negligible as the thoroughly partisan polemic of the journalist, or at most the pamphleteer, rather than the publicist, and saturated with the sectional spirit. And it was, in part at least, precisely the absence of this spirit in Lincoln, for example, that led Lowell to characterize him as "the first American." [98] Lowell's patriotism has undoubtedly this restriction.

His democracy is similarly restricted. He said some admirable things about democracy in his famous address to a public instinctively devoted to the principle of caste; he could hardly fail to call their attention to points they notoriously overlooked. But he was himself a Brahmin throughout, whereas the American democratic ideal is Brahminism in manners and tastes, not in sympathies and ideas. From the democratic point of view, either philosophic or enthusiastic, his convictions about its being "the duty of the intelligent to govern the less intelligent," and about popular government being "no better than any other form except as the virtue and wisdom of the people make it so," [99] etc., must seem rather flat, I think. It is like the defenders of the spoils system objecting to civil service examinations and insisting on the old idea of "appointing only good men to office." He had very much the political philosophy of Halifax or Macaulay plus a belief in the New England town meeting, which admirable institution unhappily has its limitations of application. But when his patriotism abandoned polemic and soared into the loftier regions of emotion, with only the broader and simpler of our truths and triumphs for a basis, he was superb. Who associates the stately measures and noble figures of "The Present Crisis" [100] with the Mexican War? And in the "Commemoration Ode" he reaches, if he does not throughout maintain, his own "clear-ethered height," [101] and his verse has the elevation of ecstasy and the splendor of the sublime.

> "O Beautiful! My Country! ours once more!
> Smoothing thy gold of war-dishevelled hair
> O'er such sweet brows as never other wore,
>   And letting thy set lips,
>   Freed from wrath's pale eclipse,
> The rosy edges of their smile lay bare." [102]

We can ask the world to match that. If Lowell had no personal "message" to deliver, in this magnificent poem he phrases ours to the world, and in the most explicit and authentic terms of beautiful and moving poetry. He will doubtless cease to be one of our superstitions, but he will always remain one of our chief glories.

HENRY JAMES

HENRY JAMES

I

IF any career can be called happy before it is closed, that of Mr. Henry James may certainly be so called. It has been a long one—much longer already than the space of time allotted to a generation. It has been quite free from any kind of mistake: there is probably nothing in it he would change if he could, except what he has been abundantly able to by a careful revision of his fiction for the definitive New York Edition,[1] in which he has made it quite as he would have it. His career has been an honorable one in a very special way and to a very marked degree. He has scrupulously followed his ideal. Neither necessity nor opportunity has prevented him from doing, apparently, just what he wanted. He has never, at any rate, yielded to the temptation to give the public what *it* wanted. The rewards of so doing are very great. Most writers in belittling them would be justly suspected of affectation. They include, for example, the pleasure of being read, and this is a pleasure usually so difficult to forego when it is attainable that Mr. James's indifference to it is striking. And—what is still more striking— he has never, as he himself expresses it somewhere in characterization of some other writer,—who must, however, have been his own inferior in this respect,—he has never "saved for his next book." Of his special order of talent fecundity is not what one would naturally have predicted, and though he has amply demonstrated his possession of it, he must have long given us his best before he could have been at all sure that he could count on matching his best to an indefinite extent. Into the frame of every book he has packed, not only the substance called for by the subject, but a substance as remarkable for containing all he could himself bring to it, as for compression. At least, if his substance has sometimes been thin, it has always been considered; however fine-spun its texture, it has always been com-

posed of thought. And his expression, tenuous as it may sometimes appear, is (especially, indeed, when its tenuity is greatest)
so often dependent for its comprehension on what it suggests
rather than on what it states as to compel the inference that
it is incomplete expression, after all, of the amount of thought
behind it.

So that he never leaves the impression of superficiality. His
material, even his result, may be as slight as his own insistent
predetermination can make it; it is impossible not to feel that
it is the work of an artist who is not only serious, but profound.
Behind his sketch you feel the careful and elaborate preliminary
study; back of his triviality you feel the man of reflection. And
this is not at all because his triviality—to call it such—is significant in itself. It often is, and the trifling feature, incident, movement, or phrase often has a typical value that makes it in effect
but the expression of a larger thing than it embodies. But often,
on the other hand, it is difficult to assign any strikingly interpretative or illustrative value to the insubstantial phenomena that
he is at the pains of observing so narrowly and recording so
copiously. And yet it can occur to no sensitive and candid intelligence to refer to the capacity of the recorder this flimsiness of
the record. One has the sense in the treatment, the technic, of
a firm and vigorous hand—such as is, in general, perhaps, needed
for the carving of "émaux et camées." [2] And still more in the
substance one perceives, as well as argues, the solidity and
dignity underlying the superficial and apparently insignificant
details with which "wonderfully"—to use a favorite word of Mr.
James—they are occupied. The sense of contrast is indeed often
piquant. Cuvier lecturing on a single bone and reconstructing
the entire skeleton from it is naturally impressive, [3] but Mr.
James often presents the spectacle of a Cuvier absorbed in the
positive fascinations of the single bone itself,—yet plainly pre-
serving the effect of a Cuvier the while. If, in a word, his work
sometimes seems superficial, it never seems the work of a
superficial personality; and the exasperation of some of his
unfriendly critics proceeds from wondering, not so much how
a writer who has produced such substantial, can also produce
such trifling, work, as how the writer whose very treatment of

triviality shows him to be serious can be so interested in the superficial.

The explanation, I think, is that to Mr. James himself life, considered as artistic material, is so serious and so significant that nothing it contains seems trivial to him. And as artistic material is, in fact, the only way in which he appears to consider it at all. In spite of his elaborations on occasion, there is no padding in his books, no filling in of general ideas or other interesting distention. His parentheses are, it is true, apt to be cognate digressions rather than *nuances* of the matter in hand. But that is a question of style, and in any case addiction to parentheses is apt to proceed from an unwillingness to stray very far from the matter in hand, to let go one's hold of it. And save for his parentheses, Mr. James holds his reader to the matter—or the absence of matter—in hand rather remorselessly. One would like more space, more air. His copiousness, too, is the result of his seriousness. If he eschews the foreign, he revels in the pertinent; and, pertinence being his sole standard of exclusion, he is bound to include much that is trivial. We have the paradox of an art attitude that is immaculate with an art product that is ineffective. It is as crowded with detail and as tight as a pre-Raphaelite picture, because there are no salutary sacrifices. It is not because he is a man, but because he is an artist, that nothing human is foreign to him. No rectitude was ever less partial or more passionless. No novelist ever evinced more profound respect for his material *as* material, or conformed his art more rigorously to its characteristic expression. Thus it is due to his seriousness that a good deal of his substance seems less significant to his readers than to him, both in itself and because (out of his own deep respect for it, doubtless) he does little or nothing to enhance its interest and importance. It is not commonly appreciated that his work is, after all, the quintessence of realism.

II

The successive three "manners" of the painters have been found in it. Mr. James has had, at any rate, two. There is a noteworthy difference between his earlier and his later fiction, though the period of transition between them is not very definite as a period. Perhaps "The Tragic Muse" comprises it. He has, however, thrown himself so devotedly into his latest phase as to make everything preceding it appear as the stages of an evolution. Tendencies, nevertheless, in his earlier work, marked enough to individualize it sharply, have developed until they have subdued all other characteristics, and have made of him perhaps the most individual novelist of his day, who at the same time is also in the current of its tendency,—Meredith (except, should one say, in regard to Woman?) standing quite apart from this in eminent isolation. It is through these tendencies, developed as they have been, that in virtue of originality as well as of excellence he has won his particular place in the hierarchy of fiction. He has created a *genre* of his own. He has the distinction that makes the scientist a savant; he has contributed something to the sum, the common stock. His distinction has really a scientific aspect, independent, that is to say, of quality, of intrinsic merit. If it should be asserted that Meredith has done the same thing,—in a way, too, not so very differently,—it can be replied that he has done so by weakening the correspondence of fiction to life, whereas Mr. James has striven hard for its intensification; it is not the construction of the scientific toy, however interesting it may be, and however much science there may be in it, that makes the savant. This flowering of Mr. James's tendencies has, in fact, been precisely what he conceives to be the achievement of a more and more intimate and exquisite correspondence with life in his art. This at least has been his conscious, his professed aim. His observation, always his master faculty, has grown more and more acute, his concentration upon the apprehensible phenomena of the actual world of men and women—and children—closer, his interest in producing his illusion by reproducing these in as nearly as possible their actual essence and actual relations, far more absorbing and complete. Indeed, he has been so interested in producing his illusion in precisely this way, that he has decidedly compromised, I think, the certainty of producing it at all.

He has parted, then, with his past,—the past, let us say, of

"The Portrait of a Lady,"—in the pursuit of a more complete illusion of nature than he could feel that he achieved on his old lines,—the old lines, let us add, observed in the masterpieces of fiction hitherto. It is true that his observation has been from the first so clearly his distinguishing faculty that his present practice may superficially seem to differ from his former merely in degree. But a little more closely considered, it is a matter rather of development than of augmentation. In the course of its exercise his talent has been transformed. He has reversed the relation between his observation and his imagination, and instead of using the former to supply material for the latter, has enlisted the latter very expressly—oh! sometimes, indeed, worked it very hard—in the service of his observation. Of what he might have achieved by pursuing a different course, I cannot myself think without regret. But instead of seeking that equilibrium of one's powers which seems particularly pertinent to the expression of precisely such an organization as his,—instead of, to that end, curbing his curiosity and cultivating his constructive, his reflective, his imaginative side, the one being already markedly preponderant and the other comparatively slender,—he has followed the path of temperamental preference and developed his natural bent. The result is his present eminence, which is, in consequence, undeniably more nearly unique, but which is not for that reason necessarily more distinguished. His art has thus become, one is inclined to say, the ordered exploitation of his experiences. The change from his earlier manner is so great that it constitutes, as I say, a transformation. It is somewhat as if a transcendentalist philosopher should become so enamored of truth as, finding it inexhaustibly manifested in everything, to fall in love with phenomena and gradually acquire an absolutely a posteriori point of view. Similarly, Mr. James may be said to have renounced the vision for the pursuit.

The most delicate, the most refined and elegant of contemporary romancers has thus become the most thoroughgoing realist of even current fiction. It is but a popular error to confound realism with grossness, and it is his complete exclusion of idealism and preoccupation with the objective that I have in mind in speaking of his realism as so marked; though of

recent years he has annexed the field of grossness also,—
cultivating it, of course, with particular circumspection,—and
thus rounded out his domain. It must be granted that his realism
does not leave a very vivid impression of reality, on the one
hand, and that, on the other, it does not always produce the
effect of a very close correspondence to actual life and character.
"The Spoils of Poynton," with its inadequate motive and aspiration after the tragic; "The Other House," with its attempt to
domesticate melodrama; "In the Cage," with its exclusion of all
the surrounding data, needed to give authenticity to an even
robuster theme; "The Awkward Age," with its impossible cleverness of stupid people, are, as pictures of life, neither very lifelike
nor very much alive. But that is a matter of artistic result. The
attitude of the artist is plainly, uncompromisingly realistic. It is
the real with which his fancy, his imaginativeness, is exclusively
preoccupied. To discover new and unsuspected phenomena in
its psychology is the aim of his divination as well as of his
scrutiny. The ideal counterpart of the real and the actual which
even such realists as Thackeray and George Eliot have constantly, however unconsciously, in mind, and the image of
which, whether or no as universal as the Platonic philosophy
pretends, is at least part of the material of the imaginative
artist,—furnishing more or less vaguely the standard by which
he admeasures both his own creation and its model, when he
has one,—this ideal counterpart, so to speak, is curiously absent
from Mr. James's contemplation. Given a character with certain
traits, suggested, no doubt, by certain specific experiences, its
action is not deduced by ideal logic, but arrived at through
induction from the artist's entire stock of pertinent general experience, and modelled by its insistent pressure. "What conduct
does my—rather unusual—experience lead me to expect of a
personage constituted thus and so, in such and such circumstances?"—one may imagine Mr. James reflecting.

Categories like realism and idealism are but convenient, and
not exact, and in the practice of any artist both inspirations must
be alternately present in the execution of detail, though one of
them is surely apt to preponderate in the general conception
and in the artist's attitude. But it is certainly true that what

may be called the ideal of realism has never been held more devoutly—not even by Zola—than it is by Mr. James. All his subtlety, his refinement, his extreme plasticity, his acquaintance with the academic as well as the actual, are at the service of truth, and that order of truth which is to be discovered rather than divined. Long ago, in speaking of George Sand's idealism, which he admitted to be "very beautiful," he observed: "Something even better in a novelist is that tender appreciation of actuality which makes even the application of a single coat of rose-color seem an act of violence." [4] The inspiration is a little different from Thackeray's "If truth is not always pleasant, at least it is best." It is more "artistic," perhaps, certainly more disinterested. And at the present day Mr. James would no doubt go farther, omit the word "tender," and for "rose-color" substitute simply "any color at all." It is an unselfish creed, one may remark in passing. Color is a variety of form, and it is a commonplace that form is the only passport to posterity. Moreover, as Mr. James concedes, even idealism at times is "very beautiful," and to be compelled to forego beauty in "appreciation of the actual" (for its actuality, that is to say, rather than its beauty) must for an artist be a rigorous renunciation.

Mr. James has renounced it for the most part with admirable consistency, and his latest works are, in effort and inspiration at least, the very apotheosis of the actual—however their absence of color or other elements of form and the encumbrances of their style (the distinction is his own) may fail to secure the desired effect of actuality for them. What Maisie knew,[5] for example, may seem to have been learned by a preternaturally precocious child, so that her actuality has not, perhaps, the relief desired by her author. But she can have no other *raison d'être*—for the supposition that even incidentally she is designed to illustrate the charm of the flower on the dunghill can be at best but a mere guess, so colorlessly is the assumed actuality of her precocity and extraordinary situation exhibited. The book, indeed, in this respect is a masterpiece of reserve. It is conspicuously free from any taint of rose-color. And in its suppression of the superfluous—such as even the remotest recognition of the pathos of Maisie's situation—it is an excellent illustration of an

order of art that *must* be radically theoretic since it could not
be the instinctive and spontaneous expression of a normally
humane motive.

III

The truth is that our fiction is in a period of transition, which
perhaps is necessarily hostile to spontaneity and favorable to
the artificial. We speculate so much as to whether fiction is "a
finer art" as practised by the little, than it was in the day of
the great, masters, that the present time may fairly be called
the reign of theory in fiction—as indeed it is in art of any kind.
And Mr. James's art is in nothing more modern than in being
theoretic. Whatever it is not, it is that. Difficult as, in many
respects, it is to characterize, it is plainly what it is by precise
intention, by system. Difficult as his theory is to define, it is
perfectly clear that his art is the product of it. It is, in a word,
a critical product. And it is so because his temperament is the
critical temperament. Now, whatever may be said of the com-
patibility or incompatibility of the critical and the creative temperaments, it is evident that in the matter of creating fiction the
critical genius will be a different kind of a practitioner from the
creative genius. The latter may be considered to produce the
"criticism of life," but the former will be likely to produce such
criticism at one remove—with, in a word, *theory* interposed.
Even supposing the creator to be also a critic, if his creative
imagination preponderates, his theory will be a theory of life,
whereas the theory of the writer in whom the critical bent
preponderates will be a theory of art. We are said to suffer
nowadays from a dearth of the creative imagination. Science,
the great, the most nearly universal of the interests of the
present time, is perhaps thought to be hostile to its entertain-
ment, its development. But science, strictly so called, with its
own speedy determination toward specialism is probably less
fatal to the imagination than is generally presumed. On the contrary, within its own range, its many ranges, it doubtless stimulates and fosters it. On the other hand, one of its incidental
phases has undoubtedly been a wholly cognate intensification
of the spirit of scrutiny in fields which, while not strictly scien-

tific, nevertheless invite inquiry and reward research. And the decline of the creative imagination in literature, in poetry, and in fiction, is, no doubt, more or less distinctly traceable to the consequent unexampled development of the philosophic and critical spirit and its inevitable invasion of the field of creative activity, the field, that is to say, of art. The contemporary artist, if he thinks at all, is compelled to think critically, to philosophize more expressly and specifically than the classic artist was. Consequently, even the creative imagination pure and simple is nowadays more rarely to be encountered than this imagination in combination with critical reflection.

But with Mr. James the case is far simpler. It would be idle to deny to the author of a shelf-full of novels and a thousand or more characters the possession of the creative imagination, however concentrated upon actuality and inspired by experience. Yet it is particularly true of him among the writers of even our own time that his critical faculty is eminently preponderant —that he has, as I say, essentially the critical *temperament*. He has never devoted himself very formally to criticism, never squared his elbows and settled down to the business of it. It has always been somewhat incidental and secondary with him. His essays have been limited to *belles-lettres* in range, and they have rarely been the rounded, complete, and final characterization of the subject from a central point of view. Such as, for example, Arnold's. They have been instead, perhaps, a little agglutinate rather than synthetic, one may say,—not very attentively distributed or organized. But this may very well be because they have more than eschewed pedantry. And certainly they have been felicity itself; each a series of penetrating remarks, an agglomeration of light but telling touches, immensely discriminating, and absolutely free from traditional or temperamental deflection, marked by a taste at once fastidiously academic, and at the same time sensitively impressionable. The two volumes "French Poets and Novelists" and "Partial Portraits" stand at the head of American literary criticism and "Essays in London and Elsewhere" next them. The "Life of Hawthorne" [6] is, as a piece of criticism, altogether unexcelled and for the most part unrivalled in the voluminous English Men of Letters series to which all the eminent English critics have contributed. One may feel that his view of the general is, in this work, too elevated to permit him always correctly to judge the specific—leads him to characterize, for instance, Hawthorne's environment as a handicap to him, whereas it was an opportunity. But to this same broad and academic view, which measures the individual by the standard of the type (and how few there are to whom this standard does not equitably apply!), we owe the most searching thing ever said about Hawthorne: "Man's conscience was his theme, but he saw it in the light of a creative fancy which added out of its own substance an interest, and I may almost say, an importance." [7] The genius itself of criticism is in the application to Tennyson's

> " 'Tis better to have loved and lost
> Than never to have loved at all," [8]

of the epithets "curt" and "reserved" by comparison with Musset's "Letter to Lamartine." The essay on Maupassant [9] is an unsurpassed critical performance. That on Emerson is, besides being subtly critical, of a curiously combined elegance and elevation with a resultant impression of a piece of art at once exquisite and noble. That on Fanny Kemble is a notable piece of sympathetic appreciation, and in places quite in the grand style itself; [10] for instance: "A prouder nature never affronted the long humiliation of life." [11] In "Daniel Deronda: a Conversation," there are more penetrating things said about George Eliot, one is tempted to say, than in all else that has been written about her. [12] And Mr. James's penetration is uniformly based on good sense. It is—perhaps ominously—never fanciful. He writes of Musset and George Sand, of Balzac and Trollope, with a disinterested discrimination absolutely judicial. His fondness for Daudet, for Turgénieff, for Stevenson, is nothing in comparison with his interest in the art they practise, the art of which he is apt to consider all its practitioners somewhat too exclusively merely as its exponents. [13] If he has a passion, it is for the art of fiction itself.

This is the theme, indeed, on which his criticism has centred, and the fact is extremely significant. It is almost exact to say that he has no other. He is actively preoccupied by it, even in the composition of his own fictions, as the Prefaces to the

New York Edition copiously attest. That is what I mean by calling his art theoretic. It carefully, explicitly, with conviction, illustrates his theory. He has an essay expressly devoted to the topic, but he has many in which it is more or less incidentally considered, and the aforesaid Prefaces, taken together, quite constitute a critical cyclopædia of it. In "The Art of Fiction" he says, "It is an incident for a woman to stand up with her hand resting on a table and look out at you in a certain way," and that "the degree of interest" such an incident has "will depend upon the skill of the painter," [14] meaning the author. In his essay on Daudet he says: "The appearance of things is constantly more complicated as the world grows older, and it needs a more and more patient art, a closer notation, to divide it into its parts;" "Life is, immensely, a matter of surface, and if our emotions in general are interesting, the *form* of those emotions has the merit of being the most definite thing about them;" "Putting people into books is what the novelist lives on;" "It is the real —the transmuted real—that he gives us best; the fruit of a process that adds to observation what a kiss adds to a greeting. The joy, the excitement of recognition, are keen, even when the object recognized is dismal." [15]

Each of these sentences—and many more might be cited— is a key to his own fiction. The last is particularly indicative. The joy of recognition is what apparently he aims at exciting in his readers; what certainly he often succeeds in exciting to the exclusion of other emotions, though the kiss he adds to his greeting—to adopt his charming figure—is oftenest, perhaps, an extremely chaste salute. It must be admitted that the pleasure we take in his characters largely depends on whether or no we have encountered them. If we have not, we are sometimes a little at sea as to the source of even his own interest in them, which, though certainly never profoundly personal, is often extremely prolonged. If we have, we experience the delight of the *aficionado* in the virtuosity with which what is already more or less vaguely familiar is unfolded to our recognition. But even in this case the recognition is something quite different from that with which we realize the actuality of a largely imaginative character. We recognize Daisy Miller, for example, differently from Becky Sharp.

For one thing, we are not so anxious to meet her again. I know of nothing that attests so plainly the preponderance of virtuosity in Mr. James's art as the indisposition of his readers to re-read his books. This would not be so true if this element of his work frankly appeared. If he himself accepted it as such, he would make more of it in the traditional way, give it more form, express it more attentively, harmonize its character and statement more explicitly. There is no difficulty in re-reading Anatole France. But Mr. James's virtuosity is not a matter of treatment, of expression, of "process," as he would say. It is an integral part of the very fabric of his conception. It is engaged and involved in the substance of his works. The substance suffers accordingly. Instead of "a closer and more intimate correspondence with life," the result of his critical theorizing about the what and the how of fiction is a confusion of life and art, which are normally as distinct as subject and statement. Virtuosity of technic is legitimate enough, but virtuosity of vision is quite another thing. And it is to this that Mr. James's study and practice of the art for which he has quite as much of a passion as a *penchant* have finally brought him. "The Sacred Fount," "The Turn of the Screw," are marked instances of it. But all the later books show the tendency, a tendency all the more marked for the virility and elevation with which it is accompanied, and perhaps inevitable in the product of an overmastering critical faculty exercised in philosophizing about, even in the process of practising, an eminently constructive art.

IV

When we predicate elusiveness of Mr. James's fiction we mean much more than that his meaning is occasionally obscure. We mean that he himself always eludes us. The completeness with which he does so, it is perhaps possible to consider the measure of his success. The famous theory that prescribes disinterestedness in art may be invoked in favor of this view. Every one is familiar with this theory, so brilliantly expounded by Taine, so cordially approved by Maupassant, so favorably viewed by Mr. James himself. Any one to whom Aristotle's dictum that virtue resides in a mean seems especially applicable to art theories, must find it difficult to accept this prescription even in theory. Even in theory it seems possible to have too little as well as too much of the artist himself in any work of art. The presence of the personality of the artist, indeed, may be called the constituting element of a work of art. It is even the element that makes one scientific demonstration what the scientists themselves call more "beautiful" than another. But in practice one may surely say that in some instances or on some occasions we do not feel the artist enough in his work. Just as on others we are altogether too conscious of him.

It is the latter difficulty that has been the more frequent in fiction up to the present age, perhaps, and in English fiction perhaps up to the present day. And very likely it is this circumstance that has led to the generalization, and the present popularity of the generalization, which insists on the attitude of disinterested curiosity as the only properly artistic attitude. Even in criticism, so much had been endured from the other attitude, Arnold—whose practice, to be sure, was quite different—observed that the great art was "to get oneself out of the way and let humanity judge." [16] We have had so much partisanship that we have proscribed personality.

Disinterested curiosity is, however, itself a very personal matter. Carried to the extent to which it is carried by Mr. James, at least, it becomes very sensible, a very appreciable element of a work of art. It is forced upon one's notice as much as an aggressive and intrusive personal element could be. To say that if you set the pieces of a work of art in a certain relative position they will automatically, as it were, generate the effect to be produced is to be tremendously sanguine of their intrinsic interest and force. Even then the artist's presence is only minimized, not excluded, one may logically observe; the pieces must be set together in a certain way, and this way will depend on the idiosyncrasy of the artist and not upon the inherent affinity of the pieces. They may have a law of combination, but to prepare them for its operation the law must be perceived by the artist as a force to illustrate rather than merely to "notate," if the result is to have an artistic rather than a scientific interest. As Mr. James himself has aptly said, "Art is merely a point of view, and genius mainly a way of looking at things." And specifically as to fiction M. Bourget reports him as agreeing with him that the truest definition of a novel is "a personal view of life." How is the "point of view," above all the "personal" point of view, to be perceived, if the artist himself eludes us completely? What is it we are looking at—the phenomena he is recording, or his view of the phenomena? But the phenomena should of themselves show his view, it may be contended. If they do, there is nothing to be said. The question at bottom is, do they?

The old practice gave us the point of view by stating it; nor could its statement even then always be called an artistic intrusion, a false note, a disillusion. It was not always imposed on the phenomena by main strength. When Thackeray was reproached with marrying Henry Esmond to Lady Castlewood, he replied, "I didn't do it; they did it themselves." [17] Some such artistic rectitude as that, recognizing the law of his own creations, is certainly to be required of the artist. But if his devotion is so thoroughgoing as to involve complete self-effacement, the practical result will be the disappearance, or at least the obscuration, of his point of view. That, I think, is the peril which Mr. James's theory and practice of art have not sufficiently recognized. Disinterested curiosity may have much of the value that has been claimed for it. It may have been too much neglected in the past. And to point out its logical self-contradiction as an absolute prescription may be conceded to savor of hair-splitting. It is, nevertheless, only valuable as a means, as an agent. When it is worked so hard as itself to become a part of the effect, its value ceases. And in Mr. James's later work what we get, what we see, what impresses us, is not the point of view, it is his own disinterested curiosity. It counts as part, as a main part, of the spectacle he provides for us. We see him busily getting out of the way, visibly withdrawing behind the screen of his story, illustrating his theory by palpably withholding from us the expected, the needful, exposition and explanation, making of his work, in fine, a kind of elaborate and complicated fortification between us and his personality.

This latter indeed he may be said to have rendered nearly proof against all attack by a device of which he has latterly made systematic use and which may be described as passing the story to the reader through the mind of one of the personages of it, thus obliterating all traces of its origin. He is thoroughly in love with this idea and nothing could more sharply attest his devotion to artistic theory than his advocacy and his practice of what in his Preface to "The Golden Bowl" he terms "the still marked inveteracy of a certain indirect and oblique view of my presented action." This oblique view is obtained, he continues, by dealing with his subject-matter "through the opportunity and the sensibility of some more or less detached, some not strictly involved, though thoroughly interested and intelligent, witness or reporter." So that the story appears "not as my own impersonal account of the affair in hand, but as my account of somebody's impression of it—the terms of this person's access to it and estimate of it contributing thus by some fine little law to intensification of interest." [18] Even as a matter of theory, one would say, this "fine little law" could only operate to intensify interest in readers who preferred the "triturate" to the "mother tincture." For even the element of how the action strikes one of the participants must be feebler than that of how it strikes not only its own author, but the author of the participant himself. There is, to be sure, a new element of interest added, but a larger one being in this very process subtracted, the net result is less interest.

And I think it works out in this way, too, in the last three novels, which are certainly wonderful and truly monumental instances of extraordinary and original literary capacity. In "The Golden Bowl" I, at least, am sensible of the presence of this artificial *âme damné* of the author as an obstruction. Why should we not know what happened except as he or she could imperfectly ascertain it, since what we wish to discover is not how it all strikes him or her, but how it strikes us. In "The Ambassadors" the alembication of the story in the crucible of the real hero's mind is a miracle of systematic art, but its result is considerably to obscure and greatly to enfeeble the story itself by concentrating the interest on this personage, who after we get over thinking of him as an obstructionist monopolizes our attention. He certainly rewards it and is indubitably one of Mr. James's most sympathetic successes. But this success is distinctly not achieved through—it is distinctly postponed by—his indirect portrayal in illustration of the artistic theory that conceives him as augmenting the interest of what he comes completely to overshadow, and as an expedient for incidentally securing the inviolability of the author's own personality.

One notable effect of this detachment in the novelist is that his characters do not seem to be *his* characters. Being the results of his observation, the fruit of his experiences, they do not count as his creations. We meet Mr. James's in life,—or we do not meet them,—as it happens; but they do not figure importantly for us in the world of art. American travellers who drift about Europe —doubtless American residents of London—encounter their counterparts from time to time, and note with a pleasure that is always more acute than permanent how cleverly, how searchingly, Mr. James has caught an individual or fixed a type. Necessarily, however, a museum thus collected has rather an anthropological than an artistic interest. The novelist's personages are not sufficiently unified by his own *penchant*, preference, personality, to constitute a society of varied individuals viewed and portrayed from one definite and particular point of view—as the characters of the great novelists do. There is not enough of their creator in them to constitute them a particular society. The society is simply differentiated by the variety and circumscribed by the limits of Mr. James's experience (and, of course, its suggestions to an extremely sensitive and speculative mind); it is not coördinated, and, as it were, organized into an ideal correlation of the actual world as conceived by a novelist of imagination, —imagination not only such as Thackeray's and George Eliot's, but such as Trollope's, even.

V

It is, however, not precise enough to say that Mr. James's mind is essentially critical, and that therefore his attitude is essentially detached. There are two sufficiently distinct varieties of the critical mind, the philosophical and the scientific. Mr. James's is the latter. And when that portion of literature which includes the works of the imagination is conceived as a criticism of life, it is so conceived in virtue of its illustrating the former—the philosophical spirit. So far as fiction is a criticism of life, it is so because it exhibits a philosophy of life, in general or in some particular. It is far more the scientific habit of viewing life and its phenomena that Mr. James illustrates. His characteristic attitude is that of scrutiny. His inspiration is curiosity. Certainly to affirm of so mature, so thoughtful, and so penetratingly observant a writer, that he has no philosophy of life would, aside from its impertinence, be quite unwarrantable. It is impossible not to feel in his fiction that he has made his own synthesis of "all this unintelligible world." [19] However impersonal and objective his art, it cannot conceal this. It is enough to be felt to give weight to his utterances, to furnish credentials for the larger correspondences and comparisons of his pictures to their moral analogies in life, to add authoritativeness to his expositions, and exorcise suspicion of their ephemeralness and superficiality. What I mean is that even in such a work as "The Sacred Fount" is to be discerned the man who has reflected on the traits and currents of existence, on their character and their implications, as well as the writer who notes the phenomena, without correlating them through the principles, of human life.

But what this philosophy is, it is idle to speculate. It is doubtless profound enough, and though one does not argue introspection of Mr. James's temperament,—unless, indeed, his work betray an effort to escape it, as the nuisance it may easily become, —he could doubtless sketch it for us if inclined, and very eloquently and even elaborately draw out for us its principles and positions. But he has no interest whatever in doing so—no interest in giving us even a hint of it. One may infer that taste plays a large part in it, the taste that some philosophers have made the foundation and standard of morals,—the taste, perhaps, that prevents him from disclosing it. He has the air of assuming its universality, as if, indeed, it were a matter of breeding, a mere preference for "the best" in life as in art, a system, in a word, whose sanctions are instinctive, and so not strongly enough or consciously enough felt to call for emphasis or exposition. No manifestation or quality or incarnation of "the best" evokes his enthusiasm. That it "may prevail" [20] is the youngest of his cares. His philosophy appears in the penumbra of his performance as a cultivated indifference, or at most a subconscious basis of moral fastidiousness on which the superstructure that monopolizes his interest is erected.

There are two sufficiently obvious results. In the first place, his work has less importance as literature, because it has significance only as art. In the next place, his individuality being as philosophically obscure as it is artistically detached, his books do not count as expressional variants of it, and are no more unified than their characters are. If they were pervaded by, or even tinctured with, some general philosophic character, they would count in the mass for far more,—his *œuvre*, as the French say, would have more relief, his position in literature would be better defined and more important. As it is, for the lack of some unifying philosophy, each one is an independent illustration of some particular exercise of his talent, and his personality is dissipated by being thus disseminated.

What is it to have a philosophy of life? In any sense in which it may be legitimately required of the artist, even of the artist who deals expressly with life,—of the poet, the dramatist, or the writer of fiction,—to have a philosophy of life certainly does not demand the possession of a body of doctrine "based on interdependent, subordinate, and coherent principles," as has been prescribed by pedantry for criticism. It is simply to be profoundly impressed by certain truths. These truths need not be recondite, but they must be deeply felt. They need be in no degree original. The writer's originality will have abundant scope in their expression. Goethe, it is true, replied to a perhaps not wholly pedantic criticism of "Wilhelm Meister": "I should think a rich, manifold life brought close to our eyes would be enough in itself without any express tendency." [21] And Goethe is probably the greatest example of the artist and the philosopher combined. This observation, however, is confined to a single work; it is impossible to think of the author of "Wilhelm Meister" as the author only of it and of works of like aim and scope. And furthermore, the life which Mr. James's books bring close to our eyes, though manifold, is not rich. It is remarkably multifarious, but "rich" is precisely the last epithet that could properly be applied to it.

It is, nevertheless, the result of observation of the most highly developed material, and if it lack vitality, it is not because it is commonplace or rudimentary. The converse is so pointedly the case as to constitute Mr. James's chief excellence. It has been said of him that he has not sounded the depths, but "charted the shallows" of life. But to say this is quite to miss the point about him. Occupy himself with the shallows he certainly often does, though quite without any attempt to chart them, any attempt at completeness. It is evident that he is not concerned to show them *as* shallows, with the inference that they compose a far larger part of life than is apprehended by current mechanical optimism. He does not deal with them in any such philosophical spirit. His scientific curiosity does not distinguish between the phenomena, all of which are inexhaustibly interesting to him. Except certain coarsenesses, which probably seem to him almost pathologic, or at any rate too ordinary and commonplace for treatment, nothing is to him, as I have said, too insignificant to be interesting, considered as material for artistic treatment. The treatment is to dignify the theme always. And in this attitude no one can fail to see, if not a deeper interest in art than in life, at least an interest in life so impartial and inclusive as to approach aridity so far as feeling is concerned. To take an interest in making interesting what is in itself perfectly colorless is, one must admit, almost to avow a fondness for the *tour de force* dear to the dilettante. Still it would be misleading to insist on this, because Mr. James's intention is, on the whole, to indicate the significance of the apparently trifling, and not to protest that an artistic effect can be got out of next to nothing. It betrays the interest of the naturalist asseverating that nothing is really trifling, since it exists.

It is easy to lose one's way in endeavoring to follow the clue of Mr. James's preoccupation, but with due attention I think it may be done. And his interest in making interesting the pose and gesture of a lady standing by a table, let me recapitulate, is not, or is only a little, to produce an artistic effect with a minimum of means; nor is it to show that of such trifles human life is largely composed; it is to show that in life itself such things are interesting not only because everything is, but also because, though slight, they are subtle and certain indications of the *character* to which they belong. In this way he can find something recondite in what is superficially very simple. And I should say that it is, in a word, to the pursuit of the recondite in life that he has come more and more to consecrate his extraordinary powers. He sees it in everything, in the simple as well as in the complicated, in the shallows as well as in the depths. That is all one can truthfully say, perhaps, though of course in seeking it in the familiar and the commonplace it is difficult to avoid the semblance of mystification.

The pursuit of the recondite, however, is quite inconsistent with much dwelling on the meaning of life as a whole. And it is owing to his taking this latter so much for granted as so largely to exclude it from his fiction, that the life which Mr. James "brings close" to us should lack the "richness" that Goethe claimed for "Wilhelm Meister." If he conceived the shallows *as* shallows and the depths *as* depths, he could hardly avoid taking a less arid view of them, and the astonishing variety of the phenomena that entertain and even absorb him would be grouped in some synthetic way around centres of coördinating feeling, instead of unrolled like a panorama of trifles hitherto unconsidered and tragedies hitherto unsuspected—exhibited like a naturalist's collection made in a country accessible to all, but heretofore unvisited by the scientist with the seeing eye.

Hence, I think, the lack of large vitality in his books, of a sensibly noble and moving effect. The search for the recondite involves the absence of direct dealing with the elemental. The passions are perforce minimized, from being treated in their differentiation rather than in their universality, as well as from being so swamped in minutiæ as largely to lose their energy. His books are not moral theses, but psychological themes, studies not of forces, but of manifestations. The latter are related as cause and effect, perhaps, but not combined in far-reaching suggestiveness. The theme has weight at times, morally considered, but it is not rendered typical, as in George Eliot, for example. It is never either ominous or reassuring. It is never brought close, in Goethe's words, to the reader. It makes him reflect, but speculatively; reason, but academically. It is an unfolding, a laying bare, but not a putting together. The imagination to which it is due is too tinctured with curiosity to be truly constructive. It has the disadvantage of never taking possession of the theme and conducting it masterfully. It is not *a priori* enough. It is held in the leash of observation and fettered by its voluntary submission to the material, to exhibit rather than to arrange which is its specific ambition. The work as a whole is thus necessarily coldly conceived. The heat is in the narration of detail. And thus the reader is impressed far more by the detail than by either the grand construction or by the general design. Above all, the characters, the portraiture of human nature, upon which the vitality of fiction depends, suffer from the recondite quality, which wars with the elemental and thus tends to eliminate the typical, the representative, which constitutes the basis of both effective illusion and significant truth. But of course all that makes types interesting is the possession of a philosophy of life. They imply classification, which is the last thing to be looked for in the *espièglerie* of the most precocious conceivable chiel among us merely occupied in taking notes.

VI

After all, the supreme test of a novelist's abiding interest is the humanity of his characters. This is certainly true of the drama. The play is not the thing without Hamlet. But as to the novel Mr. James would doubtless insist that the characters be enveloped and exhibited in an illusion of life as a distinct though not of course independent factor of the picture—a palpable general medium in which the figures exist and move. This, indeed, I take it, is his view of the peculiar province, the distinctive advantage, of the novel over other varieties of literary representation. The difficulty with this is not in the idea, but in its execution. Executed in conscious illustration of its importance the medium is apt to minimize the figures. We exchange "The School of Athens" for "The Departure for Cythera," Titian's "Entombment" for an interior by De Hooghe.[22] On the other hand, if the figures are fine the scene is extremely likely to take care of itself. Mr. James, for instance, professes a preference for "The House of the Seven Gables" over the other romances of Hawthorne because it seems to him more of a novel, because he hears more of the "vague hum" of life in it than in the other novels,— and to find or search for the hum of life [23] in Hawthorne is to have a sharp sense for it. "The House of the Seven Gables" is, however, if not the least characteristic of Hawthorne's larger productions, at least that in which the characters have the slenderest interest, the most shadowy outlines. They do not compare with those of "The Scarlet Letter." Mr. James also notes the general absence of types in Hawthorne's books, and they certainly fail in effectiveness for this reason as well as for containing so little of the hum of life. The same might be said of the personages of later and far less romantic writers. The type in fiction has become a little old-fashioned—at least the labelled and easily recognized type has. It is relegated to the stage, where, apparently, it will continue, from the limitations of the histrionic art, to be a necessity. In the novel it has largely succumbed to the conquering force of psychology, which in creating an individual and to that end emphasizing his idiosyncrasies has, almost proportionally, robbed him of his typical interest. And this is a loss for which absolutely nothing can atone in the work of the realistic novelist whose theme is actual life. It is impossible to be deeply interested in something too idiosyncratic for identification.

The list of Mr. James's novels is a long one, and his short stories are very numerous; and among them all there is not one with a perfunctory or desultory inspiration. Why is it that they in no sense constitute a *comédie humaine?* They are very populous; why is it that the characters that people them have so little relief? Taken together they constitute the least successful element of his fiction. Partly this is because, as I say, they possess so little typical quality. But why also do they possess so little personal interest? They have, seemingly, astonishingly little, even for their creator. So far from knowing the sound of their voices, as Thackeray said of his,[24] he is apparently less preoccupied with them than about the situation—the "predicament," he would aptly say—in which he places them. Apparently he is chiefly concerned with what they are to do when confronted with the complications his ingenuity devises for them,—how they are to "pull it off." These complications are sometimes very slight, in order to show, or at least showing, what trifles control destinies; sometimes they are very grave, and exhibit the conflict of the soul with warring desires and distracting perplexities. And they are never commonplace—any more than the characters themselves, each one of which is intimately observed and thoroughly respected as an individuality. But their situation rather than themselves is what constitutes the claim, the *raison d'être*, of the book in which they figure. The interest in the book, accordingly, becomes analogous to that of a game in which the outcome rather than the pieces monopolizes the attention. It cannot be said that the pieces are not attentively described,—some of them, indeed, are very artistically and even beautifully carved,—but it is the moves that count most of all. Will Densher [25] give a plausible solution to the recondite problem of how to combine the qualities of a cad and of a gentleman? Will Maisie decide for or against Sir Claude? What decision will Sir Claude himself make? Has Vanderbank ideality enough to marry Nanda? Will Chad Newsome go back to Woollett? [26] The game is very well, often exquisitely, played; and the result, which, nevertheless, from all we know of the characters, we can rarely foresee, wears—when we argue it out in retrospect as the author clearly has done in advance—the proper artistic aspect of a foregone conclusion. Mr. James rarely seems to impose it himself; except on the few occasions when, as in "The Princess Casamassima" or "The Other House," he deals in melodrama, in which he almost never succeeds in being convincing, his rectitude is so strong a reliance as to exclude all impression of perversity or wilfulness and convey the agreeable sense of sufficiently fatalistic predestination. Meantime you find out about the characters from the result. Since it has turned out in this way, they must have been such and such persons. In other words, they have not been characterized very vividly, have not been presented very completely as human beings.

At least they do not people one's memory, I think, as the personages of many inferior artists do. When one thinks of the number of characters that Mr. James has created, each, as I have said, carefully individualized, and none of them replicas,—an amazing world they certainly compose in their originality and variety,—it is odd what an effort it is to recall even their names. The immortal Daisy Miller, the sensitive and highly organized Ralph Touchett,[27] the robust and thoroughly national Christopher Newman, the gentle Miss Pynsent,[28] and a number of others that do remain in one's memory, mainly belong to the earlier novels and form but a small proportion of the great number of their author's creations. Different readers, however, would no doubt answer this rather crude test differently, and in any case it is not because they fail in precision that Mr. James's personages lose distinctness as their story, like all stories, fades from the recollection. They have a sharp enough outline, but they are not completely enough characterized.

Why? Why is it that when the American heroine of one of his stories, beautifully elaborated in detail, a perfect specimen of Dutch *intarsia,* kills herself because her English husband publishes a savage book about her country, we find ourselves perfectly unprepared for this *dénouement?* Why is it that with all the pains expended on the portrait of the extraordinary Mrs. Headway of "The Siege of London," we never quite get *his* point of view, but are kept considering the social duty of the prig who passes his valuable time in observing her attempts at rehabilitation and—no doubt most justly—exposes her in the end? There is nothing to complain of in the result, the problem is worked out satisfactorily enough, but Mrs. Headway herself does not count for us, does not hang together, in the way in which Augier's Aventurière does, or even Dumas's Baronne d'Ange.[29] It would be difficult, for example, for this reason, to make a play of "The Siege of London."

The answer to this query, the explanation of this incompleteness of characterization in Mr. James's nevertheless very precise personages, consists, I think, in the fact that he rather pointedly neglects the province of the heart. This has been from the first the natural peril of the psychological novelist, the neglect of what in the Scripture view constitutes "the whole man," just as the neglect of the mind—which discriminates and defines personalities once constituted—was the defect of the psychological novelist's predecessor. But for Mr. James this peril has manifestly no terrors. The province of the heart seems to him, perhaps, so much to be taken for granted as to be on the whole rather negligible, so far as romantic exploitation is concerned.

Incidentally, one may ask, if all the finest things in the world are to be assumed, what is there left for exploitation? Matter for curiosity mainly—the curiosity which in Mr. James is so sharp and so fruitful. The realm of the affections is that which—*ex vi termini,* one may say—most engages and attaches. Are we to be interested in fiction without liking it? And are we to savor art without experiencing emotion? The fact that few reread Mr. James means that his form, however adequate and effective, is not in itself agreeable. But it means still more that his "content" is not attaching. When Lockhart once made some remark to Scott about poets and novelists looking at life as mere material for art, the "veteran Chief of Letters" observed: "I fear you have some very young ideas in your head. We shall never learn to feel and respect our real calling, unless we have taught ourselves to consider everything as moonshine compared with the education of the heart." [30] Is it possible that Mr. James's controlling idea is a "young one"? Is his undoubted originality, after all, the exploitation of what seemed to so wise a practitioner as Scott, "moonshine"? That would account, perhaps, for the pallid light that often fills his canvas when his characters are grouped in a scene where "the human heart"—insight into which used to be deemed the standard of the novelist's excellence—has a part of any prominence to play. The voluntary abandonment by the novelist of such a field of interest as the province of the heart is witness, at all events, of an asceticism whose compensations ought in prudence to be thoroughly assured. Implied, understood—this domain! Very well, one may reply, but what a field of universal interest you neglect, what a rigorously puritanic sacrifice you make!

Thus to neglect the general field which the historic poets and romancers have so fruitfully cultivated results, however, in only a negative disadvantage, it may be contended, and Mr. James's psychology may be thought by many readers a fair compensation. It is certainly prodigiously well done. A writer with nothing more and nothing better to his credit than the group of stories assembled under the title "The Better Sort" [31] has an indisputable claim to be considered a master, whatever one may think of the tenuity of his themes and the disproportionate attentiveness of their treatment. "It is *proprement dit*, but it is pale," he makes a suppositious Frenchman say of his romance, in his clever and suggestive "The Point of View"; [32] and he frankly records his failure to interest Turgénieff in the fictions he used to send him from time to time.[33] All the same, a new *genre* is a new *genre*, and as such it is idle to belittle Mr. James's, as readers too dull to seize its qualities sometimes impertinently and impatiently do. But specifically and positively a novelist's neglect of the province of the heart involves the disadvantage of necessarily incomplete portraiture.

A picture of human life without reference to the passions, the depiction of human character minus this preponderating constituent element of it, cannot but be limited and defective. The view that half-consciously regards the passions as either titanic or vulgar, and therefore only pertinent as artistic material to either tragedy or journalism, is a curiously superficial one. The most controlled and systematized life, provided it illustrate any ideality, is inspired by them as fully as the least directed and most irregular. The diminution of demonstrativeness under the influence of civilization is no measure of the diminution of feeling; and even if we feel less than our forefathers, our feeling is still the dominant element in us. Every one's consciousness attests this, that of the ascetic as well as that of the epicurean, that of the patrician and the Brahmin as well as that of the peasant and the clown. Whether the drama of human life is of the soul or of the senses, it is equally real, universal, and the resultant of the passions. To assume that the modern man, whatever the degree of his complicated differentiation, is any more destitute of them than his autochthonous ancestor, is to leave out of consideration the controlling constituent of his nature and the mainspring of his action. All of these personages that people Mr. James's extraordinarily varied world must have them, and the circumstance that he rarely, if ever, tells us what they are, makes us feel our acquaintance with his personages to be partial and superficial. At times we can infer them, it is true. But every art, certainly not excepting the novelist's, needs all the aid it can get to make itself effective, and reliance on inference instead of statement results here in a very shadowy kind of substance.

Is it because of a certain coolness in Mr. James's own temperament that his report of human nature is thus incomplete? Does he make us weep—or laugh—so little because he is so unmoved himself, because he illustrates so imperturbably and fastidiously the converse of the Horatian maxim? [34] Candidly speaking, perhaps we have no business to inquire. Whether it is due to his theory or to the temperament responsible for his theory, perhaps it is both pertinent and proper to rest in the indisputable fact that he does leave us unmoved. After all, the main question is, does the fact have for us the compensations that evidently it has for him? Say that he deals so little with the emotions because preoccupation with them deflects and distracts from the business of presenting in all its force of singularization and relief, at whatever cost of completeness, the truths and traits of human nature that most interest him, that interest him so intensely. Say even, in other words, that to feel an emotional interest in his personages is for an author to incur the risk of a partiality inconsistent with artistic rectitude. Certainly it is impossible to be blind to this controlling rectitude in Mr. James, impossible to avoid recognizing—however easy we may suspect nature has made it for him—his unalterable fidelity to his main purpose in his fictions, which is to clothe and depict the idea he wishes to illustrate, whatever becomes of his people in the process. Say, too, that—though sometimes, in consequence, these remain very much on the hither side of realization, and though they never take possession of the scene themselves and tell or enact their own story, without, at any rate, our feeling that they rely largely on the subtlest of prompters—they nevertheless always strictly subserve the larger design of their creator. Grant all this. The salient fact remains that their creator is too much concerned with the laws of his universe, apparently, to assign them other than vicarious functions, or to take other than what is called an "intellectual" interest in them.

And this is an interest extremely difficult for an author to make his readers share. The reader is much more readily interested through his sympathies, and cannot be relied upon to attach to phenomena which exclude these the same importance as the writer who is exploiting them. He will readily respond to the author who illustrates "What a piece of work is man!" [35] and at the same time imperfectly echo the enthusiasm of the artist who exclaims, "How beautiful a thing is this perspective!" Mr. James's enthusiasm, one may fancifully say, is for the perspective rather than for the substance of human nature, and even this, of course, in taking it from him, we are obliged to enjoy at one remove; so that, even supposing our pure curiosity to equal his, we can hardly be counted on to feel the same amount for his report of life as he feels for life itself. We need something of *him* to compensate for the inevitable loss of heat involved in the process of translation. And this he is extremely chary of giving us. What chiefly we perceive is his own curiosity.

Of this, indeed, we get, I think, a surfeit. Without more warmth that he either feels or will suffer himself to exhibit, it is difficult for him to communicate the zest he plainly takes in the particular material he in general exploits. It is too special, too occasional, too recondite, at times certainly too trivial, to stand on its own merits, aided merely by extraordinary but wholly unemotional cleverness of presentation. In fact, I think one may excusably go so far as to confess a certain antipathy to the degree in which the author exhibits this curiosity. Scrutiny so searching quite excludes sympathy. "In the Cage," for instance, is a wonderful study, but so persistent and penetrating as to appear positively pitiless. How many years ago was it that Arnold complained that curiosity, which had a good sense in French, had a bad one in English? [36] For Mr. James it is not only not a defect, and not merely a quality, but a cardinal virtue. Balzac was certainly not a sentimentalist, yet Taine ascribes what he considers the superiority of Valérie Marneffe to Rebecca Sharp to the fact that Balzac "aime sa Valérie." [37] Would it ever occur to any one to suspect that Mr. James "loved" any of his characters? Ralph Touchett, perhaps; perhaps also Mr. Lewis Lambert Strether; yes, and Miss Pynsent; but surely the extraordinary attention that almost all his later personages receive from him is not an affectionate interest, and, as I say, I think the result is less completeness of presentment, less vigor of portraiture.

It is not unlikely that his frequent practice of identifying himself with one of his characters by making him narrate the tale is in part responsible for this impression of extreme coolness in the narrator that we get from the book and unconsciously refer to the author. There are a number of his stories in which the fictitious narrator exhibits his frigid curiosity with a single-mindedness that awakens discomfort as positive as that Mr. James himself complains of in reading the closing scenes of "The Newcomes." One winces at the scrutiny of defenceless personages practised by the narrators of "The Pension Beaurepas,"—a delightful sketch; of "Four Meetings,"—a masterpiece of satire and of pathos; of a dozen other tales in which some enthusiastic naturalist studies his spitted specimens. The most conspicuous instance of this is undoubtedly "The Sacred Fount," which for this reason is an unpleasant as well as a mystifying book. The amount

of prying, eavesdropping, "snooping," in that exasperating performance is prodigious, and the unconsciousness of indiscretion
combined with its excess gives one a very uncomfortable feeling,
—a feeling, too, whose discomfort is aggravated by the insipidity
of the fanciful phenomena which evoke in the narrator such a
disproportionate interest. Perhaps this nosing curiosity is itself a
trait of the "week-end" in England, and designed to be pilloried
as such. No one can know. But in this case one may wish the point
had been made plainer, even in a book where it is apparently the
author's intention to make everything obscure.

There are, moreover, many stories by Mr. James in which this
pathologic curiosity is manifested, not by the narrator,—for
whom there is a technical excuse,—but by one or more of the
characters. "The Siege of London" is an example. From this story
one might infer that the close observation of a squirming and suffering though doubtless highly reprehensible woman could really
occupy the leisure of a scrupulous gentleman. Is it true that curiosity is a "passion" of our attenuated modern life,—curiosity of
this kind, I mean; the curiosity that feeds on the conduct and
motives of one's fellows in whom one feels no other interest? It
is at all events true that it is the one "passion" celebrated with
any ample cordiality by Mr. James, though, as I say, to inquire
if he shares it be to inquire "too curiously." He himself—whom
nothing escapes that he does not exclude, one is sometimes
tempted to think—has noted the characteristic. I wish I could
put my hand on the passage—I am confident it is in one of his
earlier works—in which he speaks of a certain indiscreet closeness of observation as a disagreeable trait of a certain order of
Frenchman. Literature of course has quite other sanctions than
those of life, but surely no writer of distinction, French or other,
has ever shown this trait in such opulent profusion as it is exhibited in Mr. James's fiction, where the famous watchword, "disinterested curiosity," [38] is carried so far as to count as an element
of the fiction itself, and not merely as a guarantee of the author's
impartiality. It is "disinterested" enough in the sense hitherto intended by the epithet, but in its own exercise it is made to appear
ferociously egoistic. The author is not merely detached; his detachment is enthusiastic. One may say he is ardently frigid. The
result in these instances, I think, is the detachment of his read-

ers; certainly the elimination from the field of interest of those characters and that part of every character which, too fundamental and general to reward mere curiosity, however disinterestedly avid, nevertheless constitute the most real, the most attaching, and the most substantial elements of human life.

VII

It is possibly owing in some degree to his dispassionateness that Mr. James passes popularly for preëminently the novelist of culture. A writer so refined and so detached is inferentially the product of letters as well as of life. Less than with any other would it seem congruous to associate with him the notion of crudity in any of its aspects or degrees, the notion of nonconformity to the canon, recalcitrancy to the received. And certainly he has neglected nothing of the best that has been thought and said in the world so far as his own art is concerned. He does not look at life through books; far from it. But with the books that illustrate the problem of how art should look at life he is thoroughly familiar. On the art and in the province of latter-day fiction, at any rate, there is certainly nothing he has not read—and perfectly assimilated. No writer in any department of literature can more distinctly leave the impression of acquaintance with the modern classics of his chosen field in all languages, and with all the commentaries on them. There is, besides, in his moral attitude, his turn of phrase, his absence of emphasis, his esoteric diction, his carelessness of communication, even, his air of *noblesse oblige,* his patrician fastidiousness and manifest contentment with justification by his own standards, in the wide range of his exclusions, and—above all—in his preference for dealing with high differentiation instead of the elementary and universal,—in all this there is clearly manifest the aristocratic conformity to the conclusions of culture and of the good taste which culture can alone—even if only—supply.

There is, however, this peculiarity about his culture, considered as an element of his equipment. It is very far from being with him, as it is sometimes assumed to be in the case of the literary or other artist, a handicap on his energy, his originality—an emasculating rather than an invigorating force. It has, on the contrary, been a stimulant as well as a guiding agent in his activity. But its singularity consists in the circumstance that, though unmistakably culture, it is culture of a highly specialized kind. Prominent as Mr. James's culture is, in a word, it is precisely the lack of background, the background that it is eminently the province of culture to supply, that is the conspicuous lack in his work considered as a whole, considered with reference to its permanent appeal, considered, in brief, as a contribution to literature. Is there any other writer whose work, taken in the mass, is so considerable and marked by such extreme cleverness, so much insight, and so much real power, which is also so extremely dependent upon its own qualities and character and so little upon its relations and correspondences? It is so altogether of the present time, of the moment, that it seems almost an analogue of the current instantaneous photography. Behind it one feels the writer interested, not in Molière but in Daudet, not in Fielding but in Trollope, not in Dante but in Théophile Gautier. He writes about "Le Capitaine Fracasse," not about "Don Quixote," about the "Comédie Humaine," not about the world of Shakespeare. This is treading on delicate ground, and where the end of culture is in any wise so conspicuously achieved as it is in Mr. James, it is perhaps impertinent to inquire as to his use of the means. But where a writer's work is so voluminous as his, as well as of such a high order, it is in the interest of definition to inquire why his evident culture betrays so little evidence of interest in the classics of literature or the course of history. It is very likely true that for the writer of modern fiction an acquaintance with "Salammbô" is of more instant pertinence than saturation with the "Divine Comedy," that such an essay as Mr. James's on Maupassant—a very nearly perfect masterpiece—is more apposite than Lowell's —rather inadequate—paper on "Don Quixote." [39] I only point out that from the point of view of culture, his preoccupation with Du Maurier and Reinhart and Abbey and Stevenson and Miss Woolson indicates culture of an unusually contemporary kind. In mere point of time Mme. de Sabran is as far back as I remember his going.[40] How exquisite his treatment of these more or less current themes has occasionally been I do not need to say, or repeat. If in the last analysis there is a tincture of "journalism" in this, it is journalism of a very high class, and perhaps anything nowadays without a trace of journalism is justly to be suspected of pedantry and pretension, qualities absolutely foreign to Mr. James's genius. They are wholly absent, too, in such "journalism" as his books of travel,—the "Little Tour in France," which is curiously dependent upon "the excellent Mr. Murray" and derives from the "red-book" rather than from the library; and the "Portraits of Places," [41] which, however abounding in penetration and *justesse*,—I recall some remarkable pages about Tintoretto, for example,—is too enamored of the actual to think twice about its origins. But for a literary figure that seems and really is the antipode of some of the prominent and by no means negligible apostles of crudity of the present day, it is plain that his rather exclusive interest in the literature of the present day is a peculiarity worth remark. The man is always more than the special province in which his talent is exercised, and Mr. James's culture is such that one does not associate him with such writers of fiction as Wilkie Collins, say, so much as with Arnold and Lowell and Browning and Tennyson and Thackeray and George Eliot and Bulwer. But beside any one of these, his culture seems quite modern and current in its substance and preoccupations.

It is not, however, merely paradoxical, and therefore noteworthy, that his culture should be at once so conspicuous and so apparently partial. The circumstance is particularly significant because it is particularly disadvantageous to his impressiveness as a writer of fiction. "L'artiste moderne," says Paul Bourget, "lequel se double toujours d'un critique et d'un érudit." [42] The critic is conspicuous enough in Mr. James, but one cannot help thinking that precisely his kind of fiction would be more effective if its lining were more evidently erudite. For example, a writer interested in the "Antigone," and imbued with the spirit of its succession, would naturally and instinctively be less absorbed in what Maisie knew,—to mention what is certainly a very remarkable, but what is also, by the very perfection of its execution, shown to be a fantastic book, except on the supposition that whatever is, is important. Saturation with contemporary *belles-lettres* will no doubt suffice an artist whose talent, like that of Mr. James, is of the first class, for the production of delightful works, but to produce works for the pantheon of the world's masterpieces without a more or less constant—even if subconscious—reference to the figures already on their august pedestals, fringes the chimerical. One could wish the representative American novelist to be less interested in inventing a new game of fiction than in figuring as the "heir of all the ages." [43] For lovers of "the last new book," Mr. James's is no doubt the most important. But why should it not be an "event"—such as one of Thackeray's or George Eliot's used to be? It is certainly not because his talent is inferior; is it because his culture is limited, as well as because, as I have already said, his art is as theoretic as his philosophy of life is obscure?

To take the particular instance of "The Awkward Age," which may perhaps be called Mr. James's technical masterpiece among the later novels. I cannot better explain what I have in mind in speaking of his peculiar kind of culture than by saying that "The Awkward Age" strikes one as a little like Lilliput without Gulliver. One has only to imagine what Swift's picture of that interesting kingdom would be if the figure that lends it its significance were left out of it. Its significance, of course, depends wholly on the sense of contrast, the play of proportion. So does the significance of the corresponding Brobdingnag. And not at all exclusively in an artistic sense, it is to be borne in mind, but in a literary and human one. If the futilities and *niaiseries* of "The Awkward Age," instead of being idealized by the main strength of imputed importance, were depicted from a standpoint perhaps even less artistically detached, but more removed in spirit by knowledge of and interest in the sociology of the human species previous to its latest illustration by a wretched little clique of negligible Londoners, the negligibility of these *dramatis personæ* would be far more forcefully felt. It would constitute a thesis. As it is, the thesis apparently of an extraordinary number of pages is that a girl freely brought up may turn out a better girl than one claustrally reared. Of course this is not really all. There is a corollary—a coda: the former does not get married and the latter does. And there is a still further moral to be drawn by those expert in *nuances* of the kind. But one feels like asking brutally, in the name of literature, if this order of it is worth the lavish expenditure of the best literary talent we have. If it is, there is nothing more to be said. But it can only be so considered by the amateur of novelty, and must seem attenuated from the standpoint of culture.

It is not a matter of realism. Fielding was a realist, if ever there was one. But is it likely that without his classical culture such a realist as Fielding, even, would have depicted figures of such commanding importance and universal interest as those with which his novels are peopled? Can one fancy Gibbon praising with the same elaborate enthusiasm that he expressed for "Tom Jones" the "exquisite picture of human life and manners" [44] provided by "The Awkward Age" or "The Other House,"—supremely clever as is the art of these books and their fellows? Nor is it a question of art. Meredith, for example, is not a realist like Mr. James, but his art constantly suggests that of the younger writer. Yet it differs from Mr. James's not more in its preoccupations— with the fanciful, that is to say, rather than the real—than in its whole attitude, which, in spite of its absence of pedantry and close correspondence to the matter in hand, is obviously, markedly, the attitude of culture, the attitude of not being absorbed by, swamped in, the importance of the matter in hand, but of treating it at least enough at arm's length to avoid exaggerating its importance. He leaves the impression of a certain lack of seriousness. He has the air of the dilettante; which, to my sense, Mr. James never has. But he also leaves the impression, and has the air inseparably connected with what is understood by culture. In art of any kind at the present time, it is well known that culture is not overvalued. It is quite generally imagined that we should gain rather than lose, for instance, by having Raphael without the Church and Rembrandt without the Bible. But the special art of fiction has not yet been emancipated to this implied extent, because the general life of humanity, of which this art is *ex hypothesi* a picture, is felt to have a unity superior in interest and importance to any of its variations.

Too great an interest in the history, as well as in the present status, of mankind, therefore, can hardly be exacted of the creator of a mimic world, I will not say of Mr. James's pretensions, for he makes none, but of his powers, of which in justice too much cannot be exacted. A novelist in whom the historic sense is lacking is, one would say, particularly liable to lack also that sense of proportion which alone can secure the right emphasis and accent in his pictures of contemporary life—if they are to have any reach and compass of significance, if they are to rise very far above the plane of art for art's sake. From the point of view of culture as a factor in a novelist's production, it may be said, surely, that no one knows his own time who knows only it. Any conspectus of the sociology of the present day, in other words, that neglects its aspect as an evolution, neglects also its meaning. The life of the present day can no more be satisfactorily represented and interpreted in isolation in fiction than in history or sociology. To record its facts, even its subtlest and most recondite facts, those that have hitherto been neglected by more cursory observers, without at the same time admeasuring them, in however indirect and unconscious fashion, by reference to previous stages of the evolution, or at least the succession, to which the life of the present day belongs, is, measurably, to lose sight of their meaning, of the reason for recording them. As Buckle said, very acutely, any one who thinks a fact valuable in itself may be a good judge of facts, but cannot be of value.[45] And it is hardly too much to say that this is how Mr. James impresses us in his recent studies of English society, the studies that, taken in the mass, constitute the bulk, as in some respects they do the flower, of his work. He is an excellent judge of the phenomena—the sharp-eyed and penetrating critic for whom, in a sense, perhaps, this extraordinary and extraordinarily inept society has in fancied security unwittingly been waiting. But of their value he seems to be less a judge than an advocate. If his culture included such development of the historic sense as would present to his indirect vision the analogues of other civilizations, other societies, other *milieux*, he could hardly avoid placing as well as fixing his phenomena. And this would, I think, give an altogether different aspect and value to his work.

In illustration, I may refer to a portion—the most interesting, and, I am inclined to think, the most important though not perhaps the most "wonderful" portion—of this work itself. There was a time when Mr. James did things with obvious zest, with a freedom that excluded the notion of the theoretic; when he communicated pleasure by first feeling it himself; when, therefore, there was a strong personal note in what he wrote, and he did not alienate by his aloofness; when, indeed, one could perceive and enjoy a strain of positive gayety in his compositions. Has any reader of his, I wonder, any doubt as to the period I have in mind? I refer to the period of his studies in contemporary sociology, so to speak, the years when the contrast between America and Europe preoccupied him so delightfully. Then he produced "documents" of real value and of striking vitality. He had the field all to himself, and worked it to his own distinct profit and that of his readers. Then he portrayed types and drew out their suggestiveness. His characters were not only real, but representative. He provided material not only for the keenest enjoyment, but for reflection. His scientific curiosity resulted in something eminently worth while, something in which he excelled so notably as virtually to seem, if indeed he was not literally, the originator of a new and most engaging *genre* of romance,—to be, one may say, the Bopp of the comparative method as applied to fiction.

The literature that he produced at this period owes its superiority to his current product in general import and interest, I think, precisely to this factor of culture on which he now places so little reliance. It was inspired and penetrated with the spirit of cosmopolitanism, that is to say, culture in which the contemporary is substituted for the more universal element, and, if it does not quite make up in vividness for what it lacks in breadth, certainly performs the similar inestimable service of providing a standard that establishes the relative value and interest of the material directly dealt with. Out of his familiarity with contemporary society in America, England, France, and Italy, grew a series of novels and tales that were full of vigor, piquancy, truth, and significance. The play of the characters against contrasting backgrounds was most varied and interesting. The contrasts of points of view, of conventions and ideas, of customs and traditions, gave a richness of texture to the web of his fiction which, since it has lacked these, it has disadvantageously lost. His return to the cosmopolitan *motif* in "The Ambassadors" and (measurably) in "The Golden Bowl" is accordingly a welcome one, and would be still more welcome if the development of this *motif* were not now incrusted and obscured with mannerisms of presentation accreted in the pursuit of what no doubt seems to the author a "closer correspondence with life," but what certainly seems to the reader a more restricted order of art,—an art, at any rate, so largely dependent on scrutiny as perforce to dispense with the significance to be expected only of the culture it suggests, but does not illustrate. It is a part of Mr. James's distinction that he gives us so much as to make us wish for more, that he entertains us on so high a plane that we ask to be conducted still higher, and that his penetration reveals to us such wonders in the particular *local*, that we call upon him to show us "the kingdoms of the earth." [46]

VIII

We could readily forego anything that he lacks, however, if he would demolish for us the *chevaux-de-frise* of his later style. In early days his style was eminently clear, and at the same time wholly adequate, but in the course of years it has become an exceedingly complicated vehicle. Its complexity is probably quite voluntary. Indeed, like his whole attitude, it is even theoretic. It images, no doubt, the multifariousness of its substance, of which it follows the *nuances* and subtleties, and with its parentheses and afterthoughts and qualifications, its hints and hesitations, its indirection and innuendo, pursues the devious and haphazard development of the drama of life itself. It is thoroughly alive and sincere. It has mannerisms but no affectations. One gets tired of the frequent recurrence of certain favorite words and locutions, but the author's fondness for them is always genuine. Least of all are they perfunctory, any more than is any other manifestation of Mr. James's intellectual activity. His vocabulary is remarkable, both in range and in intimate felicity; and it is the academic vocabulary, rendered vigorous by accents of raciness now and then, the acme of literary breeding, without, however, a trace of bookish aridity. He is less desultory than almost any writer of anything like his productiveness. His scrupulous care involves often quite needless precautions, as if the reader were watching for a slip,—"like a terrier at a rat-hole," a sufferer from his superfluous concessions once impatiently observed. But his precision involves no strain. His style in general shows no effort, though it ought to be said that, on the other hand, it also shows no restraint. It is tremendously personal in its pointed neglect of conformity to any ideal of what, as style, it should be. It avoids thus most conspicuously the hackneyed traits of rhetorical excellence. And certainly the pursuit of technical perfection may easily be too explicit, too systematic. Correctness is perhaps the stupidest way of achieving artificiality. But a writer of Mr. James's rhetorical fertility, combined with his distinction in the matter of taste, need have no fear of incurring artificiality in deferring to the more elementary requirements of the rhetorical canon.

He has, however, chosen to be an original writer in a way that precludes him from being, as a writer, a great one. Just as his theory of art prevents his more important fiction from being a rounded and synthetic image of life seen from a certain centralizing point of view, and makes of it an essay at conveying the sense and illusion of life by following, instead of focussing, its phenomena, so his theory of style prevents him from creating a texture of expression with any independent interest of its own. The interest of his expression consists solely in its correspondence to the character of what it endeavors to express. So concentrated upon this end is he that he very rarely gives scope to the talent for beautiful and effective expression which occasional lapses from his rigorous practice show him to possess in a distinguished degree. There are entire volumes of his writings that do not contain a sentence like, for example, this from a brief essay on Hawthorne: "His beautiful and light imagination is the wing that on the autumn evening just brushes the dusky pane." [47] Of a writer who has this touch, this capacity, in his equipment, it is justifiable to lament that his theory of art has so largely prevented his exercise of it. The fact that his practice has not atrophied the faculty—clear enough from a rare but perfect exhibition of it from time to time—only increases our regret. We do not ask of Mr. James's fastidiousness the purple patch of poetic prose, any more than we expect from him any kind of mediocrity whatever. But when a writer, who shows us unmistakably now and then that he could give us frequent equivalents of such episodes as the death of Ralph Touchett,[48] rigorously refrains through a long series of admirable books from producing anything of greater extent than a sentence or a paragraph that can be called classic, that has the classic "note," we may, I think, legitimately complain that his theory of art is exasperatingly exacting.

And of what may be called the strategy, in distinction from the tactics, of style he is quite as pointedly negligent. The elements of combination, distribution, climax, the whole larger organization and articulation of literary presentment, are dissembled, if not disdained. Even if it be possible to secure a greater sense of life by eliminating the sense of art in the general treatment of a fiction,—which is certainly carrying the theory of *ars celare artem* very far (the first word in the aphorism having hitherto stood for "art," and the last for "artifice"),[49]—even if in attitude and construction, that is to say, the amount of life in Mr. James's books atones for the absence of the visible, sensible, satisfying element of art as art, it is nevertheless clear that in style as such there is nothing whatever that can atone for the absence of art. Skill is an insufficient substitute; it is science, not art, that is the adaptation of means to ends. And upon skill Mr. James places his whole reliance.

He is, of course, supremely skilful. His invention, for example, which has almost the force and value of the creative imagination, appears in particularly exhaustless variety in the introductions of his short stories. Each one is a study in exordiums, as skilful as Cicero's. And the way in which the narrative proceeds, the characters are introduced, and the incidents succeed one another, is most attentively considered. But no amount of skill and care compensate for the loss of integral interest in the handling, the technic, the style, that is involved in a subordination of style to content so complete as positively to seem designed to flout the traditional convention which makes the interpenetration of the two the ideal. Such an ideal is perhaps a little too obvious for Mr. James, who is as uninterested in "the obvious" as he is unconcerned about "the sublime," of which, according to a time-honored theory, the obvious is a necessary constituent.

The loss of interest involved in obscurity is, to begin with, enormous. Such elaborate care as that of Mr. James should at least secure clearness. But with all his scrupulousness, clearness never seems to be an object of his care. At least, this is true of his later work. In his earlier, his clearness was conspicuous. There are even extremely flat-footed things to be encountered in it now and then —as, for example, his reprehension of the trivial in Hawthorne, the "parochial" in Thoreau.[50] But since his later, his preponderant, and what we must consider his true, manner has been established, no one needs to be reminded that obscurity has been one of its main traits. His concern is to be precise, not to be clear. He follows his thought with the most intimate exactness—no doubt—in its subtile sinuosities, into its complicated connotations, unto its utmost attenuations; but it is often so elusive, so *insaisissable* —by others than himself—that he may perfectly express without in the least communicating it. Yet the very texture of his obscurity is composed of incontestable evidences that he is a master of expression. The reader's pleasure becomes a task, and his task the torture of Tantalus.

It is simply marvellous that such copiousness can be so elliptical. It is usually in greater condensation—such as Emerson's —that we miss the connectives. The fact attests the remarkable fulness of his intellectual operations, but such plenitude imposes the necessity of restraint in direct proportion to the unusual extent and complexity of its material. "Simplification" is a favorite word with Mr. James, but he himself never simplifies for our benefit. Beyond question, he does for his own. He has clearly preliminarily mastered his complicated theme in its centrality; he indisputably sits in the centre of the web in whose fine-spun meshes his readers are entangled. If in reading one of his fictions you are conscious of being in a maze, you know that there is an issue if you are but clever enough to find it. Mr. James gives you no help. He flatters you by assuming that you are sufficiently clever. His work, he seems to say, is done when he has constructed his labyrinth in emulating correspondence with the complexity of his model, life, and at the same time furnished a potentially discoverable clue to it. There are readers who find the clue, it is not to be doubted, and follow it in all its serpentine wanderings, though they seem to do so in virtue of a special sense—the sense, it might be called, of understandingly savoring Mr. James. But its possessors are marked individuals in every one's acquaintance; and it need not be said that they are exceptionally clever people. There are others, the mystically inclined, and therefore perhaps more numerous, who divine the significance that is hidden from the wise and prudent. But to the majority of intelligent and cultivated readers, whose appreciation constitutes fame, the great mass of his later writing is

of a difficulty to conquer which requires an amount of effort
disproportionate to the sense of assured reward.

Are the masterpieces of the future to be written in this fashion?
If they are, they will differ signally from the masterpieces of
the past in the substitution of a highly idiosyncratic *manner* for
the hitherto essential element of *style;* and in consequence they
will require a second reading, not, as heretofore, for the discovery
of "new beauties," or the savoring again of old ones, but to be
understood at all. In which case, one may surmise, they will
have to be very well worth while. It can hardly be hoped that
they will be as well worth while as those of Mr. James, and the
chances are, accordingly, that he will occupy the very nearly
unique niche in the history of fiction—hard by that of Meredith,
perhaps—of being the last as well as the first of his line. There
is no question of its eminence or of his powers. But what chiefly
distinguishes his fiction is the extraordinarily high differentiation
of his material and the complicated treatment that matches it.
His talent, his method, his point of view are extremely personal.
He is too idiosyncratic to have rivals or successors. He has a
host of imitators, it is true; he has, in a way, founded a school,
but as yet certainly this has produced no masterpieces. Has he
himself? If so, they are, at all events, not unmistakably of the
scale and on the plane suggested by his unmistakable powers,—
powers that make it impossible to measure him otherwise than
by the standards of the really great novelists and of the masters
of English prose.

NOTES

COOPER

1. "A Germanic instinct for going steadily close to the ground"—Matthew Arnold, *On The Study of Celtic Literature* (1867), chap. v. But Arnold's discussion is scarcely a eulogy. See *On the Study of Celtic Literature and on Translating Homer* (London, 1893), pp. 88–102, esp. p. 100.

2. "Homo sum; humani nihil a me alienum puto."—Terence, *Heauton Timoroumenos*, I, i, 25.

3. Thomas R. Lounsbury, *James Fenimore Cooper* (Boston, 1882), p. 242.

4. William Makepeace Thackeray, "Nil Nisi Bonum," in *Roundabout Papers*. See the Centenary Biographical Edition of Thackeray's *Works*, 26 vols. (London, 1911), XX, 214.

5. Sir Walter Scott, *Marmion*, VI, 29–30.

6. Presumably a reference to Scott's famous passage: "The Big Bow-wow strain I can do myself like any now going; but the exquisite touch, which renders ordinary commonplace things and characters interesting, from the truth of the description and the sentiment is beyond." Scott's Diary, March 14, 1826. But as the index to Lockhart's *Life of Sir Walter Scott* reveals, Scott paid Miss Austen other compliments. *St. Ronan's Well* (1823) is Scott's solitary novel of contemporary manners. The diary entry may be found in *The Journal of Sir Walter Scott from an Original Manuscript at Abbotsford*, 2 vols. (New York, 1890), I, 155.

7. See Robert Louis Stevenson, "A Gossip on Romance," *Memories and Portraits* (London, 1887).

8. For Waverley's visit see chap. xvii of *Waverley*.

9. By Charles Reade, published in 1860.

10. See the last sentence in *The Bravo*.

11. *La Dame de Monsoreau* (1846) is one of the "Valois Romances" of Alexandre Dumas *père*.

12. Chateaubriand visualizes "wild and lovely material" in many places, but the reference is presumably to his *Atala* (1800), *René* (1807), or, conceivably, *Les Natchez* (1826–27).

13. Edward A. Freeman, *History of the Norman Conquest of England* (Oxford, 1876), V, 825–839 (note W).

14. In *Oroonoko* (1668) Mrs. Aphra Behn depicts a "noble savage," but the story is based on her experiences in Surinam, not in North America. Voltaire, *L'Ingénu* (1767); Chateaubriand, *Atala* and *René*.

15. In 1881 Helen Hunt Jackson published *A Century of Dishonor*, an account of American injustice to the Indian.

16. Massasoit (d. 1601), chief of the Wampanoags, friend of the Pilgrims; Joseph Brant (1742–1807), or Thayendanege, a Mohawk leader; Osceola (1800?–1838), Seminole chieftain; Joseph, or Hinmaton-Yalakit (1840?–1904), Nez Perce chieftain.

17. On Tamenund see chap. xxviii of *The Last of the Mohicans.*

18. Wyandotte appears in the novel of that name (1843); he is the Tuscarora referred to a few lines below. Conanchet appears in *The Wept of Wish-ton-Wish* (1829).

19. George Catlin (1796–1872), famous as a painter of Western Indians.

20. Rivenoak is in *The Deerslayer;* Le Renard Subtil is one of Magua's names in *The Last of the Mohicans.*

21. Chevalier de Bussy is the hero of *La Dame de Monsoreau.*

22. The sentence by Balzac, Brownell found in Lounsbury's *James Fenimore Cooper,* p. 284.

23. Balzac reviewed *The Pathfinder* in *La Revue Parisienne,* July 15, 1840. See *Œuvres Diverses,* ed. Marcel Bouteron and Henri Longnon (Paris, 1940), vol. III.

24. See André Le Breton, *Balzac: L'Homme et l'Œuvre* (Paris, 1905), p. 80.

25. Balzac's letter is quoted in Le Breton, pp. 79–80.

26. Quoted in Le Breton, pp. 80–81.

27. Le Breton, pp. 82–83.

28. On January 12, 1905, Henry James lectured before the Contemporary Club of Philadelphia on "The Lesson of Balzac." See Leon Edel, ed., *The House of Fiction: Essays on the Novel by Henry James* (London, 1957), for a convenient edition of the lecture.

29. The quotation from Sainte-Beuve is from a review of *The Red Rover,* April 16, 1828. See *Premiers Lundis* (Paris, 1882), I, 288–294.

30. Lord Frederick Verisopht appears in Dickens' *Nicholas Nickleby;* Sam Weller is of course in *Pickwick Papers.*

31. Long John Silver, of Stevenson's *Treasure Island* (1883).

32. Dick Swiveller is in Dickens' *The Old Curiosity Shop.*

33. In a letter to Sir William Elford, March 5, 1824. See *Letters of Mary Russell Mitford,* ed. R. Brimley Johnson (London, 1925).

34. Leatherlegs appears in Thackeray's burlesque of Cooper, "The Stars and Stripes," in *Novels by Eminent Hands* (1847). See Thackeray's *Works,* VIII, 93–102.

35. Thackeray, "On a Peal of Bells," *Roundabout Papers,* in *Works,* XX, 267.

36. "trembling Felixes": cf. Acts 24:25.

37. Anthony Hope (Hawkins) published *The Prisoner of Zenda* in 1894. *Prince Otto* (1885) by Stevenson deals likewise with an imaginary kingdom.

38. *Le Capitaine Fracasse* by Théophile Gautier was published in Paris in 1863.

39. *The Three Spaniards* by George Walker, a London bookseller, first appeared in three volumes in 1800.

40. See *The Two Admirals*, chap. i.

41. Nancy and Bill Sikes are in Dickens' *Oliver Twist*.

42. See Lounsbury, pp. 280, 281.

43. See Lounsbury, p. 281.

44. "Ewig Weibliches" comes from the next to last line of Goethe's *Faust*.

45. Probably a reference to Hypatia in the novel of that name by Charles Kingsley, published in 1853.

46. "Faithful are the wounds of a friend." Proverbs 27:6.

47. William P. Trent, *A History of American Literature, 1607–1865* (New York, 1903), pp. 234–249.

48. "J'ai assez veçu pour voir que différence engendre haine"— Stendhal, *Le Rouge et le Noir*, chap. xxvii.

49. Barrett Wendell, *A Literary History of America* (New York, 1900).

50. "A chiel's amang you takin' notes,/ And faith he'll prent it"— Robert Burns, "Captain Grose's Peregrinations through Scotland" (1793).

51. Eliza Cook (1818?–1889), religious sentimentalist, whose *Journal* was published in 1849–1854. She wrote "The Old Arm-Chair" and "O why does the white man follow my path?" among other poems. But the passage was suggested by Matthew Arnold, "Irish Catholicism and British Liberalism," *Mixed Essays* (1879), in *Mixed Essays, Irish Essays and Others* (New York, 1883), pp. 103–104.

HAWTHORNE

1. Brownell apparently quoted from memory. In chap. i of *The Old English Dramatists*, James Russell Lowell wrote: "Compare it [the cathedral scene in *Faust*, part I] with Dimmesdale mounting the pillory at night, in 'The Scarlet Letter,' to my thinking the deepest thrust of what may be called the metaphysical imagination since Shakespeare." *The Works of James Russell Lowell*, Standard Library Edition (Boston, 1890–1892), XI, 209–210.

2. Author's preface to *Twice-Told Tales*, in *The Writings of Nathaniel Hawthorne*, I, liv. This is the Old Manse Edition, 22 vols. (Boston, 1900). All further references of this kind will be to this edition.

3. I.e., Charles Lamb.

4. See Emerson's "Thoreau," *Lectures and Biographical Sketches* (Boston, 1883), pp. 447–448.

5. Preface to *Twice-Told Tales*, in *Writings*, I, liv; lv.

6. The opening sentence of "The Three-fold Destiny," *Twice-Told Tales*, in *Writings*, II, 329.

7. *Mosses from an Old Manse*, in *Writings*, IV, 29.

8. The same.

9. From the preface to *Twice-Told Tales*, in *Writings*, I, liv.

10. The quoted passages are from the same preface.

11. Longfellow reviewed *Twice-Told Tales* in the *North American Review* for July 1837. See his *Outre-Mer and Drift-Wood* (Boston, 1886), pp. 360–367.

12. *Twice-Told Tales*, in *Writings*, II, 329.

13. *Mosses from an Old Manse*, in *Writings*, V, 262.

14. *As You Like It*, II, i, 17.

15. *Mosses from an Old Manse*, in *Writings*, V, 34.

16. Hawthorne was told this story by William W. Story. See *Notes of Travel*, in *Writings*, XXI, 361–362.

17. The Struldbrugs are in *Gulliver's Travels*, part iii.

18. For the description of Hilda's Tower see chap. vi of *The Marble Faun*.

19. Moncure D. Conway, *Life of Nathaniel Hawthorne* (London [1890]), pp. 162–163. The British edition of *The Marble Faun* was entitled *Transformation*.

20. Brownell erred. Sybil Dacy (not Darcy) is a character in Hawthorne's *Septimius Felton*. The sentence quoted appears in her narrative of the bloody footstep as told to Septimius, *Writings*, XIV, 198.

21. In the *Arabian Nights* Schariar or Schahriah is the husband of Scheherazade, who has resolved, because of the infidelity of an earlier wife, to marry a new woman every night and have her strangled at daybreak.

22. Henry James, *Hawthorne* (New York, 1879), pp. 123–125, 161–162.

23. By Prosper Mérimée (1803–1870).

24. The phrases by Thackeray are from "De Finibus," *Roundabout Papers*, in *Works*, Centenary Biographical Edition, 26 vols. (London, 1911), XX, 261.

25. Matthew Arnold, preface to *Poems of Wordsworth* (London, 1882), p. xxiv.

26. I.e., Louise de la Ramée (1839–1908). The passage is from James, *Hawthorne*, pp. 42–43.

27. Thackeray so calls Alexandre Dumas *père* in his essay, "On a Lazy Idle Boy," in *Roundabout Papers*. The statement about drama usually appears as: "Two trestles, four boards, three actors, and a passion." The next quoted sentence, from Taine, I cannot locate, but it sets forth the doctrine of "convergence" in H. Taine, *The Ideal in Art*, trans. J. Durand (New York, 1874).

28. Cf. *The Merchant of Venice*, act III, scene ii.

29. Cf. Brownell's essay, "Carlyle," *Victorian Prose Masters* (New York, 1901), p. 60.

30. William Ellery Channing (1780–1842), Edward Everett (1794–1865), Amos Bronson Alcott (1799–1888). Channing was of course

the poet-friend of Thoreau; Everett was the orator and statesman (and president of Harvard College) greatly admired by Emerson; and Alcott was noted as an educator and "mystic," the friend of Emerson.

31. Conway, *Life of Nathaniel Hawthorne*, p. 156.

32. See the article so entitled in *Revue des Deux Mondes*, XXVIII (3): 668–703 (August 1860).

33. Julian Hawthorne, *Nathaniel Hawthorne and His Wife*, 2 vols. (Boston, 1884), I, 214.

34. Evidenced in *The Life of Franklin Pierce* (Boston, 1852).

35. In *The Sketch-Book* (1819–20).

36. This passage and the quoted letter from Hawthorne to Longfellow below are from Conway, *Hawthorne*, p. 84, n., and p. 57.

37. "Wakefield," *Twice-Told Tales*, in *Writings*, I, 181.

38. Arnold's definition of the function of culture: "To know the best that has been thought and said in the world." See, *inter alia*, the preface to *Literature and Dogma* (London, 1873).

39. In the chapter "Leamington Spa," *Our Old Home*, in *Writings*, XI, 63.

40. *The Life and Voyages of Columbus* (1828).

41. In 1854 George Henry Lewes abandoned his wife, a former Miss Jervis, to form a union with Marian Evans (George Eliot).

42. William Wetmore Story (1819–1895), the sculptor.

43. See *Notes of Travel*, in *Writings*, XXI, 332.

44. Richard Holt Hutton, *Essays Theological and Literary*, 2 vols. (London, 1871), II, 437. The essay is reprinted in *Essays in Literary Criticism* (1876) and *Literary Essays* (1888).

45. *Notes of Travel*, XXI, 204–205, 271–272. In this whole discussion Brownell follows Henry James. See James's *Hawthorne*, p. 156.

46. Cf. chap. vii of *The Marble Faun*.

47. In *Hawthorne*, pp. 155–156.

48. Conway, *Hawthorne*, p. 181.

49. On Hawthorne's acquaintance with Mrs. Jameson see *Notes of Travel*, in *Writings*, XXI, 354–355.

50. *Mosses from an Old Manse*, in *Writings*, IV, 11.

51. *The Dolliver Romance and Kindred Tales*, in *Writings*, XIV, 87.

52. *Notes of Travel*, in *Writings*, XXI, 212.

53. *Notes of Travel*, XXI, 140.

54. *Notes of Travel*, XXI, 319.

55. *Notes of Travel*, XXI, 133.

56. *Our Old Home*, in *Writings*, XI, 141–142.

57. *Notes of Travel*, in *Writings*, XI, 142f; XIX, 177. The reference to Sidney Lee (later Sir Sidney Lee) presumably concerns his *Life of William Shakespeare* (London, 1888, often reprinted, a new and enlarged edition appearing in New York in 1909).

58. I.e., Paolo and Francesca.

59. *The Scarlet Letter*, in *Writings*, VI, 281–282.

60. *The Scarlet Letter,* VI, 371–372.

61. John 8:11.

62. James, *Hawthorne,* p. 113.

63. *Henry Esmond,* book I, chap. xiii, the last paragraph.

64. Exodus 9:29.

65. *The Scarlet Letter,* in *Writings,* VI, 282–283.

66. Arnold's phrase, recurrent in his critical prose.

EMERSON

1. James Russell Lowell, "Ode Recited at the Harvard Commemoration," l. 208.

2. "The world is too much with us"—Wordsworth, "Miscellaneous Sonnets," XXXII, l. 1.

3. "Goethe," *Representative Men,* in *The Complete Works of Ralph Waldo Emerson* (Centenary Edition, New and Revised), IV, 282. All references to Emerson will be to this edition, published in Boston in twelve volumes, 1903–1904.

4. Cf. Luke 23:4.

5. "Goethe," *Representative Men,* in *Works,* IV, 276.

6. H. Taine, *The Ideal in Art,* trans. J. Durand (New York, 1874), p. 11.

7. Psalms 37:37.

8. "The Fugitive Slave Law," *Miscellanies,* in *Works,* XI, 217.

9. Cf. Genesis 27:22.

10. I suppose this to be: "To preach well you must speak the truth," *Journals,* April 14, 1823, but it may be elsewhere in Emerson's works also.

11. "Goethe," *Representative Men,* in *Works,* IV, 284.

12. In the *Wolfenbüttle Fragmente.*

13. Cf. "The American Scholar," *Nature, Addresses and Lectures,* in *Works,* I, 81–116.

14. Cf. n. 29 to "Hawthorne."

15. "My reasoning faculty is proportionally weak," *Journals,* April 18, 1824.

16. Emerson writes: "Art . . . was defined by Aristotle, 'The reason of the thing, without the matter.'" "Art," *Society and Solitude,* in *Works,* VII, 39.

17. ". . . he taught them as one that had authority, and not as the scribes." Mark 1:22.

18. Ecclesiastes 12:13.

19. Tennyson, *The Princess,* pt. vii, song, st. 3.

20. Panentheism, or the doctrine that all things are in God, is especially associated with the German philosopher Karl C. F. Krause (1781–1832).

21. "Self-Reliance," *Essays: First Series,* in *Works,* II, 53.

22. "A foolish consistency is the hobgoblin of little minds, adored

by little statesmen and philosophers and divines."—"Self-Reliance," *Essays: First Series*, in *Works*, II, 57.

23. Marie Dugard, *Ralph Waldo Emerson: Sa vie et son œuvre* (Paris, 1907), p. 117.

24. "Beauty," *Nature*, in *Works*, I, 22.

25. "Uses of Great Men," *Representative Men*, in *Works*, IV, 10.

26. "In like manner our moral nature is vitiated by any interference of our will."—"Spiritual Laws," *Essays: First Series*, in *Works*, II, 133.

27. James Elliot Cabot, *A Memoir of Ralph Waldo Emerson*, 2 vols. (Boston, 1887), I, 276–278.

28. Luke 2:49.

29. Brownell apparently found this in Cabot, *Memoir*, I, 361.

30. "Divinity School Address," *Nature, Addresses and Lectures*, in *Works*, I, 129.

31. "Literary Ethics," *Works*, I, 182.

32. George Edward Woodberry, *Ralph Waldo Emerson*, English Men of Letters (New York and London, 1907). See especially pp. 196–197.

33. Matthew Arnold, *Literature and Dogma* (New York, 1873), p. 22.

34. "Literary Ethics," *Nature, Addresses and Lectures*, in *Works*, I, 183.

35. "Self-Reliance," *Essays: First Series*, in *Works*, II, 50.

36. For this favorite Biblical phrase of Brownell's see "Arnold," in *Victorian Prose Masters*, p. 180.

37. Woodberry, *Ralph Waldo Emerson*, pp. 117, 137.

38. "He only earns his freedom and existence who daily conquers them anew"—Goethe, *Faust*, pt. ii, ll.11575–11576.

39. Wordsworth, "Ode: Intimations of Immortality from Recollections of Early Childhood," l. 152.

40. "Swims into his ken"—Keats, "On First Looking into Chapman's Homer," l. 10.

41. "Where there is no vision, the people perish." Proverbs 29:18.

42. Woodberry, *Emerson*, p. 73; but cf. Ralph L. Rusk, *The Life of Ralph Waldo Emerson* (New York, 1949), p. 402.

43. Cf. "Divinity School Address," *Nature, Addresses and Lectures*, in *Works*, I, 130–131.

44. "Plato; or, The Philosopher," *Representative Men*, in *Works*, IV, 43.

45. Presumably Brownell is referring to John William Burgess, *The Civil War and the Constitution, 1859–1865*, 2 vols. (New York, 1901). This was published by Charles Scribner's Sons, for whom he served as editor.

46. "Initial, Daemonic, and Celestial Love," *Poems*, in *Works*, IX, 118.

47. *Representative Men*, in *Works*, IV, 4.

48. According to the *Mirror of Perfection* (*Speculum Perfectionis*),

an early fourteenth-century speculation, chap. cxiv, St. Francis appealed to the emperor to protect the ass and the ox. Brownell apparently borrowed this from Arnold's essay, "Pagan and Mediaeval Religious Sentiment," *Essays in Criticism*, 2d. ed. (London, 1869), p. 202.

49. "Voluntaries," sec. iii, *Poems*, in *Works*, IX, 207.

50. "Literary Ethics," in *Works*, I, 179.

51. Brownell apparently found this in Matthew Arnold's essay on Shelley, *Essays in Criticism: Second Series*. But Arnold uses it elsewhere.

52. "Self-Reliance," *Essays: First Series*, in *Works*, II, 50.

53. Brownell seems to have got this from Woodberry's *Emerson*, p. 88.

54. "Self-Reliance," *Essays: First Series*, in *Works*, II, 51. The repeated words following are from the same source; see n. 21.

55. "Spiritual Laws," *Essays: First Series*, in *Works*, II, 133.

56. J. A. Froude, *Bunyan* (New York, 1880), p. 41.

57. Arnold's citation from Bishop Wilson in "Doing as One Likes" (*Culture and Anarchy*, 1869): "Firstly, never go against the best light you have; secondly take care that your light be not darkness." *Culture and Anarchy and Friendship's Garland* (New York, 1912), p. 69.

58. "Success," *Society and Solitude*, in *Works*, VII, 304–305.

59. See chap. i of *Representative Men*, in *Works*, IV.

60. *A Memoir of Ralph Waldo Emerson*, I, 290.

61. Cf. Woodberry, *Emerson*, p. 109 and reference.

62. Hawthorne's *Our Old Home* was published in 1863. Brownell found this opinion of it in Arnold's lecture on Emerson, *Discourses in America* (London, 1885), pp. 173–174.

63. See the essay on Napoleon in *Representative Men*, in *Works*, IV.

64. Brownell seems to have picked this up from Woodberry, *Emerson*, p. 92.

65. "So careful of the type she seems,/ So careless of the single life."—Tennyson, *In Memoriam*, LV, st. 2.

66. Matthew 10:39.

67. Goethe, *Faust*, pt. I, l. 1549. "Thou shalt do without."

68. An oblique reference to "The Chambered Nautilus" by Oliver Wendell Holmes, first published in *The Autocrat of the Breakfast Table*, when that work ran serially in the *Atlantic Monthly*, 1857–1858.

69. "And the individual withers and the world is more and more."—Tennyson, "Locksley Hall," l. 142.

70. "Considerations by the Way," *Conduct of Life*, in *Works*, VI, 248. The next sentences are from "Worship," in the same work, p. 238.

71. *Nature, Addresses and Lectures*, in *Works*, I, 22.

72. Psalms 110:4.

73. Shakespeare, *Sonnets*, 66, 12.

74. See Goethe, *Dichtung und Wahrheit,* part I, book I.

75. Henry James Sr., *Literary Remains,* ed. William James (Boston, 1885), p. 293.

76. "Swedenborg," *Representative Men,* in *Works,* IV, 138.

77. Rudolf Christoph Eucken, 1846–1926. He won the Nobel Prize in literature (1908).

78. For "The Problem" see *Poems,* in *Works,* IX, 6–7. Henley's "Invictus" was first published in 1888.

79. Both Henley and Stevenson were "Scribner authors." "Invictus," originally entitled "I.M.R.T.Hamilton Bruce (1846–1899)," is the fourth poem in "Echoes" in William Ernest Henley, *Poems* (New York, Scribner, 1905); and the doctrine of *"gaudium certaminis"* or the joy of battling against odds is set forth in *"Æs Triplex," Virginibus Puerisque and Other Papers,* vol. XIII of the Author's Edition of Robert Louis Stevenson (New York, Scribner, 1895).

80. The statement about Socrates and Zion is taken over from Arnold, "Hebraism and Hellenism," in *Culture and Anarchy.*

81. "Fall like sweet strains or pensive smiles"—"The Problem," *Poems,* in *Works,* IX, 6.

82. James Fitzjames Stephen, *Liberty, Equality, Fraternity* (London, 1874), pp. 353–354.

83. Herbert Spencer, *The Philosophy of Style* (New York, 1872, often reprinted).

84. Wendell Phillips (1811–1884), abolitionist and orator.

85. Edward Everett (1794–1865), orator, president of Harvard, governor of Massachusetts, minister to England, secretary of state, and U.S. senator. He was the formal orator at the dedication of the Gettysburg Cemetery.

86. *Lectures and Biographical Sketches,* in *Works,* X, 331, 334.

87. The same, pp. 331–332.

88. Cf. "Goethe," *Representative Men,* in *Works,* IV, 287–288.

89. *Nature, Addresses and Lectures,* in *Works,* I, 23.

90. The same, pp. 24, 8, 15, 52, 8.

91. I.e., Claude Lorraine (1600–1682), whose landscapes were much admired as expressing "ideality."

92. Henry James, "Emerson," *Partial Portraits* (London, 1888), p. 30.

93. Brownell apparently picked this up from Henry James's "Emerson," p. 29.

94. "Goethe," *Representative Men,* in *Works,* IV, 270.

95. Dugard, *Ralph Waldo Emerson.* The problem of the study is essentially one of intellectual history.

96. Woodberry, *Emerson,* p. 158.

97. This is apparently from the introduction by Richard Watson Gilder to *Power, Success and Greatness,* selections from Emerson (New York, 1908). But I have been unable to consult a copy of this work.

98. "Here once the embattled farmers stood"—"Concord Hymn," *Poems*, in *Works*, IX, 158; "Musketaquid," pp. 141–144.

99. "Ode Inscribed to W. H. Channing," *Poems*, in *Works*, IX, 78.

100. *Twelfth Night*, II, iv, 113.

101. See n. 97 above.

102. "Under her solemn fillet saw the scorn."—"Days," *Poems*, in *Works*, IX, 228.

103. Milton, "Lycidas," l. 11.

104. "Woodnotes II," *Poems*, in *Works*, IX, 54.

105. "Love," *Essays: First Series*, in *Works*, II, 173–174.

106. "Love," p. 172.

107. "Friendship," *Essays: First Series*, in *Works*, II, 195.

108. Byron, *Don Juan*, canto I, st. 74.

109. "Love," *Essays: First Series*, in *Works*, II, 174, 175.

110. In *Works*, II, 169–188.

111. "Swedenborg," *Representative Men*, in *Works*, IV, 128.

112. Browning, "The Last Ride Together," *Dramatic Romances*.

113. This may be somewhere in Emerson but it may also be a reminiscence of "Let's contend no more, Love," the first line of "A Woman's Last Word" in Browning's *Dramatic Lyrics*.

114. Not found.

115. ". . . my stress lay on the incidents in the development of a soul: little else is worth study. I, at least, always thought so . . ." Letter to J. Milsand, prefixed by Browning to the 1863 reprint of *Sordello*.

116. *Sortes Vergilianae*, a method of determining choice by opening a copy of Virgil at random and reading the first line that met one's eyes.

117. Oliver Wendell Holmes, *Ralph Waldo Emerson* (Boston, 1884), p. 381.

118. "Plato," *Representative Men*, in *Works*, IV, 56.

119. See the conclusion of Arnold's essay on Emerson in *Discourses in America*, pp. 196ff.

POE

1. Ishmael: cf. Genesis 6:12.

2. Johann Joachim Winckelmann (1717–1768). It is difficult to know what Brownell has specifically in mind, but see Hanna Koch, *Johann Joachim Winckelmann: Sprache und Kunstwerk* (Berlin, 1957), particularly the passages cited on pp. 71f.

3. See Poe's "Dickens's 'Barnaby Rudge,'" *The Works of Edgar Allan Poe*, VII, 39–64. This edition in ten volumes edited by Edmund Clarence Stedman and George Edward Woodberry (Chicago, 1894–1895), will be referred to hereafter as *Works*.

4. M. C. Auguste Dupin is the "detective" in "The Murders in the

Rue Morgue," *Works*, III, 53–98, and other detective stories by Poe.

5. See "The Philosophy of Composition," *Works*, VI, 31–46.

6. *The Letters of Robert Browning and Elizabeth Barrett Barrett, 1845–1846*, 2 vols. (New York, 1899), I, 429.

7. Wordsworth, "Lines Composed a Few Miles Above Tintern Abbey."

8. Presumably Wordsworth's "Ode on the Intimations of Immortality Recollected from Early Childhood." The other poem is of course by Keats.

9. *Letters of Robert Browning and Elizabeth Barrett Barrett*, I, 429. However, in a letter to Richard Hengist Horne, she says: "The rhythm acts excellently upon the imagination, and the 'nevermore' has a solemn chime with it." *Letters of Elizabeth Barrett Browning Addressed to Richard Hengist Horne* (New York, 1889), p. 307.

10. "Memoir of Edgar Allan Poe," in *Poems of Edgar Allan Poe* (New York, 1875), p. 37. But Brownell may be referring to some of Stoddard's magazine articles about Poe.

11. William Dean Howells, *Literary Friends and Acquaintance* (New York, 1900), p. 63.

12. See p. 179. The next sentence refers presumably to Gautier's *History of Romanticism* (1874).

13. Philippians 4:8.

14. In "Sterne and Goldsmith," the last unit in *The English Humourists of the Eighteenth Century*.

15. Charles Dickens, *Pickwick Papers*, chap. viii.

16. For Arnold's estimate of Kinglake see "The Literary Influence of Academies," *Essays in Criticism*, First Series (ed. London, 1893), pp. 75f. (The *Essays* first appeared in 1865. But Brownell is apparently paraphrasing from memory.)

17. Sir John Mandeville is the putative author of a book of travels composed after the middle of the fourteenth century. The *Travels* of Baron Munchausen (1785) is by Rudolph Erich Raspe. Both books are bywords for incredible adventures.

18. This seems to be a reminiscence of Matthew Arnold on the Celt—"always ready to react against the despotism of Fact . . . the description a great friend of the Celt gives of him." A footnote refers to Henri Martin, *Histoire de France*. The passage from Arnold is in *On the Study of Celtic Literature* (1867), in *On the Study of Celtic Literature and on Translating Homer* (London, 1893), p. 77.

19. Acts 9:5.

20. Poe's own phrase.

21. Thoreau, *A Week on the Concord and Merrimack Rivers* (1849), in *The Writings of Henry David Thoreau* (Boston, 1893), I, 121. On the Oriental prototypes of *Zadig* see the introduction to the edition by Verdun L. Saulnier (Paris, 1946).

22. *The London Spectator*, 102 (January 23, 1909): 122–123.

H. Rider Haggard published *She* in 1887. The subsequent allusion to H. G. Wells presumably concerns such books as *The Time Machine* (1895).

23. "Guy de Maupassant," in Jules Lemaitre, *Les Contemporains: Etudes et Portraits Littéraires, Première Serie* (Paris, 1887), p. 310.

24. The usual form of this legal saw is: If you have a weak case, abuse the other side.

25. Presumably the reference is to the fact that "Kubla Khan" came to Coleridge in a dream, and that when he was interrupted in writing down the poem, he could not recover the rest of it.

26. Cf. Jules Lemaitre, *Impressions de Théatre, Première Serie* (Paris, 1888), pp. 126–139 ("Je ne demandais ce que fût devenu le même sujet entre les mains de Racine").

27. Arnold's famous phrase.

28. Shakespeare, Sonnet no. 111.

29. The "tarn" is close to the house of Usher in Poe's tale; "Tale of the Ragged Mountains" is in *Works*, I, 283–296; shrieking water-lilies seems a generalized term, though lilies "loll" in l. 10 of "The Sleeper"; "rank miasma" is a phrase from "The Fall of the House of Usher," *Works*, I, 150.

30. The professional detective in the mystery stories of Emile Gaboriau (1835–1873). *Monsieur Lecoq* appeared in 1869.

31. Marie Tussaud (1760–1850) transferred her noted wax models of famous and infamous personages to London in 1802, and the institution still exists. Mrs. Jarley in Dickens' *The Old Curiosity Shop* is the proprietress of a traveling show of waxworks.

32. Ernest Theodor Amadeus Hoffmann (1776–1822), author of macabre and eccentric fiction in German, of which the *Phantasiestücke* (1814–1815) is representative.

33. The classification "Tales of Conscience" is set up in the Stedman-Woodberry edition, *Works*, II.

34. Thackeray's *Novels by Eminent Hands* (originally *Punch's Prize Novelists*, 1847) contains "George de Barnwell," a burlesque of Bulwer-Lytton, and "Codlingsby," a burlesque of Disraeli. See the Centenary Biographical Edition of Thackeray's *Works*, 26 vols. (London, 1911), VIII, 3–34.

35. "Count" Alessandro Cagliostro (1743–1795), whose real name was Giuseppe Balsamo, was a charlatan involved in the famous "Diamond Necklace" affair, of which Marie Antoinette was the intended victim.

36. Thackeray makes this remark of Congreve in the lecture on Congreve and Addison in *The English Humourists of the Eighteenth Century*.

37. Isaac Disraeli, *Curiosities of Literature* (1791, 1793, 1823).

38. This is somewhat unnecessarily complicated. Ishmael and the Bedouin are types of wanderers; Isaac, the younger brother of Ishmael, has all the domestic virtues. I suppose the Brahmin is opposed to the

Bedouin not only because of the Brahmin's high rank in the caste system but also because of his stability. Boeotian of course means dull or clownish.

39. For two characteristic comments by Poe on Longfellow see "Longfellow's Ballads" and "A Reply to 'Outis,'" *Works*, VI, 120–198.

40. For Poe's statement that Emerson is no more than an imitator of Carlyle see *Works*, VII, 248–249.

41. "Poe at West Point," *Harper's New Monthly Magazine*, 35 (November 1867): 756.

42. *Works*, VII, 130.

43. *Works*, VII, 309–310; VI, 27.

44. *Works*, VII, 128.

45. "Le bon critique est celui qui reconte les aventures de son âme au milieu des chefs-d'oeuvre."—Anatole France, preface, *La Vie Littéraire* (1888–1892).

46. This may be somewhere in Poe, but the New English Dictionary credits it to *Punch*, May 17, 1879. For the following phrase cf. Dryden, "Cymon and Iphigenia," 1. 84. "He whistled as he went for want of thought."

47. The passage from Bacon ("Lord Verulam") appears several times in Poe, e.g., in "Ligeia," *Works*, I, 183–184.

48. Stedman supplies a number of the introductory essays in the *Works*, notably the one to the criticism (VI, xi–xxvi) and that to the poems (X, xiii–xxxv).

49. Emerson, "Goethe; or, The Writer," *Representative Men*, in *The Complete Works of Ralph Waldo Emerson*, Centenary Edition, 12 vols. (Boston, 1903–1904), IV, 277.

50. Brownell carried this over from his *French Art* (new and enlarged edition 1908, but the original edition was 1892), p. 15.

51. For Gautier's discussion of Poe see the essay on Charles Baudelaire, in *Portraits et Souvenirs Littéraires* (Paris, 1875), esp. sec. vii.

52. For Swinburne's estimate of Baudelaire see, besides the famous elegy, "Ave atque Vale," the essay-review, "Charles Baudelaire" (1861), in *The Complete Works of Algernon Charles Swinburne*, Bonchurch Edition (London and New York, 1925–1927), XIII, 417–427. For the opinion of Edmond Scherer see *Etudes sur la Littérature Contemporaine*, 4th series (Paris, 1873), pp. 279–289. Henry James's essay on Baudelaire is in *French Poets and Novelists* (London, 1878).

53. Presumably the *Histoire de la Littérature Française* by Emile Faguet, which reached a sixth edition in 1900–1901 in Paris.

54. Henry James, "Charles Baudelaire," *French Poets and Novelists*, p. 76: "An enthusiasm for Poe is the mark of a decidedly primitive stage of reflection."

55. *Works*, I, 3–87.

56. The references are to the New Variorum edition of Shakespeare under the editorship of H. H. Furness, begun in 1871; the standard edition of Bacon (1857–1874) edited by J. Spedding, R. L. Ellis and

D. D. Heath; and the life of Milton in six volumes (1859–1880; index, 1894) by D. Masson.

57. "The noble pleasure of praising"—Swinburne, "Notes on Poems and Reviews," *Prose Works*, in *Complete Works*, VI, 372.

58. "Hear the mighty stream of tendency"—William Wordsworth, *The Excursion*, bk. IX, l. 87. But the phrase is also used by Hazlitt, Arnold, and Emerson.

59. This sentence is in Thackeray's lecture on Swift, in *The English Humourists of the Eighteenth Century*.

60. Thackeray makes a point of Swift's "daring" to inscribe on his tombstone, "Ubi saeva indignatio ulterius cor lacerare nequit." ("Where savage indignation cannot further lacerate his heart.")

61. *Works*, IX, 135. ("No thinking being lives, who at some luminous point of his life of thought, has not felt himself lost amid the surges of futile efforts at understanding or believing that anything exists *greater than his own soul*.")

62. Thomas Carlyle, *Reminiscences* (London, 1881).

LOWELL

1. "The Place of the Independent in Politics," *The Works of James Russell Lowell*, Standard Library Edition, 12 vols. (Boston, 1890–1892), VI, 190–221. Hereafter referred to as *Works*, these volumes are also sometimes called the Riverside Edition. Lowell's address was delivered before the Reform Club of New York at Steinway Hall April 13, 1888.

2. George William Curtis (1824–1892), essayist, editor, and reformer.

3. The second series of *The Biglow Papers*, No. II ("Mason and Slidell: A Yankee Idyll") dated January 6, 1862, has some harsh things to say about Great Britain.

4. "A Fable for Critics," *Works*, IX, 85.

5. Cf. Schiller's *Letters upon the Aesthetic Education of Man*, XV and XXVI (various translations).

6. "That queer duality in Lowell"—Ferris Greenslet, *James Russell Lowell: His Life and Work* (Boston, 1905), p. 82.

7. *The Biglow Papers*, in *Works*, VIII, 46.

8. "Beaumont and Fletcher," *The Old English Dramatists*, in *Works*, XI, 288.

9. "Coleridge," *Literary and Political Addresses*, in *Works*, VI, 70.

10. "James Gates Percival," *Literary Essays*, in *Works*, II, 148, 155.

11. William Dean Howells, *Literary Friends and Acquaintance: A Personal Retrospect of American Authorship* (New York, 1900), *passim* but esp. pp. 212–250; Henry James, *Essays in London and Elsewhere* (New York, 1893), pp. 44–80.

12. James, *Essays in London*, p. 45.

13. "Ode Recited at the Harvard Commemoration, July 21, 1865,"

Poetical Works, vol. IV: *War Poems, Heartsease and Rue, etc.,* in *Works,* X, 24.

14. "New occasions teach new duties; Time makes ancient good uncouth"—"The Present Crisis," *Poetical Works,* vol. I: *Earlier Poems, The Vision of Sir Launfal, etc.,* in *Works,* VII, 184.

15. *The Old English Dramatists,* in *Works,* XI, 198.

16. *Essays in London,* p. 30.

17. "He should have served under Nelson . . . He hates a Frenchman as he does the devil."—Arnold, *Culture and Anarchy and Friendship's Garland* (New York, 1912), p. 224.

18. *Essays in London,* p. 58.

19. Edward A. Freeman's principal historical masterpiece is *The History of the Norman Conquest* (1867–1876); Bishop William Stubbs, *Constitutional History of England* (1874–1878); Thomas Babington Macaulay, *History of England from the Accession of James II* (unfinished, 1848–1860); James Anthony Froude, *History of England from the Fall of Wolsey to the Defeat of the Armada* (1856–1869); David Hume, *The History of England* (1754–1762); John Richard Green, *A Short History of the English People* (1874).

20. Thackeray, in *The Four Georges: Sketches of Manners, Morals, Court, and Town Life:* "George the First," the seventh paragraph.

21. *Essays in London,* p. 49.

22. "St. Francis could not have looked with more benignity on her (Poverty) whom he chose, as Dante tells us, for his bride." "Don Quixote," *Literary and Political Addresses,* in *Works,* VI, 119.

23. Presumably pp. 121f in "The Rebellion: Its Causes and Consequences, 1864," *Political Essays,* in *Works,* V. And see *Henry Esmond,* chap. i.

24. "Dante," *Literary Essays,* in *Works,* IV, 237.

25. "Dante," p. 140.

26. "Harvard Anniversary: Address Delivered in Sanders Theatre, Cambridge, November 8, 1886, on the Two Hundred and Fiftieth Anniversary of the Foundation of Harvard University," *Literary and Political Addresses,* in *Works,* VI, 177.

27. Winslow Homer (1836–1910), American artist. Homer's virtual withdrawal from social intercourse in his later years gives force to Brownell's "I remember."

28. This is repeated from *French Traits* (1890), p. 74, and comes originally from Emerson, "Uses of Great Men," *Representative Men.*

29. "Others abide our question. Thou art free"—"Shakespeare," in Matthew Arnold, *The Strayed Reveller, and Other Poems* (London, 1849).

30. Arnold, "Guide to English Literature," *Mixed Essays* (1879), in *Mixed Essays, Irish Essays and Others* (New York, 1883), p. 145.

31. These various phrases are from Carlyle, "The Hero as Poet. Dante; Shakespeare," in *Heroes, Hero-Worship and the Heroic in History,* of which there are numerous editions.

32. "On a Certain Condescension in Foreigners," *Literary Essays,* in *Works,* III, 233.

33. Matthew Arnold, preface to *Essays in Criticism,* 2d. ed. (London, 1869), p. ix.

34. Whatever the source of this anecdote, it does not appear in the lengthy account of Porson's final illness and death in John Selby Watson's *The Life of Richard Porson* (London, 1861), pp. 318–330. Porson seems to have been in a stupor.

35. See the preface to *Literature and Dogma.* The phrase also appears in *Culture and Anarchy.*

36. This is obviously William James (1842–1910), but I have not been able to find the passage.

37. Bacon, "Of Beauty," *Essayes* (ed. 1625), no. XLIII.

38. Richard Bentley published his notorious "improved" edition of *Paradise Lost* in 1732.

39. See "Chaucer," *Literary Essays,* in *Works,* III, 298.

40. This Latin tag was a favorite with Arnold. See, e.g., "Pagan and Mediaeval Religious Sentiment," *Essays in Criticism,* First Series.

41. See "Thoreau," *Literary Essays,* in *Works,* I, 361–381.

42. According to Greenslet, it was "eight unbroken hours." For the use to which Lowell put this poem see "Spenser," *Literary Essays,* in *Works,* IV, 269–270.

43. "Library of Old Authors," *Literary Essays,* in *Works,* I, 248–348.

44. James, *Essays in London,* pp. 62–63.

45. "On a Certain Condescension in Foreigners," *Literary Essays,* in *Works,* I, 233.

46. "Dante," *Literary Essays,* in *Works,* IV, 142.

47. For these various passages on Michelangelo, domes, etc., see "A Few Bits of Roman Mosaic," part of "Leaves from My Journal," *Literary Essays,* in *Works,* I, 205–206.

48. Champfleury is Jules Fleury (1821–1889), a voluminous writer of fiction and literary commentary. I have not found the phrase Brownell quotes, but *cocodète* (*sic*) is defined as a woman of the middle-class world affecting a toilet and tastes incompatible with her modest position. The word has a mildly scandalous implication. See Lucien Rigaud, *Dictionnaire d'Argot Moderne* (Paris, 1888), p. 103.

49. See particularly the essays in *Literary Essays,* in *Works,* III and IV.

50. "On a Certain Condescension in Foreigners," *Literary Essays,* in *Works,* III, 239.

51. "No brain but had its private maggot, which must have found pitiably short commons sometimes."—"Thoreau," *Literary Essays,* in *Works,* I, 362. For "The Pickens-and-Stealin's Rebellion," see *Political Essays,* in *Works,* V, 75–91.

52. "You write with ease to show your breeding,/But easy writing's vile hard reading."—Richard Brinsley Sheridan, "Clio's Protest." This

is quoted in Thomas Moore's *Life of Sheridan* (London, 1825), I, 55.

53. James, *Essays in London*, pp. 48–49.

54. Brownell repeats this from his essay on Arnold, *Victorian Prose Masters* (New York, 1901), p. 165.

55. "Omnis definitio periculosa est."—Erasmus, *Adagia*.

56. "Dante," *Literary Essays*, in *Works*, IV, 140.

57. Greenslet, *Lowell*, p. 277.

58. "A Moosehead Journal," *Literary Essays*, in *Works*, I, 21.

59. In *Victorian Prose Masters* Brownell employs this phrase of Arnold's to establish his own theory. See pp. 157–158 in that volume.

60. "There is not a college in America in whose literary courses Lowell's is not a name to conjure with."—Greenslet, *Lowell*, p. 298.

61. These various allusions, quotations, and references are to be found as follows: that on Sir Thomas Browne in "Shakespeare Once More," *Literary Essays*, in *Works*, III, 3; on Hawthorne, "Thoreau," *Literary Essays*, in *Works*, I, 365; on Milton, the essay by that name in *Literary Essays*, in *Works*, IV, 117; on Donne, the essay on "James Gates Percival," *Literary Essays*, in *Works*, II, 160; on Dante, the essay by that name in *Literary Essays*, in *Works*, IV. I do not know where Lowell calls French "the most feminine of tongues."

62. For the statement on Marvell's "Horatian Ode" see the essay on Dryden, *Literary Essays*, in *Works*, III, 116; for that on the conclusion of the "Paradiso" see the address on Wordsworth, *Literary and Political Addresses*, in *Works*, VI, 105 ("the sublimest reach to which poetry has risen, the conclusion of the 'Paradiso'"); on the ranking of Chaucer see the conclusion of the essay of that name, *Literary Essays*, in *Works*, III, esp. p. 364: the distich from a Spanish Ballad is in "The Study of Modern Languages," *Works*, XI, 150. For Lowell's opinion of English as a literary medium see especially the essay on "Shakespeare Once More," *Literary Essays*, in *Works*, III, 1–94.

63. Miss Rossetti is Maria Francesca Rossetti; her book: *A Shadow of Dante, Being an Essay towards Studying Himself, His World and His Pilgrimage*, an American edition being published in Boston in 1872.

64. "Dante," *Literary Essays*, in *Works*, IV, 191, 190.

65. Matthew Arnold, "Dante and Beatrice." This essay first appeared in *Fraser's Magazine* (May 1863), and is collected into *Essays in Criticism . . . and Five Other Essays Now for the First Time Collected* (London, 1914).

66. Arnold, "Pagan and Mediaeval Religious Sentiment," *Essays in Criticism*, First Series (ed. London and New York, 1893), p. 221.

67. The various statements about Greek drama and the Christian ethic are to be found in the essay on Dante, *passim*, beginning p. 232.

68. Brownell repeats this from *French Traits* (New York, 1899), p. 76.

69. Stendhal published his *Histoire de la Peinture en Italie* in two volumes in 1817; his *Promenades dans Rome* in two volumes in 1829.

70. Brownell's remark that Lowell had no speculative side seems to be an oblique reference of the passage in Henry James, "James Russell Lowell," that Lowell's "imagination lighted up but scantily in the region of analysis and apology," *Essays in London,* p. 60. Faguet is August Emile Faguet (1847–1916), French critic.

71. "The Life and Letters of James Gates Percival," *Literary Essays,* in *Works,* II, 140f, *passim.*

72. In the lecture on John Webster, *The Old English Dramatists,* in *Works,* XI, 253.

73. For "A Moosehead Journal" see *Works,* I, 1ff. "On a Certain Condescension in Foreigners" is in *Works,* III, 220ff.

74. From "A Fable for Critics," *Works,* IX, 65.

75. Buffon, *Discours sur le Style,* the third paragraph. The *Discours* was originally printed in 1753. There are many reprints.

76. *Essays in London,* p. 75.

77. *Essays in London,* pp. 75–76.

78. *La Périchole,* comic opera by Jacques Offenbach (Paris, 1868). Lowell quotes one of Piquillo's saucy lines.

79. Slightly misquoted. See *The Old English Dramatists,* in *Works,* XI, 201.

80. In *The Arabian Nights.*

81. From "Thoreau," *Works,* I, 361.

82. "Thoreau," *Works,* I, 362.

83. "And rosy years that stood expectant by/ To buckle the winged sandals on their feet"—"Agassiz," *Works,* X, 116.

84. This is in Keats's letters, but Brownell probably picked it up from Arnold's essay, "John Keats," *Essays in Criticism: Second Series* (London, 1888), p. 109.

85. "The Legend of Brittany" is in *Works,* VII, 78–104.

86. "The Vision of Sir Launfal," *Works,* VII, 291–304.

87. "Auf Wiedersehen," *Works,* IX, 212–213.

88. Brownell means Matthew Arnold's "Isolation," of which the quoted line is the last line, in *Empedocles on Etna, and other Poems* (1852).

89. "The First Snow-Fall," *Works,* IX, 166–167.

90. From "Under the Willows," *Works,* IX, 151.

91. From "The Vision of Sir Launfal," *Works,* VII, 293.

92. From *The Biglow Papers,* in *Works,* VIII, 333.

93. Shakespeare, *Richard II,* II, i, 46, 50.

94. "Ode Recited at the Harvard Commemoration," *Works,* X, 17–31.

95. "Agassiz," *Works,* X, 101–120.

96. By "The Bridge and the Moniment" Brownell means "Mason and Slidell: A Yankee Idyll," *The Biglow Papers,* in *Works,* VIII, 240–270.

97. "The Election in November," *Political Essays,* in *Works,* V, 25–26.

98. "Ode Recited at the Harvard Commemoration," *Works*, X, 24.

99. "On a Certain Condescension in Foreigners," *Works*, III, 249.

100. "The Present Crisis," *Works*, VII, 178–184. This poem is dated "December, 1844."

101. "Clear-ethered height" is from the second line of the "Ode Recited at the Harvard Commemoration," *Works*, X, 17.

102. From the final section of the "Ode Recited at the Harvard Commemoration," *Works*, X, 31.

HENRY JAMES

1. *The Novels and Tales of Henry James* (1906–1917), in 26 volumes, was the first collected American edition. Additional titles appeared in the London edition of this set (1921–1923). The New York edition was published by Scribner.

2. Théophile Gautier published a book of poems, *Emaux et Camées,* in 1852. The poem "L'Art" in this collection demands a perfectly chiseled work of art.

3. The anecdote concerning Baron Georges Cuvier (1769–1832) is widely diffused, but I do not know the source of it.

4. Henry James, *French Poets and Novelists* (London, 1878), p. 236.

5. James published *What Maisie Knew* in 1897.

6. *French Poets and Novelists,* 1878; *Partial Portraits,* 1888; *Essays in London and Elsewhere,* 1893; *Hawthorne,* 1879.

7. James, *Hawthorne* (New York, 1879), p. 183.

8. *In Memoriam,* XXVII, st. 4.

9. In *Partial Portraits* (London, 1888), pp. 243–290.

10. In *Essays in London and Elsewhere* (London, 1893), pp. 81–120.

11. "A prouder nature never affronted the long humiliation of life, and to few persons can it have mattered less on the whole how either before or after death the judgment of men was likely to sound," *Essays in London,* p. 83.

12. "Daniel Deronda: A Conversation," *Partial Portraits,* pp. 65–96.

13. The essays on Musset, George Sand, and Balzac (two) are in *French Poets and Novelists;* those on Trollope, Daudet, Turgénieff, and Stevenson in *Partial Portraits.* But James has other discussions of some of these writers.

14. "The Art of Fiction," *Partial Portraits,* p. 393.

15. These various sentences are from the essay, "Alphonse Daudet," *Partial Portraits,* beginning on p. 206, and extending to p. 217.

16. This is repeated from *French Art* (ed. 1908), p. 66.

17. See John Taylor Brown, *Dr. John Brown* (Edinburgh, 1903), pp. 96–97.

18. Preface to *The Golden Bowl,* vol. I (New York Edition, 1909), pp. v–vi.

19. Wordsworth, "Lines Composed a Few Miles Above Tintern Abbey," l. 40.

20. From "Doing as One Likes" in *Culture and Anarchy*. But the idea recurs in Arnold in many places.

21. *Conversations of Goethe with Eckermann and Soret*, trans. John Oxenford, rev. ed. (London, 1892), p. 110.

22. "The School of Athens" is by Raphael, "The Departure for Cythera" by Watteau. "De Hooghe" seems to be a slip for Pieter de Hooch, inasmuch as Romeyn de Hooghe is not notable for interiors, and de Hooch is.

23. "That vague hum, that indefinable echo, of the whole multitudinous life of man, which is the real sign of a great work of fiction"— *Hawthorne*, p. 130.

24. Thackeray, "De Finibus," *Roundabout Papers*, in *Works*, Centenary Biographical Edition, 26 vols. (London, 1911), XX, 255.

25. In *The Wings of the Dove* (1902).

26. Maisie and Sir Claude are of course in *What Maisie Knew*. Vanderbank and Nanda are in *The Awkward Age* (1899). Newsome is in *The Ambassadors* (1903).

27. Ralph Touchett is in *The Portrait of a Lady* (1881).

28. Christopher Newman is in *The American* (1877); Miss Pynsent is in *The Princess Casamassima* (1886).

29. Emile Augier, *L'Aventurière* (Paris, 1870). Baronne Suzanne d'Ange appears in *Le Demi-Monde* by Dumas *fils* (Paris, 1855).

30. John Gibson Lockhart, *Memoirs of the Life of Sir Walter Scott*, 5 vols. (Boston and New York, 1902), IV, 310.

31. *The Better Sort* (1903).

32. "It is *proprement écrit*, but it's terribly pale."—"The Point of View," in *The Siege of London, The Pension Beaurepas, and The Point of View* (Boston, 1883), p. 277.

33. "Ivan Turgénieff," *Partial Portraits*, p. 298.

34. Presumably the reference is to the famous "nine years pondered lay."

35. "What a piece of work is a man!"—*Hamlet*, act II, sc. 2.

36. Arnold remarks that curiosity has a good sense in "other languages," not French alone. "The Function of Criticism at the Present Time," *Essays in Criticism*, First Series (ed. London and New York, 1893), p. 16.

37. Hippolyte Taine, *History of English Literature*, "The Novel—Thackeray," sec. viii. There are many editions.

38. "Disinterested curiosity" is recurrent in Matthew Arnold.

39. The James essay is in *Partial Portraits*. The reference to Lowell is to his "Don Quixote: Notes Read at the Workingmen's College, Great Ormond Street, London," *Literary and Political Addresses*, in *The Works of James Russell Lowell*, Standard Library Ed., 12 vols. (Boston, 1890–1892), VI, 114–136.

40. James wrote on George De Maurier, Robert Louis Stevenson,

and Constance Fenimore Woolson in essays collected in *Partial Portraits*. He wrote essays on Edwin A. Abbey and Charles S. Reinhart collected in *Picture and Text* (1893). "Madame de Sabran" is in *French Poets and Novelists*, pp. 359–389.

41. *A Little Tour in France* (Boston, 1885); *Portraits of Places* (London, 1883).

42. Probably in Paul Bourget, *Essais de Psychologie Contemporaine*, 2 vols. (Paris, 1899).

43. Tennyson, "Locksley Hall," 1. 178.

44. Edward Gibbon, *Autobiography* (Everyman's Library), p. 4. But Gibbon's phrase is merely "that exquisite picture of human manners."

45. This is in the opening chapters of Henry Thomas Buckle, *Introduction to the History of Civilization in England* (London, 1857–1861). The Bopp referred to a little later in the text is Franz Bopp (1791–1867), whose famous comparative grammar appeared first in 1833.

46. "Kingdoms of the world"—Matthew 4:8.

47. "Hawthorne," *Library of the World's Best Literature*, ed. Charles Dudley Warner (New York [c.1896–c.1898]), XII, 7061.

48. In *The Portrait of a Lady*.

49. The full form of the phrase is *ars est celare artem* and is an Ovidian direction to the seducer to conceal the means of seduction. As a Latin tag it has come to have the meaning in Brownell's text. Hence, his distinction between "art" and "artifice."

50. "I have said that Hawthorne was an observer of small things, and indeed he appears to have thought nothing too trivial to be suggestive." Thoreau "was worse than provincial—he was parochial . . ." James, *Hawthorne*, pp. 40, 97.

THE JOHN HARVARD LIBRARY

The intent of
Waldron Phoenix Belknap, Jr.,
as expressed in an early will, was for
Harvard College to use the income from a
permanent trust fund he set up, for "editing and
publishing rare, inaccessible, or hitherto unpub-
lished source material of interest in connection
with the history, literature, art (including minor
and useful art), commerce, customs, and man-
ners or way of life of the Colonial and Federal
Periods of the United States . . . In all cases
the emphasis shall be on the presentation of the
basic material." A later testament broadened this
statement, but Mr. Belknap's interests remained
constant until his death.

In linking the name of the first benefactor
of Harvard College with the purpose of this
later, generous-minded believer in American
culture the John Harvard Library seeks to
emphasize the importance of Mr. Belknap's
purpose. The John Harvard Library of the
Belknap Press of Harvard University Press
exists to make books and documents
about the American past more readily
available to scholars and the
general reader.